Educating the Developmentally Disabled

Educating the
Developmentally Disabled
Meeting the Needs of Children
and Families

Jan S. Handleman
Sandra L. Harris

Rutgers
The State University of New Jersey
New Brunswick

College–Hill Press, San Diego, California

College-Hill Press
A Division of
Little, Brown and Company (Inc.)
34 Beacon Street
Boston, Massachusetts   02108

Library of Congress Cataloging in Publication Data
Main entry under title:

Handleman, Jan S.
  Educating the developmentally disabled.

  Includes index.
  1. Developmentally disabled children — Education —
United States. 2. Developmentally disabled children —
Care and treatment — United States. 3. Developmentally
disabled children — United States — Family relationships.
4. Developmentally disabled children — Teacher training —
United States. I. Harris, Sandra L. II. Title.
HV894.H36   1986   371.9   86-18859

ISBN 0-316-342971

Printed in the United States of America

This book is dedicated to families:
to Emma and Samuel Handleman
and Felice Harris, and in memory of William Harris,
who first taught us about life in families,
and to the families of the children at the
Douglass Developmental Disabilities Center,
who taught us about courage in confronting some
of life's most painful moments.

CONTENTS

PREFACE

This is a book for teachers and for teachers-in-training who wish to specialize in work with developmentally disabled children. It is our hope that the educator who reads this book will emerge with a sense of the special needs of these youngsters, how one adapts the educational curriculum to meet these needs, what life is like in the family of a developmentally disabled child, and how the family's experiences affect the education of the child.

We have worked together for the past 14 years, collaborating in a variety of educational, administrative, and research projects aimed at serving developmentally disabled children and their families. Because one of us is a special educator (JSH) and the other a clinical psychologist (SLH), we have brought different but compatible views to bear on the many issues that have confronted us in the supervision of a university-based program for the treatment of autism. Out of those different perspectives has emerged a book that attempts to describe the development of an educational curriculum in a context that encompasses the needs of all developmentally disabled children in both the school and the home.

Our own program, the Douglass Developmental Disabilities Center, is a Rugters University day school for 30 children with autism. Beyond its fundamental goal of educating children the Douglass Center has a number of other diverse functions, including training undergraduates to work with the developmentally disabled, providing specialized graduate training in this area, and conducting an ongoing research program to improve current technology for the treatment and understanding of autism and related disorders.

The content of this book reflects an attempt to distill some of the important principles that have emerged for us in our work with developmentally disabled youngsters. Thus, the Douglass Center is behaviorally based, and so this book reflects our conviction that a curriculum anchored in behavioral techniques has the firmest empirical support of any treatment approach now available. Similarly, we have found over the years that active family involvement is important to the progress of our students, and we have therefore attempted to share with the reader a strong sense of the importance of family involvement along with one's work in the classroom.

One of the most encouraging developments we have witnessed in our years in the field of developmental disabilities is the continuing growth of educational technology. There now exists a substantial body of literature that documents persuasively that these children and adults can benefit in measurable ways from intensive educational experiences. There are techniques available with the potential to make a significant impact on the life of very nearly every person with a developmental disability. The challenge now is to make that knowledge part of the professional skills of every teacher who works with the developmentally disabled. It is the intention of this book to contribute to such a dissemination of knowledge.

ACKNOWLEDGMENTS

This book was made possible through the efforts of many people. The staff at the Douglass Developmental Disabilities Center helped to shape our thinking about the many educational issues that have arisen over the years. We owe special thanks to Maria Arnold, Leisa Bass, Robert Carlson, Lorraine Carpenter, Pattey Fong, Mary Jane Gill, Rita Gordon, Barbara Kristoff, and Ellen Murphy. Some of these staff members drafted the sample programs that illustrate important aspects of curriculum in this book.

Linda Hoffman and Diane Johnson spent many hours patiently typing endless pages of manuscript and references and attending to the myriad other details involved in the preparation of this book. We also owe thanks to our many colleagues at Rutgers University who created an atmosphere in which the Douglass Center could flourish and our scholarly efforts go forward. Jean L. Burton, Ruth S. Schulman, and Peter E. Nathan were particularly facilitative of our work. Florence Veniar and Larry Taft made important clinical contributions.

Our work would have been impossible without the gracious cooperation of hundreds of families over the years. Their willingness to collaborate with us in the education of their children, and to share a sense of the realities of their lives, taught us much of what we understand about the human issues that underlie life with a handicapped child.

Writing a book rarely stops at the end of the day. We owe special thanks to Elaine and Lauren Handleman for supporting their husband/father in this effort and for being so very patient regarding the many hours that had to be spent at the computer.

New Brunswick, NJ
March 1986

Chapter 1

Nature and Needs of the Developmentally Disabled

Case Report: Jake

It was late in the afternoon of the third day of the administrative hearing to determine Jake Long's appropriate educational classification and placement. The due process hearing had been initiated by Jake's parents, with representation from the state office of the public advocate. The first 2 days of the hearing had included testimony by child study personnel from the school district, who argued that Jake was a 5-year-old child best classified as eligible for day training and whose educational needs would be appropriately met at the county day training center. Independent professionals retained by the state office of the public advocate were preparing on this third day to testify that Jake was an autistic youngster who required a specialized program for the autistic.

Laying the groundwork for the evidence she was about to present, Jake's attorney offered an opening statement to the hearing officer. She emphasized that Jake was one of many children whose educational needs could not be reflected appropriately by a single classification. She indicated that she was prepared to demonstrate that as an autistic child Jake should be classified as multiply handicapped. She added that in the absence of an educational classification of autism the multiply handicapped category, although not totally accurate, was the most appropriate the state classification system had to offer.

The first professional called to the stand was a psychologist. Based on his observations and evaluation, he reported that Jake displayed many behaviors consistent with the diagnosis of autism. The onset of Jake's symptoms was before 30 months of age: he exhibited a relative indifference to other people, he had a severe language impairment, and he showed peculiar interest in inanimate objects. The psychologist stated that Jake was a child who needed considerable structure, a highly individualized program, and a curriculum focused on instructional control and language development.

During cross-examination, the attorney representing the school district tried to argue that Jake's primary handicap was his severe retardation. The psychologist replied by describing the differences between the autistic and the retarded with regard to etiology, deficits, and most importantly, educational needs.

The next professional to testify was a neurologist. She summarized the results of her neurological examination and stated that based on soft signs she diagnosed Jake's handicap as a neurological impairment with the characteristics of infantile autism. The neurologist emphasized that Jake should be immediately placed in an appropriate program. After the direct testimony the school-district attorney's cross-examination included questions about the appropriateness of the classification of neurological impairment in the absence of hard neurological evidence.

The final testimony, provided by the learning consultant, confirmed the diagnosis of autism and emphasized Jake's specialized needs. The consultant's outline of educational considerations included a highly structured one-to-one student-teacher ratio, a behavioral curriculum, and provision for parent involvement and year-round programming. During cross-examination the attorney attempted to redirect the discussion to classification rather than programming issues.

Summary statements were provided by both sides that afternoon. The school district confirmed their commitment to the classification of eligible for day training, whereas Jake's attorney continued to emphasize the difficulties of differential diagnosis and supported the multiply handicapped classification.

Case Commentary. Although the child is different in each case, the scenario just presented is a familiar one to administrators, clinicians, and teachers working with the developmentally disabled. Jake represents all youngsters who cannot readily be placed along the continuum of categories and classifications. In Jake's case his specific diagnosis of autism did not have an educational counterpart. The unfortunate result of such a gap in classification is the often lengthy due process procedure needed to classify and appropriately place developmentally disabled students.

As a consequence of the growing recognition of the difficulty in establishing differential diagnoses for handicapped children, more attention is being given to the concept of noncategorical educational placement. Furthermore, most professionals would agree that after sifting through the myriad of educational descriptions, the most important issue is an effective educational program and not the labeling of the child.

INTRODUCTION

Teachers, administrators, and other professionals are faced with the complex task of assessing developmentally disabled children to make educational plans. The task is especially challenging in light of the specialized needs of these students.

This chapter presents diagnostic criteria for developmental disabilities and focuses attention on the problem of differential diagnosis, specifically with the severely developmentally disabled. A delineation of behavioral characteristics is followed by a discussion of the needs of this population. School, home, and community needs are presented, and discussions include the issue of providing comprehensive programming through mainstreaming, extended-year programming, and parent training.

Although the following pages focus on specific handicapping conditions, an attempt is made to dissolve the boundaries between these conditions to facilitate a clearer view of needs as opposed to clinical descriptions. Within this framework it is hoped that assessment can follow a functional path and that attention can focus on educational programming.

HISTORICAL OVERVIEW

The current concept of developmental learning disabilities includes those cognitive or physically handicapping conditions that originate in early life and interfere with developmental progress. Most descriptions of developmental disabilities address the multiple handicaps of these youngsters and the comprehensive special education services necessary to support maximum growth (Powers and Handleman, 1984).

The success of President Kennedy's Panel on Mental Retardation in 1961 accelerated professional and public interest in the developmentally disabled. For example, the 1960s witnessed the allocation of federal funds for the creation of programs for the mentally retarded. Eventually, political and professional interest expanded to include other related handicapping conditions beyond mental retardation.

In 1974 the term *developmental disabilities* was legalized in Public Law 94-103. This legislation defined the condition as a disorder attributable to autism, cerebral palsy, epilepsy, or mental retardation. Four years later in 1978 Public Law 95-602 abandoned the categorical definition and described developmental disabilities in terms of functional limitations. According to the 1978 definition, the term *developmental disability* refers to a severe, chronic disability that

- is attributable to a mental or physical impairment or combination of mental and physical impairments;
- is manifested before the person attains age 22;
- is likely to continue indefinitely;
- results in substantial functional limitation in three or more of the following areas of major life activity: (i) self care, (ii) receptive and expressive language, (iii) learning, (iv) mobility, (v) self-direction, (vi) capacity for independent living, and (vii) economic sufficiency; and
- reflects the person's need for special services that are lifelong or extended duration and are individually planned and coordinated. (PL 95-602)

Throughout the early 1970s legislative activity regarding the developmentally disabled continued to grow. As the result of increasing parent advocacy during this period, a variety of developmentally disabled children with diverse severe and profound handicaps were loosely grouped. The Bureau of Education for the Handicapped of the U.S. Office of Education offered the following description:

> Severely handicapped children are those who, because of the intensity of their physical, mental, or emotional problems or a combination of such problems, need education, social, psychological, and medical service beyond those which are traditionally offered by regular and special education programs, in order to maximize their full potential for useful and meaningful participation in society and for self-fulfillment. Such children include those classified as seriously emotionally disturbed (schizophrenic and autistic), profoundly and severely mentally retarded, and those with two or more serious handicapping conditions such as the mentally retarded-blind and the cerebral palsied-deaf.
>
> Such severely handicapped children may possess severe language and/or perceptual cognitive deprivations and evidence a number of abnormal behaviors including: failure to attend to even the most pronounced social stimuli, self-stimulation, self-mutilation, manifestation of durable and intense temper tantrums, and the absence of even the most rudimentary of forms of verbal control, and may also have an extremely fragile physiological condition. (PL95-602,121.2,1974)

Originally, the term *severely and profoundly handicapped* was used to describe a population of children excluded from traditional programs because of their extensive deficits (Van Etten, Arkell, and Van Etten, 1980). Because of their diverse educational needs, there is increasing interest in placing these children along a continuum of developmental disabilities and in referring to them as the severely developmentally disabled (Handleman, 1986; Powers and Handleman, 1984).

THE CONTINUUM OF DEVELOPMENTAL DISABILITIES

The concept underlying the term *developmental disabilities* is multidimensional. The interaction of etiology, age of onset, and deficit results in various levels of functioning (Thompson and O'Quinn, 1979). These varied manifestations support the 1978 functional definition as opposed to categorical descriptions.

Whether primary or secondary, retarded functioning is characteristic of all developmentally disabled persons (Handleman, in press). Although the widely used classification system of the American Association on Mental Deficiency (Grossman, 1983) classifies these individuals as mentally retarded, the same notion of a continuum of intellectual functioning can be applied to other developmentally disabled learners. There are those children with seizure disorders who are fully mainstreamed, children with cerebral palsy who are placed in classes for the educable mentally retarded, and autisticlike youngsters attending day training facilities. Focusing attention on the specific learning deficits and assets of the developmentally disabled can facilitate individualized, needs-based educational programming.

Of recent interest are those children who represent the severe portion of the continuum. As a result of confusion over terminology regarding children with impairments diagnosed as autism, severe mental retardation, and multiple handicaps, many professionals have opted to group these youngsters as *severely developmentally disabled* (Handleman, 1986; Powers and Handleman, 1984). The inclusion of these children under the umbrella of developmental disabilities has clarified understanding of these students and has allowed assessment and educational planning to be linked in a more meaningful way.

The behaviors of severely developmentally disabled children may be influenced by environmental or organic factors that are different from those that influence the behaviors of other developmentally disabled children (Powers and Handleman, 1984). The varied descriptions of these youngsters suggest that the population is behaviorally heterogeneous, and professionals tend to view the disorder as a constellation of common characteristics shared by a particular group of children and not as a separate diagnostic entity (Powers and Handleman, 1984).

Although the fields of psychology and education continue to develop effective strategies for educating the severely developmentally disabled, biomedical research is expanding the understanding of these youngsters (Cohen and Shaywitz, 1982). For example, the cause of severe developmental disability is probably multifactorial (Coleman, 1976; Fish and Ritvo, 1978) and includes factors such as prenatal and postnatal trauma, metabolic diseases, and viral infections (Ciaranello, Vandenberg, and Anders, 1982). Many of the characteristics of these children probably reflect central nervous system dysfunction (Ciaranello et al., 1982; Maurer and Damasio, 1982). The recent detection of high serotonin levels in some retarded and autistic children (Young, Kavanagh, Anderson, Shaywitz, and Cohen, 1982) and the possibility of genetic and cogenital influences (Meryash, Szymanski, and Gerald, 1982) has also attracted interest.

DIAGNOSIS AND DIFFERENTIAL DIAGNOSIS

Because of the behavioral heterogeneity of the developmentally disabled population, diagnosis is an intricate process (Johnson and Koegel, 1982; Shea and Mesibov, 1985). Age of onset, organicity, and environmental influence all enter into diagnostic decision making. Furthermore, the child's lack of speech, negativistic responding, and noncompliant behavior make assessment difficult.

Diagnosis is facilitated when a specific organic cause can be determined (Powers and Handleman, 1984). Developmentally disabled children with cerebral palsy, spina bifida, or other cogenital or acquired physiological conditions can be recognized fairly easily. Similarly, children with viral histories such as maternal rubella (German measles) or genetic conditions such as tuberous sclerosis or fragile X syndrome can often be identified prenatally (DeLaCruz, 1985). Nonetheless, it is the majority of children with unknown causes who challenge a professional's diagnostic skills.

Developmentally disabled children with subtle neurological dysfunction, for example, have historically challenged the diagnostic process (Swanson and Watson, 1982). Those youngsters with clear neurological trauma or dysfunction (Coleman, Romano, Lapman, and Simon, 1985; Garreau, Barthelemy, Sauvage, Leddet, and LeLord, 1985) can be easily identified. However, those children with "soft" neurological signs have met various responses from the medical community. Some neurologists will classify a child as neurologically impaired on the basis of soft signs such as hyperactivity and distractibility, whereas others will rely only on hard evidence such as a brain lesion. These inconsistencies in labeling behaviorally similar children create placement and programming difficulties.

The severely developmentally disabled present additional challenges for the diagnostician. Specifically, there is concern about the exact boundaries of disorders such as severe mental retardation, autism, and multiple handicaps (Powers and Handleman, 1984). For example, professional discussions on autism are marked by varied opinions regarding primary diagnostic criteria (Rutter, 1979; Tinbergen and Tinbergen, 1972). This confusion is also seen in clinical accounts of different problems attributed to the severely developmentally disabled population.

According to some authors, there is a valid distinction between disorders such as autism and mental retardation (Powers and Handleman, 1984); many others suggest that these conditions coexist and share many similarities (Lockyer and Rutter, 1969; Schopler, 1966). For example, diagnosis with both populations is problematic and both groups exhibit a variety of psychological and physical characteristics (Snell and Renzaglia, 1982). Also, few retarded and autistic children have a single handicap, and it is difficult to determine precise causes for many of the children (Van Etten et al., 1980).

The close legal relationship between autism, mental retardation, and multiple handicapping conditions created by the 1974 federal definition of developmental disabilities has resulted in an appreciation of the many similar needs of these children. Although there are numerous discussions about the accurate diagnosis of autism and mental retardation, concerns have been reduced somewhat by including these conditions under the more general category of severe developmental disabilities (Handleman, 1986; Powers and Handleman, 1984). Lovaas (1981) reported that severely developmentally disabled children share deficits in communication, social, and cognitive areas. Focusing attention on the functional characteristics of these children can facilitate more precise assessment and promote more accurate educational programming.

DIAGNOSTIC CRITERIA

Examination of the prominent views on developmental disabilities and the 1978 federal definition suggest four general areas of learning deficits (Powers and Handleman, 1984): (1) communication disorders, (2) problems of interpersonal responsiveness and social development, (3) information processing difficulties, and (4) developmental delays and associated cognitive disorders. Table 1-1 presents a summary of general and specific diagnostic criteria.

Table 1-1.   Summary of Diagnostic Criteria for Developmental Disabilities

Communication Disorders
  Disorders of articulation
  Disorders of voice
  Absence of speech
  Echolalic speech
  Reversals of word order
  Sing-song speech patterns
  Pronoun reversals
  Receptive language deficits

Problems of Interpersonal Responsiveness and Social Development
  Lack of motivation
  Limited interest
  Poor impulse control
  Resistance to change
  Avoidance of eye contact
  Self-stimulatory behavior
  Aggressiveness
  Self-injury
  Tantrums
  Little curiosity

Information Processing Difficulties
  Discrimination difficulty
  Memory problems
  Association difficulties
  Perseveration
  Overselective responding
  Self-stimulation
  Self-injurious behavior
  Insensitivity to pain

Developmental Delays and Associated Cognitive Disorders
  Developmental delays
  Toilet training delays
  Poor self-help abilities
  Limited play

Communication Disorders

The difficulties that developmentally disabled children demonstrate with the acquisition and development of communication skills is well documented (Harris, 1975; Lovaas, 1981; Tager-Flushberg, 1985). The literature provides many accounts of the various degrees of difficulty with both the structural and interpersonal aspects of communication by the developmentally disabled (Powers and Handleman, 1984). These children typically have problems with the mechanics of speech or the more complex skills of comprehension.

There are three major categories of communication disorders displayed by developmentally disabled learners. Many youngsters demonstrate disorders of articulation in which distortions, substitutions, additions, or omissions may characterize their speech (Kirk and Gallagher, 1979). Disorders of voice such as vocal pitch, voice quality, and volume are also prominent among these students (Carrow-Woolfolk and Lynch, 1982). The third category of communication disorders includes those difficulties that are associated with the interpersonal aspect of communication and that affect the sharing and exchange of information (Carrow-Woolfolk and Lynch, 1982; Kirk and Gallagher, 1983).

Common language deficits of the severely developmentally disabled include the complete absence of speech, echolalic speech, singsong speech patterns, word order reversals, and pronoun reversals (Hinerman, Jenson, Walker, and Petersen, 1982). Many retarded and multiply handicapped youngsters demonstrate difficulty with both the semantic and syntactic elements of language (Cromer, 1981) and have problems generalizing within language classes such as plural formations and descriptive adjectives (Handleman, 1979a, 1981b, 1986). Those who develop speech display language disorders in such areas as emotional expression, speech delivery, inflection, sequencing, abstraction, and memory (Lockyer and Rutter, 1969; Rutter, 1970, 1979).

Problems of Interpersonal Responsiveness and Social Development

The difficulties that developmentally disabled students demonstrate with communication are often compounded by problems with interpersonal relationships and other social experiences (Thompson and O'Quinn, 1979). Issues regarding motivation, impulse control, and interpersonal attending are also important for this population. In addition, behavior management and social skills training are often essential components of educational plans.

Deficits in social and interpersonal development are endemic to the severely developmentally disabled population (Powers and Handleman, 1984). For example, it is not uncommon for severely developmentally disabled children to exhibit maladaptive behaviors (Johnson, Baumeister, Penland, and Inwald, 1982). Many of these youngsters insist on environmental sameness (Baumeister, 1978; Birnbrauer, 1979), avoid eye contact (Harris, 1975; Howlin, 1978), or prefer objects to people (O'Gorman, 1967).

Most severely developmentally disabled children also lack interest in socially appropriate activities (Johnson and Koegel, 1982; Powers and Handleman, 1984). There are many reports that describe these children as being unmotivated (Carr, E. G., 1985), preferring self-stimulatory activities such as rocking or hand waving (Devany and Rincover, 1982), and engaging in self-injurious behaviors (Edelson, 1984; Wiesler, Hanson, Chamberlain, and Thompson, 1985). In addition, the developmentally disabled student usually demonstrates little curiosity (Koegel and Schreibman, 1976).

Self-injurious behavior (SIB), a matter of great concern, has been linked to interpersonal attention (Lovaas and Simmons, 1969) or avoidance (Carr, Newsom, and Binkoff, 1976). In severely developmentally disabled children SIB is considered by many as the most dangerous form of psychopathology (Cataldo and Harris, 1982; Russo, Carr, and Lovaas, 1980; Schroeder, Schroeder, Rojahn, and Mulick, 1981). The self-injurious acts of these children range from head banging to self-hitting and self-scratching.

Information Processing Difficulties

Considerable attention has been directed toward the information processing deficits of the developmentally disabled (Kirk and Gallagher, 1983; Koegel, Dunlap, Richman, and Dyer, 1981). Developmentally disabled children may experience difficulty with processing auditory or visual information and translating that sensory input into vocal or physical responses. These information processing deficits have been linked to the children's academic difficulties (Chalfant and Scheffelin, 1969).

The skills of discrimination, awareness, association, and memory are problematic for most developmentally disabled students. There are many reports of the difficulties that mentally retarded youngsters demonstrate with memory tasks (Kirk and Gallagher, 1983), and the central processing deficits of the multiply handicapped are well documented (Van Etten et al., 1980). Also, the difficulty of processing complex environmental stimuli by severely developmentally disabled children is widely recognized (Powers and Handleman, 1984).

Inconsistent response to sensory stimulation is considered a primary characteristic of autistic and other severely developmentally disabled children (Powers and Handleman, 1984; Schopler, 1978). The phenomenon of stimulus overselectivity, for example, is a manifestation of difficulty in responding to environmental stimuli. Severely developmentally disabled learners who show this characteristic may perseverate on a single stimulus to the exclusion of others (Boucher, 1977; Hermelin, 1971) or respond to a narrow range of informational input (Kolko, Anderson, and Campbell, 1980; Lovaas, Koegel, and Schreibman, 1979). Inconsistent responding is also exemplified by the pervasive deficits in generalization demonstrated by these children (Handleman, 1979a, 1981b; Rincover and Koegel, 1975). The inability to transfer learning from one situation to another is often observed with novel instructors or new settings or from the school to the home (Handleman, 1979a, 1981b; Powers and Handleman, 1984).

The difficulties that the severely developmentally disabled display with information processing have also been related to self-stimulation and self-injury. Many authors have reported the educationally disruptive effects of self-stimulatory acts (Devany and Rincover, 1982; Eason, White, and Newsom, 1982), and some researchers have suggested that this behavior is controlled by sensory consequences (Rincover, 1978; Rincover, Newsom, and Carr, 1979). Self-injurious behavior (Baumeister and Forehand, 1973; Favell, McGimsey, and Schell, 1982) and the insensitivity to pain exhibited by some severely developmentally disabled children (Johnson and Koegel, 1982) have also been described as forms of sensory stimulation.

Developmental Delays and Associated Cognitive Disorders

The 1978 definition of developmental disabilities highlights the learning problems of these children. The developmentally disabled learner may have difficulty integrating perceptual and cognitive processes. Such deficits have been manifested on paired associate tasks, in short- and long-term memory and in concept formation (Carter, Alpert, and Stewart, 1982). The severely developmentally disabled student may also demonstrate developmental delays and discontinuity (Donnellan, Gossage, LaVigna, Schuler, and Traphagan, 1977; Powers and Handleman, 1984).

The severely developmentally disabled demonstrate many skill deficiencies (Johnson and Koegel, 1982), and as these children grow older the discrepancy between chronological age and developmental level tends to increase (Brown, Branston, Hamre-Nietupski, Pumpian, Certo, and Gruenwald, 1979). Many of these children are not toilet trained when they enter school, lack self-help capabilities, and fail to engage in appropriate play. Although severe developmental disabilities are typically associated with retarded functioning, splinter skills in various areas may be evident (Donnellan et al., 1977).

NEEDS OF THE DEVELOPMENTALLY DISABLED

Service delivery to developmentally disabled students is an intricate task. Their diversity of needs extends beyond traditional educational concerns to include the home environment and community settings. A summary of educational, home, and community needs is presented in Table 1-2.

Educational Needs

The need for a comprehensive service delivery system for the developmentally disabled is well documented (Janicki, Lubin, and Friedman, 1983; Thompson and O'Quinn, 1979). The specialized educational requirements of these children necessitate attention from an array of highly specialized professionals. This multidisciplinary approach to diagnosis, assessment, and planning allows educational programming to focus on the individual needs of the student.

The range of possible functional limitations of the children outlined by the 1978 federal definition of developmental disabilities requires multidisciplinary input for assessment. Medicine, speech and language, occupational therapy, physical therapy, social work, psychology, and education are some of the contributors to educational decision making and assessment. Each area plays a vital role in diagnostic and assessment practices and determines the parameters of curriculum, teaching strategies, and educational materials.

Within the broad category of developmental disabilities, the severely developmentally disabled student requires further specialized attention (Powers and Handleman, 1984). Active and structured programming is often suggested to promote optimal progress (Powers and Handleman, 1984; Schreibman and Koegel, 1981), and a curriculum that includes instructional control, communication, academics, self-help, and daily living is characteristic of many programs (Devany and Rincover, 1982; Lovaas, 1981). Furthermore, behavioral techniques are typically used to facilitate learning and to manage the disruptive behaviors demonstrated by many severely developmentally disabled students (Carr, E.G., and Durand, 1985; Koegel and Williams, 1980).

Although the effectiveness of behavioral techniques for teaching severely developmentally disabled children has been widely documented (Powers and Handleman, 1984; Harris, 1975), there remain certain educational challenges. For example, it is recognized that it is difficult to teach these youngsters to communicate spontaneously (Bricker and Bricker, 1979; Stremel, 1972). Current programming efforts to increase spontaneity focus on reducing a child's reliance on verbal prompts from others and attempt to enhance the child's use of cues in the physical environment for speech (Sosne, Handleman, and Harris, 1979).

Table 1-2. Needs of the Developmentally Disabled

Educational Needs
Comprehensive services
Multidisciplinary planning
Structured programming
Special techniques
Home Needs
Parent training
Advocacy
Family support services
Community Needs
Mainstreaming opportunities
Community participation
Respite care

Another educational concern involves the pervasive problem that many severely developmentally disabled students demonstrate with generalization and maintenance of behavior (Egel, Shafer, and Neef, 1985; Haring, T., 1985). Early reports described these children as bound to the physical elements of the teaching structure and therefore unable to transfer learning from one situation to another or maintain behavior changes (Hamilton, 1966). Although generalization and maintenance by severely developmentally disabled children may not be automatic, there are techniques that can enhance the transfer of learning and durability of responding. For example, providing a child with a variety of instructors can increase generalization to novel teachers (Garcia, 1974; Kale, Kaye, Whelan, and Hopkins, 1968) and using varied teaching settings can enhance the transfer of learning to new instructional situations (Griffiths and Craighead, 1972; Jackson and Wallace, 1974). The results of recent research have indicated that generalization to settings such as the home and new educational placements can be facilitated by teaching in a variety of settings (Handleman, 1979a, 1981b; Handleman and Harris, 1980, 1983). Improved maintenance of responding has been facilitated by the use of continuous review, the use of parent tutors, and the manipulation of schedules and reinforcement during training (Koegel and Rincover, 1977; Lancioni, 1983).

The last two decades have witnessed an increase in the availability of basic educational services for the severely developmentally disabled student. Current attention is now focused on the provision of more comprehensive educational programming. For example, although recent legal decisions and research have argued that there is a compelling need for a year-round educational program for these children (*Armstrong v. Kline*, 1979; *Battle v. Commonwealth*, 1980), many educators and administrators are struggling with the implementation of this concept (Handleman and Harris, 1984; Lehr and Haubrich, 1985). Similarly, administrative and educational discussions have turned to issues of preschool education and full-day programming (Powers and Handleman, 1984).

Home Needs

Parents of developmentally disabled children play many roles. In an environment of improving services parents often assume the role of advocate to ensure their child's rights and access to effective programs. Parents of the developmentally disabled are also partners in an increasingly complex and intricate service delivery network. In addition, they often play the role of teacher, attempting to maximize the educational opportunities for their children.

Teaching parents of the developmentally disabled to work with their children at home can directly reinforce school programming and facilitate the teaching of self-help and daily living skills (Eheart and Nakamura, 1984; Kozloff, 1975). Home programming also facilitates the transfer of treatment gains from the school to the home (Handleman, 1979a).

The home needs of the severely developmentally disabled child extend to all family members (Lobato, 1983; Vadasy, Meyer, Fewell, and Greenberg, 1985). The disruption to normal family functioning and added stress placed on the family create a need for comprehensive family services (Harris, 1983; Powers and Handleman, 1984). Support, training, and educational services can provide the framework for a service delivery system that is sensitive to the complex needs of the family.

The families of the severely developmentally disabled are a valuable resource that can provide the extensive review, repetition, and reinforcement of behavior that is crucial to educational efforts (Harris, 1983; McClannahan, Krantz, and McGee, 1982). Parents can extend and support programming in many curricular areas and provide experiences necessary for the practical application of skills in home and community settings.

Community Needs

Public Law 94-142 has directed attention toward community-based services for the developmentally disabled. Concepts such as least restrictive placement, mainstreaming, and normalization are common in the literature and reflect the philosophy that all handicapped learners have the right to the most normalized community-based educational placement possible (Deno, E.N., 1973; Wolfensberger, 1975).

The mainstreaming movement is as important for the developmentally disabled learner as it is for any other student (Handleman and Harris, 1983). Although mainstreaming may be difficult (Poorman, 1980), viewing the concept in terms of integrating the handicapped with less handicapped learners extends participation to all developmentally disabled children (Handleman and Harris, 1983). This broadened view of mainstreaming can also allow the severely developmentally disabled student access to less structured and more normalized educational environments. Designing strategies for the preparation of developmentally disabled children for placements previously deemed inappropriate because of the nature of their difficulties must therefore become a goal of programming (Handleman, 1979b; Jenkins, Speltz, and Odom, 1985).

Community-based services are enhancing the lives of a growing number of developmentally disabled individuals (Gilhool, 1978). Additional support for this movement is evidenced by the increasing consensus that community-based residential settings are more appropriate than institutional placements (Ferleger and Boyd, 1979; Seltzer and Krauss, 1985). Also, recent years have witnessed a growth in respite care services for the developmentally disabled to support continued community participation and possibly avoid institutionalization (Townsend and Flanagan, 1976; Upshur, 1982a).

SUMMARY

The diagnosis, assessment, and treatment of developmentally disabled children are among the more challenging issues facing educators, administrators, and clinicians. As described in the case of Jake Long that opened this chapter, the range of professional descriptions for the population often burdens the classification and placement process. The diversity of educational needs demonstrated by the developmentally disabled complicates the full range of service delivery from identification to educational programming.

The 1978 federal definition of developmental disabilities refocused professional thinking on the functional limitations of the students. The notion of a continuum of disabilities provides a framework for describing the heterogeneity of the population. Increasing support for the umbrella term *severe developmental disabilities* has created a grouping of individuals, whose impairments traditionally were diagnosed differentially, that is beginning to facilitate more appropriate diagnosis and treatment.

Although diverse in their limitations, the developmentally disabled appear to share common characteristics. Deficits in communication and interpersonal relationships are demonstrated by most students, and information processing difficulties and developmental delays are displayed by many developmentally disabled learners. This emphasis on the functional aspects of the disability allows educational placement to be guided by instructional planning.

The needs of the developmentally disabled are many and varied and extend beyond the school to both the home and the community. The intricacies of educational planning require input from many professionals with specialized training, and educational planning needs to be cooperative and comprehensive. An important partner in this process is the parent who serves both as advocate and as teacher. As mainstreaming opportunities for the developmentally disabled have grown, attention has also focused on providing these individuals with the resources necessary to support community participation.

As the history of developmental disabilities continues to evolve, the outcome of situations for students like Jake Long may change. For example, the growing interest in noncategorical service delivery is beginning to affect educational decision making by emphasizing the child's needs rather than classification. As a result of this shift in focus, educational planning has a better chance of remaining in the schools and out of the courtrooms.

Chapter 2

Service Options for the Developmentally Disabled

Case Report: Brenda

All of the evaluations on Brenda Rotter were completed and the child study team had convened a meeting with Brenda's parents to discuss placement options. Brenda, a 5-year-old developmentally disabled youngster, had recently moved to the school district after completing a state operated preschool program

The meeting began with brief summaries from the participating professionals. The school psychologist described Brenda as a student of borderline intellectual potential who had difficulties with social interactions. Some immaturity was reported, along with occasional outbursts of temper. The learning consultant confirmed Brenda's adjustment problems and estimated an approximately 12-month delay in achievement. Additional deficits in verbal expression and fine motor abilities were described. The report of the neurological examination indicated no evidence of neurological dysfunction.

The school social worker indicated that the team members felt Brenda required a structured educational environment rich in academic and social experiences. Important considerations included small groupings with opportunity for individualized instruction and availability of interactions with less handicapped students. It was also noted that Brenda's behavioral difficulties would best respond to behavior modification.

The school social worker reviewed the various school visits with Mr. and Mrs. Rotter. The advantages and disadvantages of an in-district self-contained class were compared with those of a class in a nearby community. Although the children in the district's class were somewhat lower functioning than Brenda, the classroom was housed in the same school as the team's office, which would allow for closer monitoring. The teacher of the class was also well trained in the use of behavior management techniques, and the school psychologist would be readily available for consultation.

A possible placement at a local private school was also discussed. A lengthy discussion about the private placement focused on the low student to teacher ratio that could be offered Brenda. The school psychologist, while confirming the advantage of the smaller grouping, expressed concern for the segregated programming and limited contact with less handicapped peers. Transitional services were just being developed for the program, and it would take a few years to organize appropriate community contacts.

Mrs. Rotter asked the team to elaborate on the related services Brenda would receive in the district class. After describing the curriculum for the class, the learning consultant discussed the type of experiences Brenda would have in the resource room. Brenda would visit the resource room daily and work with the teacher individually on academic readiness activities and on fine motor development. The learning consultant also indicated that Brenda would meet with the speech pathologist three times per week. In addition, the psychologist said that he would meet with Brenda's teacher weekly to discuss behavior management strategies.

A decision was reached to place Brenda in the district's self-contained class. There was agreement that the placement would offer Brenda the comprehensive services that could be closely monitored by the child study team. Although it was believed that the private program might provide a more tightly structured program, the segregated nature of that setting was viewed as a limiting factor. Future consideration of the private class would be made if Brenda experienced difficulties in the district class.

Case Commentary. The events surrounding Brenda's placement are familiar to most parents of the developmentally disabled and to those professionals responsible for making decisions about educational planning. The complexity of diagnosis and assessment discussed in Chapter 1 typically results in an elaborate placement process. Many variables need to be considered when securing appropriate placements; curriculum, student to teacher ratio, and related services are among the many elements that enter into the decision-making process. As depicted in Brenda's situation, parent input and participation are also important components.

The complex needs of the developmentally disabled may necessitate programming demands that exceed those services available in the public schools. For those students the private sector may provide the comprehensive educational programming that is required. There are many factors to assess when considering a private placement. In Brenda's case the final decision was based on careful consideration of her individual needs.

INTRODUCTION

The developmentally disabled student continues to challenge the educational system with regard to placement. As the result of the diversity of need, the placement options are many. Successful and appropriate placement requires careful planning and the cooperation of professionals and parents.

The developmentally disabled are provided services in many settings. This chapter describes a continuum of services offered in both public and private settings. Discussions include rationale for private placements and the problems and pitfalls of public education. Attention also focuses on the least restrictive placement option and on strategies to facilitate mainstreaming and transition from highly structured environments to more normal educational settings. The parent-professional partnership is repeatedly cited as an important feature of the placement process.

In the arena of educational placements the severely developmentally disabled child continues to require special attention. Location, staffing, and related services are among the variables that need to be considered by administrators and educators. This chapter addresses those special considerations and provides guidelines for the selection of an appropriate placement.

A CONTINUUM OF SERVICE OPTIONS

The concept of a continuum of special education services is well documented (Kirk and Gallagher, 1979). Probably the most popular of the service delivery models is E. N. Deno's (1973) "cascade of education services." Deno's (1973) presentation of service options provides a framework from which to assess mainstreaming and normalization experiences for exceptional children. Most importantly, the continuum of services presented by E. N. Deno and others offers a menu of placement options for these children. Table 2–1 presents the range of educational settings available to the developmentally disabled student.

Full-Time Regular Class Placement

Some developmentally disabled students can benefit from the diverse range of educational experiences offered in the regular class. The child's learning or behavioral difficulty can be comfortably addressed with traditional staffing patterns, curriculum, and teaching methodology. Occasional assistance and monitoring by child study

Table 2-1.   Service Options for Developmentally Disabled Students

Full-time regular class
Part-time regular class
Part-time special class
Full-time special class
Special school
Community-based residential program
Segregated residential program

personnel might be necessary to support successful full-time class placement.

Part-Time Regular Class Placement

For some developmentally disabled youngsters the regular classroom can provide normalized educational challenges with the appropriate supportive services. For example, a particular student might require supplemental or resource room instruction for the remediation of learning deficits. This blend of instructional settings can support regular class placement and provide needed individualized instruction.

Part-Time Special Class Placement

The specialized learning needs of many developmentally disabled students require educational programming that goes beyond the regular classroom. The need for smaller groupings and special teaching methodologies may result in primary placement in a self-contained special education classroom. There are a group of students, however, who can benefit to different degrees from partial integration in the regular education mainstream. This participation can take the form of resource room instruction or attendance in some portion of the regular curriculum such as physical education or reading instruction.

Full-Time Special Class Placement

There is a group of developmentally disabled children who exclusively require the specialized attention offered by a special education classroom. Lower student to teacher ratios, special teacher training, and methodologies are some of the components of the self-contained classroom that best support the needs of this group of children. The special education class within the public school setting can also provide the student with exposure to less restrictive education and possible participation in normalization activities.

Special School Placement

When the learning requirements of the developmentally disabled student are very specialized, a special school placement might be necessary. This type of educational setting can provide an environment that is entirely supportive to the needs of the student. Curriculum, professional consultation, and supportive services can all be specifically designed for the school population. Many severely developmentally disabled children require the specialization that this type of environment can offer. For many children the special school can provide a springboard to less segregated and more normalized settings.

Community-Based Residential Placement

A decision to place a child in a residential setting is multifaceted. Age of child, educational needs, family considerations, and finances are some of the major variables that enter into the decision. Once a decision is made, the community-based residence has become a very attractive option to both parents and professionals. The group home setting can provide a 24-hour specialized supportive environment. This combination of effective day programming and residential life has successfully supported community participation by many severely developmentally disabled individuals.

Segregated Residential Placement

There are some developmentally disabled children whose multiple handicaps and environmental conditions dictate alternative placements. For the child with extensive medical requirements, homebound or hospital instruction might be necessary. In those situations in which a community-based residence is not available or possible, placement in a residential school might be sought. Also, for reasons ranging from lack of appropriate resources to state guardianship, some severely developmentally disabled children are placed in state schools or hospitals.

MOVEMENT ALONG THE CONTINUUM: THE ISSUES OF MAINSTREAMING AND TRANSITION

An important aspect of E. N. Deno's (1973) cascade is the provision for upward movement to other placement levels according to educational need. This component adds flexibility to a service delivery model that traditionally has been rigid with regard to the boundaries of instructional placements and movement within the system. A service delivery system that is based on changing educational needs can be more responsive to the requirements of developmentally disabled students (Handleman, 1984).

The least restrictive placement option mandated by PL 94–142 and the normalization principle proposed by Wolfensberger (1975) provide useful criteria for assessing movement along the service delivery continuum (Powers and Handleman, 1984). Planning for appropriate integrative experiences, therefore, becomes as important as other curricular considerations for developmentally disabled students. The foundation of a mainstreaming effort is cemented when the need for normalization is recognized and community participation is encouraged.

Although mainstreaming is widely discussed and has been successful with many populations of exceptional children including the emotionally disturbed (Vac, 1968), mildly retarded (Gallagher, 1972), and learning disabled (Glass and Meckler, 1972), difficulty has been encountered when attempting to apply the mainstreaming concept to severely developmentally disabled learners (Handleman, 1984; Koegel, Rincover, and Russo, 1982). The learning and behavioral difficulties demonstrated by these children may preclude mainstreaming in the traditional sense of the concept. Broadening the notion of mainstreaming, however, to be the integration of the handicapped learner with less handicapped as opposed to normal students can increase the implementation of the concept for all children (Handleman, 1984; Stainback, Stainback, Courtnage, and Jaben, 1985). Although many professionals wish to view the severely developmentally disabled as normally as possible, the physical integration of such students into the most normal mainstream remains problematic (Poorman, 1980).

Because severely developmentally disabled children require treatment components such as low student to teacher ratios and behavioral technology, many students are being served in specialized facilities (Handleman, 1981a). The systematic nature of programming has often resulted in distancing these programs from the mainstream of the community. Concern for the eventual reentry of the severely developmentally disabled student into the mainstream of public opportunity is, therefore, shared by many service providers (Harris and Handleman, 1980; Koegel, Rincover, and Russo, 1982). Many authors encourage the adoption of the normalization principle and the design of transition strategies when planning mainstreaming experiences for these students (Handleman, 1984).

Although the behavioral approach has been successful in teaching severely developmentally disabled learners a variety of skills, their problems of generalization, particularly to novel settings, remain (Powers and Handleman, 1984). Consequently, the transition of such students to more normal educational placements becomes an intricate task. The severely developmentally disabled child needs to be weaned from the intensive teaching structure to more normal environmental contingencies (Harris, 1975), and other strategies need to be designed to prepare them for less structured settings (Handleman, 1979b).

The framework for a mainstreaming effort for severely developmentally disabled children can be set in place with a highly individualized and increasingly diverse curriculum (Handleman, 1984; Harris and Handleman, 1980). Variables such as complexity of curriculum, number of staff, and reinforcement can be manipulated systematically as a student progresses through a carefully designed program (Powers and Handleman, 1984). For example, a child could be taught instructional control and basic skills in a tightly controlled entry level structure. After mastery of entry level skills the child could enter an intermediate level structure and be exposed to a less intensified and more normalized curriculum. Ultimately, the child could enter a transitional structure that provides a more diversified program and approximates a more normalized, community-based placement. Table 2–2 presents a variety of guidelines to consider when planning transitional experiences.

Preparation of severely developmentally disabled children for educational placements previously determined as inappropriate must be systematically planned and considered in the overall programming for each student (Handleman, 1979b, 1984). Those professionals currently involved with the child are often the best coordinators of the transition process. When a child begins the transitional year, attention can be directed toward the identification and selection of a new school program. Once a program has been selected, efforts focus on preparing both the child and the placement for the transition. For example, the current staff can begin to approximate the new environment and the new staff can familiarize themselves with effective methods and strategies for working with the child. The ultimate support of both administrators and professionals, however, will directly affect the success of the mainstreaming attempt (Handleman, 1984; Martin, 1974).

FINDING AN APPROPRIATE PLACEMENT

Securing an appropriate placement for a developmentally disabled student is an intricate, multilevel process requiring the cooperation

Table 2-2.   Guidelines for Transitional Programming

Transition From Entry to Intermediate Program
1. Can sit in a group of two for at least one 15-minute work session and remain seated during intertrial intervals
2. Can sustain a 3- to 4-second gaze upon request
3. Can maintain visual contact with various environmental objects for 3 to 4 seconds
4. Shows increase behavior to at least one primary or secondary reinforcer
5. Does not demonstrate life-threatening behaviors, and interfering behaviors respond to special intervention
6. Can respond to simple, one-step instructional commands
7. Can discriminate simple gross motor and a few fine motor movements.
8. Can identify concrete environmental objects
9. Can imitate sounds or sign movements
10. Can indicate some basic needs
11. Can demonstrate beginning self-help skills and responds to a diaper-free toileting schedule
12. Can orient to a greeting by an adult
13. Can occupy self constructively for short periods

Transition From Intermediate to Transition Program
1. Can sit in a two-student group and remain seated with no competing or disruptive behaviors for 25 minutes
2. Can orient to various classroom mediums, such as blackboards and work sheets
3. Can consistently sustain attention to task
4. Can respond to the earliest stages of a token economy
5. Does not require individual supervision
6. Can follow basic classroom commands
7. Can identify simple pictorial representations of objects
8. Can imitate simple words, signs, or gestures
9. Can identify simple nouns and verbs
10. Can consistently indicate basic needs
11. Can self-feed and undress completely and is accident-free on periodic toileting schedule
12. Can greet an adult and accept brief physical contacts from others without pulling away
13. Can complete simple matching, sorting, or completion tasks with limited prompting

Criteria for Out-of-Agency Placement
Criteria for transition will vary, depending on the selected placement. Size of group, contingencies for motivation and management, and independent functioning requirements are some variables to consider.

of parents and professionals (Handleman, 1984; Johnson and Koegel, 1982). Each of these very important partners in the placement process is interested in the student's well-being and committed to securing the most appropriate education. The search for a placement must be a well-tuned process and one flexible enough to accommodate opinions that are generated from different perspectives. Possible settings must be identified and visited and a placement selection agreed upon after a careful review and assessment of information. Once the placement is selected, the often lengthy admissions process can begin.

Although agreement regarding the most appropriate placement is important, it may be difficult to obtain. The placement process, although guided by state mandates, must be sensitive to the intricate interpersonal relationship between the school and the home. Mutual respect and understanding are important adjuncts to bureaucratic proceedings. Under conflicting circumstances the due process procedure mandated by PL 94-142 can assist resolution. Table 2–3 provides a glimpse at some of the elements of due process.

A classification report that includes program suggestions is needed to guide the placement search. Typically created by a child study team with input from parents, the classification report summarizes the findings of contributing professionals, indicates an educational classification, and offers placement and program recommendations. The program parameters set forth in the report are needed to assist the placement process and program development.

Identification of Possible Placements

The identification process involves gathering information about existing programs and visiting those that seem compatible with the needs of the individual student (Handleman, 1979b, 1984). Reviewing state or county generated lists of approved programs can provide a starting point. Similarly, consulting with state or national professional and parent organizations can help to focus the search. After a reading of school brochures and a reflection on phone contacts, a list of placement options can be generated.

Although policies regarding school visits may vary, it is helpful to arrange a visit that allows opportunity to observe classrooms and possibly meet with staff. Table 2–4 provides a checklist of important elements to consider when visiting a potential program. Information gathered from school visits can provide the foundation for selecting the appropriate program.

Selection of Educational Placement

Securing an optimal child-placement match is the goal of the placement process (Handleman, 1984). Analyzing the information gathered from pamphlets, meetings, and visits according to variables such as classification, class size, staff ratio, and curriculum priorities can help to narrow the range of program possibilities. Whenever possible having the child spend some time in a potential placement can assist in selecting an appropriate program.

There are a group of developmentally disabled students whose needs extend beyond the services provided within the public schools.

Table 2–3.   Due Process: Sequence of Events

Child study team review
District administration review
County review
Prehearing conference
Due process hearing

In an attempt to meet the needs of these students and provide specialized services to low-incidence populations, the private school community has grown. Guided by very specific regulations in many states, the private school has become a viable option for many developmentally disabled children. An important issue to consider when assessing the merits of a particular private program involves the provisions that are offered for eventual community participation.

Program Admissions

Once an appropriate program is agreed upon, the admissions process can be initiated. Although procedures vary across programs, in most instances the first step is completing an application. Parents of developmentally disabled students quickly become skilled at filling out various forms. Family background, birth history, and developmental background are common elements of most applications or intake forms. Many parents have found it useful to keep a notebook of important facts to assist this often lengthy, repetitive task.

An important component of the admissions process for many programs is a family interview and child evaluation. During the interview items on the intake form are clarified and a preliminary assessment of educational and family needs is initiated. The evaluation of the child provides the staff with a sample of the applicant's abilities and a glimpse at deficiencies. Recognizing that a novel setting is stressful for many children, some programs also include an observation of the child in a more comfortable setting such as the home or current placement.

The limited nature of the intake process does not always support the formation of an entirely accurate picture of a child. As a result of the limited time and scope of this initial evaluation, it is important to ensure optimal conditions during an intake process. A preevaluation introduction to school can be useful, as can having the child accompanied by a familiar professional to facilitate maximum performance.

Table 2-4.   Potential Placement Considerations

Program Information
Orientation: academic versus prevocational
Availability of long-term placement (e.g., vocational)
Programming more comprehensive than that offered at present placement
Population of students: presence of peer models to provide increased language stimulation and socialization
Class size and student to teacher ratio
Availability of ancillary services: physical therapy, speech and language therapy, occupational and recreational therapy

Administration
Willingness to assist in a smooth transition by providing opportunities for the student and teacher to interact in targeted setting
Willingness to cooperate in postplacement follow-up and evaluation
Provision of support systems for staff

Teaching Staff
Training, understanding, and willingness to provide individualized programming in academics, language, social skills, and life skills
Training, understanding, and willingness to use behavior modification techniques
Low staff turnover rate, especially in targeted class

Parental Involvement
Availability of family services (e.g., parent training, support groups)

SELECTING AN APPROPRIATE PROGRAM FOR THE SEVERELY DEVELOPMENTALLY DISABLED STUDENT

The complex needs of the severely developmentally disabled student dictate special considerations when selecting appropriate educational programs (Lovaas, 1981; Powers and Handleman, 1984). The ongoing interplay between school, home, and community concerns necessitates programming that is highly individual, yet diverse enough to meet the often immediate and changing needs of the students (Johnson and Koegel, 1982). These special education requirements are increasingly being met in very specialized programs (Handleman, 1984).

There are numerous discussions addressing the effective treatment of severely developmentally disabled children (Johnson and Koegel, 1982; Lovaas, 1981). Curriculum, staffing, methods, and materials are a few of the variables that are considered important to discussions of appropriate programming. A very useful collection of criteria for identifying appropriate programs is presented by the New Jersey Task Force on Autism (Appendix 2-A). These guidelines focus on the important program components that support comprehensive and intensive educational programming required by severely developmentally disabled students.

Specialized Services

The severely developmentally disabled student requires very specialized services (Handleman, 1986; Wing and Wing, 1971). The curriculum of the program must be highly individualized and must include activities that are appropriate to the student's needs. It is also important that necessary ancillary services such as speech or physical therapy be available to individual students.

Intensive Programming

Autistic and other severely developmentally disabled children require intensive, prolonged, and uninterrupted education (Handleman, 1984; Powers and Handleman, 1984). Full-day programming ensures maximal intervention and extended-year schooling provides the continuity necessary to avoid regression during the summer months (Handleman and Harris, 1984).

Data-Based Treatment

The efficacy of data-based treatment for severely developmentally disabled children is well documented (Koegel, Russo, Rincover, and Schreibman, 1982; Powers and Handleman, 1984). Ongoing measurement and record keeping maintain a high level of accountability and facilitate performance monitoring.

Family Involvement

The involvement of families of severely developmentally disabled children promotes maximal intervention and insures program continuity (Harris, 1983). Furthermore, the active participation by families helps facilitate generalization of newly acquired skills (Handleman, 1979a).

Accreditation

Adhering to standardized criteria and legal guidelines demonstrates a professional posture regarding the provision of services to the severely developmentally disabled. Accreditation by the department of education or another state agency can help ensure program accountability. Also, an effective governing body can further enhance program administration.

Staff Training

An experienced and appropriately credentialed staff promotes effective education for the severely developmentally disabled student (Handleman, 1984). Ongoing training and supervision help keep staff members informed of research and aware of new developments in programming.

Community Service

Programs that train and educate students and volunteers increase community awareness and sensitivity to the needs of the severely developmentally disabled (Handleman, 1981a). Enlisting the efforts of these community members can also help to lower the student to teacher ratio and facilitate program individualization (Powers and Handleman, 1984).

A MODEL FOR A SELF-CONTAINED CLASS FOR SEVERELY DEVELOPMENTALLY DISABLED CHILDREN

The passage of PL 94–142 has increased pressure to provide more comprehensive services for severely developmentally disabled children (Handleman, 1981a; Van Etten et al., 1980). The nature of the learning difficulties demonstrated by these children has often led to their exclusion from the mainstream of public education. As a result of their complex learning and behavioral needs, many severely developmentally disabled students are placed in specialized programs (Handleman, 1981b).

Higher numbers of identified youngsters and the limited space in available programs have increased pressure to provide services for the severely developmentally disabled within the public school (Handleman, 1981b). Although the highly specialized program has been discussed repeatedly and described as preferable for many severely developmentally disabled learners, community-based classrooms are beginning to be looked upon as viable alternatives (Handleman, 1981b; Powers and Handleman, 1984).

Examination of programs for the severely developmentally disabled reveals the following commonalities that could serve as components for a generic self-contained class: (1) teacher, (2) assistant, (3) tutors, (4) children, (5) classroom, and (6) comprehensive program. Many of these components are accessible to most public school and community settings, and the remaining could be arranged in many situations with careful planning and some reorganization.

The Teacher

The limited number of teacher training programs in developmental disabilities has resulted in a very small number of experienced professionals (Handleman, 1981a). To provide for the most experienced staff, selection of a teacher should be made, if possible, from a group of individuals who have demonstrated ability in (1) individualization of instruction, (2) basic child management, (3) social and language development, (4) paraprofessional supervision, and (5) parent training.

The Assistant

The classroom assistant can be instrumental in individualizing instruction and in lowering the student to teacher ratio. Ideally, selection of an individual with abilities similar to those of the teacher would maximize educational programming. At a minimum a graduate from a program for special education assistants would ensure a sensitivity to the needs of the severely developmentally disabled.

Tutors

Local universities and colleges can provide a valuable resource of instructional tutors. The classroom can provide unique personal and professional experiences for students from the fields of special education, speech, and psychology. In areas with limited access to colleges and universities service organizations and high schools can provide alternative resources.

The Children

A low student to teacher ratio can maximize educational experiences for the severely developmentally disabled student (Handleman, 1981b). Depending on the number of available professionals, a class consisting of no more than six children can blend the needed one-to-one and small group programming. Also, grouping children according to similar needs can facilitate greater program effectiveness.

The Classroom

The characteristics of the classroom are no different from those for the typical self-contained class. The size should be conducive to both individual and small group instruction, and adjacent bathroom facilities would enhance training in self-help areas.

Comprehensive Program

There are a variety of components of an effective program for severely developmentally disabled children that are useful to consider.

Specialized Curriculum

Severely developmentally disabled children require a program that focuses on their communication, social, and cognitive needs.

Full-Day, Year-Round Program

The severely developmentally disabled student requires intensive programming. Without an extended school year many children would regress during the summer months.

Low Student to Teacher Ratio

During the beginning phases of instruction many severely developmentally disabled children require one-to-one instruction. As the child learns to respond, this ratio can be gradually increased.

Family Involvement

The best way to maximize educational efforts is to enlist the cooperation of the family. The severely developmentally disabled child places added demands on the family, and as a result the educational placement needs to provide supportive as well as educational services to families.

Transitional Services

After intensive early efforts many severely developmentally disabled children are able to function in less structured special education settings. Active transitional programming is often necessary to bridge the gap between programs.

Behaviorally Based Program

Most professionals agree that the behavioral model of instruction is the treatment of choice for the severely developmentally disabled student. Included in this approach are a comprehensive data base and ongoing staff training.

Many authors write about the application of behavioral techniques within the public schools (Handleman, 1981; Powers and Handleman, 1984); however, little attention has focused on the implementation of such techniques with the severely developmentally disabled student. The need for intensive programming, added staff, and specialized techniques often differs from general practices in public education. The decision to implement a behavioral approach, however, can be based on repeated empirical and experiential success (Lovaas, 1981; Powers and Handleman, 1984). Training in the behavioral model has become increasingly accessible to many professionals (Handleman, 1981b). In-service training seminars, professional conferences, and various manuals are a few of the many resources available to educators and administrators. Also, ongoing consultation can be provided by experienced child study personnel.

SUMMARY

Although placement options for the developmentally disabled student are growing, the process of securing appropriate services is a complicated one. The variables of curriculum, methodology, and staffing addressed in the case of Brenda, which opened this chapter, are only a few of the many issues that need to be considered. The initial creation of a comprehensive student needs assessment often guides a lengthy placement search and program negotiations.

Securing an appropriate student-placement match for the developmentally disabled is facilitated by the various placement options that are available. A wide range of instructional settings provides some leeway for efforts to identify the most appropriate learning environment. Options ranging from the regular class to specialized programs often support an individually tailored placement.

The least restrictive placement option mandated by PL 94-142 is an important consideration for all developmentally disabled students. Although mainstreaming experiences are easier to plan for less disabled learners, they are equally as important for the severely developmentally disabled. Maintaining a flexible service delivery system and ongoing transitional planning will often facilitate upward movement along the continuum of services.

The placement of a developmentally disabled student is an intricate process that requires the cooperation of professionals and parents. Identification, selection, and admissions are some of the events that necessitate careful consideration and agreement by all participants. Placing a severely developmentally disabled child further complicates the process. Programs that can meet the specialized educational needs of children with multiple handicaps are much more limited and difficult to find.

The developmentally disabled population includes students with different needs. Often the more severe the learning deficit is, the more complicated the service delivery. An effective partnership of parents and professionals is necessary to assess educational need, identify and secure appropriate services, and when needed, act as advocates on behalf of the developmentally disabled student.

Appendix 2–A

Guidelines to Assist Families and Professionals When Looking for Programs and Services for Children and Adults with Autism (New Jersey Task Force on Autism)

Fact
Individuals with autism require specialized services that are distinct from services required by other populations. However, among those with autism there are individual differences. It is, therefore, important for the educational setting to have services that are appropriate for your child.

Questions
Is the program appropriate for your child?
Are there other students who seem to have similar learning problems?
Are ancillary services provided (occupational therapy, speech therapy, physical therapy) that your child might need?
Are there activities that are appropriate for your child's needs?
Is a full-day preschool program available?

Fact
All children require individualized planning to ensure appropriate treatment. Research has repeatedly demonstrated the efficacy of data-based treatments. Data allow for accountability—considering the often slow progress of children with autism, it provides an objective means of evaluation.

Questions
Is the program individualized to meet the unique needs of each student?
Is there evidence of systematic implementation of the children's individualized education plan (IEP)?
What is the staff to student ratio? Is one-to-one available when necessary? Are the children under instructional control?
Is there objective (data-based) observation (or other good records), measurement, and evaluation of the children's behavior and of the effectiveness of their programs? How are the data used?

Fact
The involvement of families of children with autism in the educational process promotes program continuity and generalization of the child's newly acquired skills.

Question
Is there comprehensive home programming, including
• Parent training activities, enabling parents to serve as home therapists?
• A plan for home visits by the staff?
• Parent support programs?
• Follow-up services to assure continued success after the child leaves the program?

Fact
Accreditation ensures adherence to standardized basic and legal guidelines (e.g., building characteristics, fire drills, balanced lunches) and demonstrates a professional attitude regarding provision of services.

Question
Is the school accredited by the department of education or is it a member of an organization whose guidelines you can refer to?

Fact
An experienced staff ensures effective treatment. Unusual challenges presented by children with autism necessitate experience in teaching this type of population.

Questions
Is the staff experienced and credentialed?
Is in-service training available?

Fact
Accountability is enhanced when there is a good system of organization and supervision of teachers. Knowledge of the chain of command (whom the staff is responsible to) is important, especially in emergency situations.

Questions
Is it evident that teachers are supervised through observation?
Is the staff working appropriately with the children?
Is the chain of command evident? Is an organizational chart available?

Fact
Each school's program should be consistent in its approach to autism, but there are many different approaches. It is important for parents, guardians, and professionals to explore what exists and make placement decisions on what is best for the child.

Questions
Is there a central philosophy of education throughout the school?
• Can the teachers explain and support it?
• Can you as a parent support it?
• Does the school have a policies and procedures manual?
• Is there a discipline policy? A child welfare policy?
• Is the policy, as presented, observable?

Fact
Programs that prepare high school and college students and community volunteers to provide services to children with autism increase the possibility of a high teacher to student ratio and reflect a dedication to informing the community regarding the needs of individuals with autism.

Questions
Are there programs that prepare high school and college students and community volunteers to provide services to autistic children?
Are there internship programs that prepare graduate students to serve children with autism?

Fact
It is important that teachers be informed of research that is being conducted and of new approaches that are being used.

Questions
Are there teacher training and consulting services (based on research being done at the particular school or a knowledge of credible research elsewhere) provided that
• Promote awareness of the problems and needs of children with autism?
• Contribute to the service provider's knowledge of effective programs for children with autism?
• Contribute to developing new programs that are needed but not available?

Fact
Children with autism require intensive, prolonged, and uninterrupted education.

Question
Is an extended school year or 12-month program offered?

Fact
Observation allows you to watch techniques at work and facilitates using them at home. Accountability is increased when the school has nothing to hide.

Question
Is there openness?
• Are you able to observe in various classes?
• Is there a pleasant, positive atmosphere?

Fact
It is important to have an effective governing body that enhances communication and ensures accountability.

Question
Is there a governing body?
• What is its role?
• Do you have access to it?

Chapter 3

Early Steps of Educational Programming

Case Report: Bruce

The learning consultant, Bruce's teacher and Bruce's parents, Mr. and Mrs. Quinn, met to discuss Bruce's individualized education plan (IEP) for the new school year. At 6 years old, Bruce was beginning his second year in a private school. He was in a class of six communication handicapped youngsters that was staffed by a teacher and an assistant and that stressed traditional academic development.

The first part of the IEP conference focused on Bruce's slow rate of progress during the previous year. The learning consultant shared the findings of her end-of-the-year report and expressed concern for Bruce's difficult classroom adjustment. Bruce was described as highly distractable, difficult to focus, and impulsive in his response cycle. He continued to present management and instructional challenges, in spite of frequent supplemental assistance.

Mr. and Mrs. Quinn shared their difficulties with home management and confirmed the learning consultant's concern for Bruce's slow progress. They had hoped Bruce would respond better to the small classroom groupings and supplemental instruction. Mr. Quinn described how hard it was to get Bruce to focus his attention and to engage in short independent tasks. Both parents expressed their hope for a better school year.

The conference next focused on the identification of goals and objectives for the new school year. Everyone agreed that attention should be placed on instructional control and school life behaviors. The learning consultant presented a list of objectives that included remaining in seat during instruction and attending to the teacher during individual and small group lessons. Mr. and Mrs. Quinn asked that an overall goal of increased compliance with classroom instructions remain in the IEP. Their request was slightly modified to reflect an objective regarding consistent response to daily routines.

Mr. and Mrs. Quinn and the learning consultant agreed that goals and objectives concerning academic development were secondary to instructional control. It was recognized that if Bruce could not attend to educational efforts, the pursuit of academic demands would be futile. All of the participants expressed their frustration that Bruce was not achieving to his potential and emphasized their commitment to a comprehensive effort to modify his behavior.

When it came time to discuss the instructional guide portion of the IEP, the learning consultant suggested that the district consult with a behavioral specialist to assist in designing an appropriate program for Bruce. It was hoped that if attention could be placed on motivation and systematic teaching, improvement would be fostered. The Quinns expressed their appreciation for both the support and sensitivity offered by the school district.

Discussion also focused on the issue of home programming and the importance of school and home consistency. The learning consultant indicated that efforts would be maximized if there were ongoing communication between the teacher and the family and reinforcement of school efforts at home. The Quinns agreed that frequent communication would be useful and suggested that a daily notebook be used to communicate school and home events.

Toward the end of the conference Mrs. Quinn asked if Bruce would benefit from occupational therapy. She said that a friend had read an article suggesting that children with attention deficits benefit from occupational therapy. The learning consultant indicated that the team had not considered occupational therapy for Bruce but that they could pursue an evaluation. She asked the Quinns to give her a few days to investigate the issue and said that she would get back to them by the end of the week.

The meeting concluded with optimism expressed by all participants. The learning consultant suggested that a meeting with the team be scheduled shortly after the first of the year to formally assess Bruce's progress to facilitate program monitoring and future planning.

Case Commentary. As the case of Bruce Quinn illustrates, planning a student's curriculum is a multilevel process. After an initial assessment by an interdisciplinary team, results of the evaluations are shared by parents and professionals to generate specific goals and objectives. This input from all involved parties ensures that educational programming is sensitive to school, home, and community needs.

The IEP conference should serve to regularly monitor and adjust educational programming. For example, Bruce's slow progress was a major focus of the meeting, and as a result, modifications of programming were discussed. Ongoing assessment by school professionals and Bruce's parents facilitated the fine tuning that was necessary to adjust the curriculum to Bruce's needs.

Many developmentally disabled students require extensive instruction in foundation skills. Bruce's progress was hampered by his difficulty with basic attending and instructional control. His inability to focus on materials and follow classroom and home instructions was interfering with the acquisition of more complex tasks. Redirecting programming to focus on these basic skills is often needed to foster school progress.

INTRODUCTION

The complex needs of the developmentally disabled student pose a challenge to educational planning. The diversity of school, home, and community needs necessitate an individualized and comprehensive planning process. The successful execution of the educational plan requires input and monitoring by both school professionals and the family.

Curriculum development for the developmentally disabled typically focuses on the following areas: (1) instructional control, (2) basic skills, (3) readiness, (4) cognitive, communication, and social development, and (5) life skills. These skill categories serve as a useful framework for educational assessment and programming. This chapter surveys the areas of instructional control and basic skills. The remaining categories are discussed in Chapter 4.

Accounts of students encountering learning difficulties as a result of attention deficits confirm the relationship between instructional control and educational progress. Even more than other students the developmentally disabled learner requires instruction in those early skills necessary for academic success. Skill deficiency in this area may prevent or interfere with the learning of more complex tasks.

This chapter focuses on the acquisition of early foundation skills by the developmentally disabled learner. An emphasis is placed on establishing basic instructional control through activities designed to increase a student's ability to attend to the educational environment. Specific teaching methodologies are presented, and a discussion of the important programming issues of natural and functional instruction is included. In addition, the chapter places a special focus on severely developmentally disabled students and their pervasive difficulties with generalization and maintenance. The discussion that follows will enable the teacher to make broad curriculum plans for the developmentally disabled student and to find existing support resources for detailed program development.

DEVELOPING FOUNDATION SKILLS

Any discussion about the early phases of education for the developmentally disabled starts with the question, When should a child's schooling begin? There is growing agreement that the earlier a handicapped child receives professional services, the sooner learning can begin. Early education, particularly for the severely handicapped student, is the cornerstone of the educational process (Sailor and Guess, 1983). Recognition of the need for early intervention for the developmentally disabled student can bring the benefits of professional attention at a very young age (Fenske, Zalenski, Krantz, and McClannahan, 1985; Simeonsson, 1985; White and Casto, 1985).

Regardless of age of intervention the pages of curriculum textbooks are filled with guidelines for teaching academic tasks to handicapped and nonhandicapped youngsters. Chapters on methods and materials dominate these texts, and the careful reader can emerge feeling comfortable with academic instruction. Less often the education student or teacher encounters comprehensive discussions about teaching basic skills to developmentally disabled children. Most special educators are familiar with the importance of prerequisite learning skills for the learning disabled student (Kirk and Gallagher, 1983); however, these discussions have only slowly been extended to other populations of exceptional children.

Because educational progress may be hampered when a child is unable to attend to the environment and follow directions (Dunlap and Egel, 1982; Sailor and Guess, 1983), instruction in foundation skills must focus on student motivation, instructional control, and other school life behaviors. Once a child's receptivity to educational efforts is increased, more complex teaching can be introduced.

Student Motivation

Motivation has traditionally been viewed as an intrinsic internal drive that initiates behavior or activity (Fantino, 1973). Recently, many educators and scientists have questioned this mentalistic description and have adopted a more behavioral interpretation (Dunlap and Egel, 1982). Within a behavioral framework motivation is defined operationally with an emphasis on response characteristics such as the child's frequency or latency of responding.

Motivation of the developmentally disabled learner has been widely discussed (Thompson and O'Quinn, 1979; Wacker, Berg, Wiggins, and Cavanaugh, 1985). There is concern about selection of appropriate materials, teaching strategies, and effective rewards to stimulate the performance of children with mild and moderate handicapping conditions (Kirk and Gallagher, 1983). This issue is most pressing for severely developmentally disabled students (Pace, Ivancic, Edwards, Iwata, and Page, 1985; Powers and Handleman, 1984). The general unresponsiveness of the severely developmentally disabled and their lack of curiosity add to the difficulty of motivating these children (Dunlap and Egel, 1982; Luiselli, Myles, Evans, and Boyce, 1985). For example, natural reinforcers such as praise and affection may not interest the severely developmentally disabled student. As a result creative ways to increase and maintain student motivation become an important focus of early educational efforts.

The idiosyncratic response styles of severely developmentally disabled children often complicate the selection of effective reinforcers (Murphy, 1982; Rincover and Newsom, 1985). For example, the early stages of instruction for the severely developmentally disabled child typically include the use of primary reinforcement to condition more naturally occurring rewards. Once the child's responsiveness to secondary reinforcers increases, individualization becomes the most successful strategy for motivating student performance.

There are a variety of issues to consider when selecting potential reinforcers. Rincover and Koegel (1977) suggested that consideration be given to the naturalness of the reinforcer in order to foster normalization and integrative experiences. The use of variety in reinforcement delivery may also serve to maintain reward potency (Koegel and Felsenfeld, 1977). In an effort to assist teachers in the selection of reinforcers, Gelfand and Hartmann (1980) offered the following suggestions:

1. A reinforcer should be practical.
2. A reinforcer should be administered in small units.
3. A reinforcer should be administered immediately after the occurrence of the desired behavior.
4. A reinforcer should be preferred.
5. A reinforcer should be compatible with the treatment program.

Familiarity with the student through daily observation and interaction is the first step in identifying potential reinforcers (Powers and Handleman, 1984). Preferred toys, activities, and naturally occurring high-rate behaviors are useful clues. Talking to parents and other professionals can also be informative in the selection process. Requesting that all partners in the child's education list the child's favorite foods, toys, and activities may provide a core of potential reinforcers. Finally, having the student sample from a menu of items can reveal a pattern of preferred rewards.

Reinforcement is defined in terms of an increase in the targeted behavior. The test of a potential reward, therefore, is the effect it has on performance. The teacher can quickly assess the effectiveness of reinforcement by monitoring frequency (response) or duration (time). This objective approach to evaluation can assist in modifying the treatment plan and can enhance individualization of instruction (Powers and Handleman, 1984).

Instructional Control

The ability to attend to the instructional environment and respond to the variety of classroom stimuli is fundamental to the education of developmentally disabled students. Many educators and researchers consider that being able to focus on educational events is a prerequisite to learning (Cook, Anderson, and Rincover, 1982; Lovaas, 1981). In addition, the ability to sit quietly in the classroom, to refrain from behaviors that interfere with learning, and to follow routine instructions provides a framework for progress in communication and academic areas.

Establishing eye contact is considered by many to be the most fundamental of attending behaviors (Altman and Krupshaw, 1982). This very important interpersonal skill is critical to the reception of auditory and visual information and necessary for the interpretation of social cues (Harris, 1975). Increasing spontaneous eye contact may be especially valuable because when a student orients to a speaker without prompting, more natural speech and communication patterns are approximated (Sosne, Handleman, and Harris, 1979). Table 3–1 presents a sample program for increasing eye contact.

Although establishing eye contact is necessary for students to receive information or imitate behavior, it is also important for them to focus on environmental objects and actions (Lovaas, 1981). For example, teaching a child to attend to an object presented for labeling is a critical prerequisite skill. A suggested program for teaching environmental attending is presented in Table 3–2.

A student's ability to follow routine directions reflects an understanding of language and sets the stage for learning more complex tasks (Harris, 1975). Initially, compliance with commands such as

Table 3–1.   Sample Program for Increasing Eye Contact

Target Behavior
Eye contact

Operational Definition of Behavior
Upon presentation of the S^D "(Name), look at me," child will establish eye contact within 2 seconds of the S^D and maintain it for 5 seconds.

Description of Program
Establish appropriate sitting.
S^D: "(Name), look at me."
Response: Child will establish eye contact within 4 seconds for designated length of time.
Consequence: Reward eye contact with appropriate reinforcement. If child responds incorrectly, prompt child as needed to establish eye contact for designated length of time. Provide social reinforcement.
Step 1: Use food prompt: Hold small piece of food between eyes when presenting S^D.
Step 2: Prompt by pointing toward your eyes when presenting S^D.
Step 3: Present S^D only (no prompting).
Set 1: Child must provide eye contact within 4 seconds.
Set 2: Child must provide eye contact within 3 seconds for 2 seconds.
Set 3: Child must provide eye contact within 3 seconds for 3 seconds.
Set 4: Child must provide eye contact within 2 seconds for 4 seconds.
Set 5: Child must provide eye contact within 2 seconds for 5 seconds.

Data
+ = correct response.
− = incorrect response.
Criterion: 85% or better over 2 consecutive days

Comments
Do Steps 1 and 2 for Set 1 *only.* After Step 3 of Set 1, proceed to Step 3 of Set 2, and so forth.

"come here" and "sit down" demonstrates basic comprehension and provides the foundation for teaching multiple commands. Following directions, like attending behaviors, is an important prerequisite skill for academic, vocational, and daily living activities. The strategies outlined in Table 3–3 are designed to increase a student's compliant behavior.

Ensuring that a child is sitting quietly and not engaging in competing behaviors such as throwing a tantrum, engaging in self-stimulation, or being aggressive is basic to establishing instruction control (Powers and Handleman, 1984). Teaching a child to sit quietly for increasing periods of time may be accomplished by using strategies similar to those presented in Table 3–4. Designing an educational plan that focuses on the reduction of disruptive and competitive behaviors is more complex and initially includes the identification of appropriate consequences for the target behavior (Powers and Handleman, 1984).

Table 3-2.   Sample Program for Teaching Environmental Attending

Target Behavior
Establish eye contact with an object or picture

Operational Definition of Behavior
The child will establish 3 to 5 seconds of eye contact with an object or picture when cued verbally by the teacher.

Description of Program
Establish appropriate sitting and attending.
S^D: "(Name), look at (object or picture)."
Response: Direct eye contact with object or picture when cued (3 to 5 seconds).
Consequence: Reward appropriate response with appropriate reinforcement.
Step 1: Place an object that makes a noise in front of the child and give the S^D while making the noise.
Prompt: Gently guide the child's chin so that the object is in the direct line of sight.
Step 2: Same as Step 1 except no prompting is used.
Step 3: Use an interesting object or picture in random locations (e.g., right, left, up, and down). Give S^D with no prompting.

Data
+ = correct response.
− = incorrect response.
Criterion: 85% or better over 2 consecutive days

Comments
Visually interesting objects or pictures are important to the success of this program. If objects or pictures of interest for the child are not readily known, try to determine some by observation or those identified by parents. For example,
• Bounce an object around to see if the child follows it once the child has looked at it.
• Vary voice quality, loudness, pitch, or a combination of these to attract attention to the object when presenting the verbal cue.
• Vary placement of object or picture to stimulate a search by the child.

The efficacy of behavior reduction programs is well established (Adams, Sternberg, and Taylor, 1982; Lovaas, 1981). Techniques such as time out, response cost, and overcorrection have been used successfully in various settings to decrease self-stimulatory behavior, aggressiveness, and a multitude of other disruptive behaviors (Harris and Wolchick, 1979; Luiselli, 1984; Singh and Winton, 1985). Although behavior management techniques are widely used, implementation requires intensive training, supervision, and monitoring.

Other School Life Behaviors

In addition to demonstrating the ability to sit, attend, and follow directions, the developmentally disabled student must be able to respond to small group instruction. The more normalized the educa-

Table 3–3.   Strategies to Increase Compliant Behavior

Target Behavior
Following directions — Actions

Operational Definition of Behavior
When presented with a one-step direction, child will perform the correct behavior within 5 seconds of the S^D.

Description of Program
Establish good sitting and attending.
S^D: For example, "Clap hands" or appropriate direction.
Response: Child will respond by performing appropriate behavior within 5 seconds of the S^D.
Consequence: Reward correct response with appropriate reinforcement. If child does not respond or responds incorrectly, physically prompt or model behavior. Provide social reinforcement only.
Step 1: Present S^D and model behavior.
Step 2: Present S^D but *do not* model behavior.

Data
+ = correct response.
− = incorrect response.
Criterion: 85% or better over 2 consecutive days

tional setting is, the greater reliance that is placed on group instruction. Teaching children to sit still, wait turns, and respond when asked are important skills for overall school adjustment.

Individualized instruction has been recommended for maximal educational gains and is generally regarded as the most effective method of teaching severely developmentally disabled children (Harris, 1975; Powers and Handleman, 1984). Recent years have also witnessed the success of small group programming (Handleman and Harris, 1983). Teaching children basic school life behaviors in a group of two to three can set the groundwork for the instruction of other skills. Whether accomplished by slowly fading a child into the group (Rincover, Koegel, and Russo, 1978) or by shaping group behaviors by systematic reinforcement, group programming provides an alternative to individualized instruction, particularly in those settings in which staff are limited.

Once the group is established, a two-pronged approach can be implemented by the teacher and classroom assistant. Some of the students can be provided with group instruction while others receive individualized attention. This approach is implemented in many self-contained special education classes. Not only can the group provide effective programming, but also there is growing evidence that group exposure enhances socialization (Handleman, 1981b).

Table 3–4.   Strategies for Teaching a Child to Sit Quietly

Target Behavior
Sitting

Operational Definition of Behavior
Upon presentation of S^D "Sit quiet," child will demonstrate appropriate sitting within 4 seconds of S^D and maintain it for 5 seconds. *Sitting* is defined as both buttocks in chair, body oriented forward, feet on floor, and hands in lap or on desk.

Description of Program
S^D: "Sit quiet."
Response: Child will establish appropriate sitting and maintain for designated length of time.
Consequence: Reward good sitting with appropriate reinforcement. If child responds incorrectly say, "No, this is quiet sitting" and physically prompt child to sit in chair for designated length of time. Provide social reinforcement.
Step 1: Place child in appropriate sitting position. As you release hands, present S^D. Child must maintain sitting for designated length of time. (See comments.)
Step 2: Present S^D. Child must establish appropriate sitting within 4 seconds and maintain for designated length of time.
Set 1: Child must maintain sitting for 1 second.
Set 2: Child must maintain sitting for 2 seconds.
Set 3: Child must maintain sitting for 3 seconds.
Set 4: Child must maintain sitting for 4 seconds.
Set 5: Child must maintain sitting for 5 seconds.

Data
+ = correct response.
− = incorrect response.
Criterion: 85% or better over 2 consecutive days

Comments
Step 1 should be done for Set 1 only. Upon reaching criterion for Step 1 of Set 1, proceed to Step 2 of Set 1 and then to Step 2 of Set 2, and so forth.

TEACHING STRATEGIES TO HELP LAY THE GROUNDWORK

Resources for teachers of the developmentally disabled continue to be expanded and refined. In addition to a number of manuals and handbooks (Harris, 1975; Lovaas, 1981; Schopler, Reichler, and Lansing, 1980), there are a variety of teaching strategies designed to analyze the task, identify deficient skills, and systematically present the material. Task analysis, for example, is widely used by teachers to assess educational goals and plan instructional experiences. The techniques of prompting, shaping, and chaining are also useful for teaching complex and difficult tasks. In addition, the discrete trial method of instruction is being adopted by many educators as a framework for systematic teaching.

Task Analysis

Task analysis is an important part of curriculum development for developmentally disabled students (Powers and Handleman, 1984; Van Etten et al., 1980). This approach grew from the assumption that a student's failure with a particular task is related to an inability to perform some prerequisite skill (Bijou, 1973). The technique involves breaking learning tasks into subskills and sequencing them into an appropriate learning progression (Bijou, 1973; Gold, 1976). Task analysis facilitates careful identification of teaching objectives and fine tuning of educational programming (Powers and Handleman, 1984).

A variety of approaches to task analysis are presented in the literature. One method is to observe a student performing a particular task and record each component behavior. Such observation assists in determining specific skill deficits and in adjusting educational programming (Resnick, Wang, and Kaplan, 1973). A more precise approach to task analysis has been presented by Williams (1975) who described a "question-recording" technique: The teacher attempts to identify prerequisite skills for each component of the task and then determines subtasks for each prerequisite skill. For example, if the behavior of getting ready for bed were task analyzed, the first breakdown would include undressing, bathing, and dressing. The next level of analysis would reduce each component into necessary skills such as adjusting water or placing hands through sleeves of pajama top.

Two listing formats are typically discussed with regard to task analysis (Smith, Smith, and Edgar, 1976). Vertical listing refers to the arrangement of component tasks into a single list, and lattice listing presents an analysis according to level and subtask. With regard to the exact sequencing of tasks, N. G. Haring (1982) distinguished between a "teaching" sequence and a "natural" sequence. Haring (1982) stated that the natural progression may not always be the most beneficial for developmentally disabled students and suggested that the exact skill sequence be based on individual needs.

Prompting, Shaping, and Chaining

The techniques of prompting, shaping, and chaining have been widely used in day-to-day instruction to teach new skills to developmentally disabled and nonhandicapped learners (Walker and Shea, 1980). These strategies enable the educator to approach teaching in a systematic fashion and to better link assessment to remediation (Powers and Handleman, 1984).

Prompting is useful for teaching new skills and is referred to as an offer of assistance. For example, a verbal prompt is used when initial sounds of words are presented to children during reading. Similarly, lightly supporting a child who is learning to skate is an example of a physical prompt. To foster independent performance, however, prompting must be decreased. Systematically fading the use of instructional prompts is often necessary to reduce initial prompt dependence.

The technique of shaping refers to breaking down a behavior into smaller steps and beginning instruction with the easiest step. By using shaping a child could be taught to sit quietly by first requesting quiet sitting for only a few seconds and slowly increasing the amount of time. Shaping can also be used to teach a child to eat with a spoon or to imitate words. In each example the easiest step is taught first (e.g., touching spoon, saying m for "mom") and then demands are systematically increased.

Chaining is similar to shaping in that behavior is reduced to component parts and instruction proceeds in a systematic fashion from least difficult to more complex. Chaining is most useful in the teaching of complex tasks that can be broken down into independent behaviors. For example, the task of getting dressed includes the behaviors of putting on undergarments, shirt, pants, etc. Each component behavior can be taught independently and linked together by sequentially chaining the individual behaviors. Chaining can be used to teach other complex behaviors such as food preparation and difficult prevocational tasks.

Discrete Trial Teaching

One of the most successful contributions to the educational technology for developmentally disabled learners is the discrete trial teaching format (Donnellan, Mesaros, and Anderson, 1985). Discrete trial teaching presents instructional material according to a clearly defined sequence and attempts to reduce irrelevant or redundant information. This successful approach has been repeatedly applied to many instructional areas such as speech (Harris, 1975), reading (Rosenbaum and Brieling, 1976), and play (Koegel, Firestone, Kramme, and Dunlap, 1974).

There are four components to a discrete teaching trial. The first component is the discriminative stimulus or S^D. The term S^D refers to instructions, commands, directives, or requests that are made to the student. The S^D serves as the initiator of the "response" or the second component of the discrete trial. The third component includes the variety of consequences for student responses such as rewards, instructional feedback, or corrections. The final component, the intertrial interval, provides opportunity to record student performance and prepare for the next trial.

ISSUES IN THE EARLY PHASES OF EDUCATING SEVERELY DEVELOPMENTALLY DISABLED STUDENTS

Laying the early foundation for learning is vital to the education of the severely developmentally disabled (Powers and Handleman, 1984). The literature repeatedly addresses the importance of establishing instructional control and facilitating motivation for the student with a severe developmental disability (Harris, 1975; Lovaas, 1981). Many teachers of the autistic or severely mentally retarded can describe countless trials devoted to teaching attending or compliance training.

Most of the attention in curriculum development for the severely developmentally disabled has focused on communication, social, and cognitive development (Lovaas, 1981; Powers and Handleman, 1984). There is also growing concern for a variety of issues that underscore the teaching of basic skills, academic tasks, and prevocational activities. For example, concern exists for the pervasive difficulty that the severely developmentally disabled student demonstrates with generalization and maintenance of behavior (Handleman, 1979a, 1981a). In addition, increasing interest is being expressed for the importance of functional and naturalistic instruction (Donnellan et al., 1985) and the sanctity of the developmental model (Handleman, Powers, and Harris, 1984).

Generalization

Applying information outside the instructional setting is vital to the durability of learning. Without the ability to transfer learning, behavior becomes situation specific and of limited use to the student. Many severely developmentally disabled learners are bound to the teaching situation and are restricted in their ability to generalize learning across materials, settings, and persons (Hamilton, 1966; Handleman, 1979a; Rincover and Koegel, 1975).

Generalization refers to a student's ability to employ information beyond the teaching situation. Two important forms of generalization are stimulus generalization and response generalization. Stimulus generalization occurs when behavior is demonstrated under conditions different from those present during training (Lovaas, Koegel, Simmons, and Long, 1973) and includes the transfer of skills to new people (Stokes, Baer, and Jackson, 1974) and new settings (Wahler, 1969). Response generalization occurs when changes in untrained responses co-vary with changes in trained behaviors (Garcia, 1974). Severely developmentally disabled students have difficulty with both types of generalization (Handleman, 1979a, 1981a).

Discussions of response generalization by severely developmentally disabled learners have focused primarily on the formation of response classes. Wheeler and Sulzer (1970) stated that a generalized response class exists when all responses in a particular class show an effect of a manipulation that is made in relation to only a few members of the class. The creation of a response class is reflected by the appearance of novel responses for which direct training has not been given and offers an alternative to teaching the infinite number of responses that a student might be expected to use each day (Baer and Guess, 1971; Garcia, Guess, and Byrnes, 1973; Guess and Baer, 1973). For example, a child might master the response class of descriptive adjectives and be able to use adjectives in novel contexts without training (Hart and Risley, 1968).

Once a skill has been mastered in the teaching setting, attention must be placed on extending performance to other people and settings (Harris, 1975). Most educators recognize the importance of generalization of learning, but it is not always recognized that generalization does not automatically occur when a skill is acquired in the classroom (Browning, 1983; Stokes et al., 1974). The issue of stimulus generalization by the severely developmentally disabled learner has received extensive attention (Borkowski and Varnhager, 1984; Handleman, 1981b; Simic and Bucher, 1980).

Functional performance has been described in terms of the control of behavior in situations different from those in which training occurred (Garcia, 1974). Over the last two decades extratherapy generalization has received increased attention. Research has indicated that transfer of learning does not usually take place without special intervention (Adubato, Adams, and Budd, 1981; Rincover and Koegel, 1975; Walker and Buckley, 1972). Transfer of treatment gains was viewed as the exception rather than the rule and as a process that needed to be programmed for by the use of varied settings

(Griffiths and Craighead, 1972; Jackson and Wallace, 1974) and varied teachers (Garcia, 1974; Kale et al., 1968).

An assumption of earlier approaches to the education and treatment of the severely developmentally disabled was that changes in the teaching situation would generalize to the natural environment (Wulbert, 1974). The results of limited work in this area once again confirmed the lack of generalization by these students (Birnbrauer, 1968; Wahler, 1969). Recent investigations have suggested that the transfer of learning from school to home can be facilitated by using a variety of instructors and teaching settings (Handleman, 1979a; Handleman and Harris, 1980). The usefulness of varied teachers and settings has also been documented for increasing rates of generalization from a student's current educational placement to novel school programs (Handleman, 1981a; Handleman and Harris, 1983).

Educators and psychologists urge that transfer of learning be planned rather than assumed to follow as a consequence of teaching (Kazdin and Bootzin, 1972). It has been argued that generalization of behavior should be a fundamental criterion for assessing the success of treatment (Handleman and Harris, 1980; Rhode, Morgan, and Young, 1983). Because of the important role generalization plays with all types of learning, a student's deficiency with generalization should be assessed and remediated (Powers and Handleman, 1984). Using a variety of materials, different teachers, and different instructional settings has proven to be a powerful teaching tool.

Response Maintenance

Maintaining behavior change or acquired skills over time increases the utility of learning. Response maintenance complements a student's ability to generalize skills and strengthens responding (Powers and Handleman, 1984). Although the need for response maintenance by severely developmentally disabled students has been experimentally documented (Dunlap and Koegel, 1980; Lancioni, 1982; Rusch and Kazdin, 1981), the issue has received relatively little professional attention.

The degree to which educational gains are maintained over time in extratherapy settings often depends on the similarity of conditions in teaching and nontraining settings (Egel, 1982; Marholin and Siegel, 1978; Sowers, Rusch, Connis, and Cummings, 1980). Performance by severely developmentally disabled students seems to be maintained for longer periods when conditions such as reinforcement and other contingencies are consistent across settings. Koegel and Rincover (1977) have reported limited response maintenance when a student is able to discriminate between the presence or absence of performance contingencies.

Educational strategies for increasing response maintenance by severely developmentally disabled students have focused on reducing the discriminability of contingencies across situations (Egel, 1982; Sowers et al., 1980). A well-endorsed approach includes employing similar methods and contingencies in nontreatment settings (Lancioni, 1982; Powers and Handleman, 1984). Other successful strategies that have been employed include the use of peer tutors (Patterson and Anderson, 1964; Solomon and Wahler, 1973), parent trainers (O'Leary, O'Leary, and Becker, 1967), and the leaning of reinforcement schedules during maintenance (Kazdin and Polster, 1973; Koegel and Rincover, 1977).

Naturalistic or Functional Interaction

The combined effects of Wolfensberger (1975) and PL 94-142 have been responsible for normalizing professional attitudes regarding the severely developmentally disabled. The quality of education has improved since the early 1970s, and the availability of services has increased. Topics such as mainstreaming, which were initially limited to less disabled students, are increasingly discussed for the student with a severe and profound handicapping condition (Handleman, 1984). The severely developmentally disabled student is finally being afforded the same right to appropriate education and access to community participation as other exceptional children.

The need to provide normalizing experiences for the severely developmentally disabled student confronts many administrators and educators. The growing shift away from traditional to more functional skill training, particularly in academic areas (Kirk and Gallagher, 1983), reflects this concern. An increase in available community group homes and adult activity programs has also enhanced more normalized community activities. In addition, successful transition efforts from highly specialized programs to less structured educational environments have been described (Handleman, 1979b, 1984).

Regardless of educational placement, there is growing agreement that curricular planning for the severely developmentally disabled should reflect the following considerations:

1. Educational experiences should be individualized.
2. Programming should include opportunity for functional application of skills (e.g., sorting clothing).

3. Tasks should be age appropriate.
4. Opportunity should be provided for performance of skills in natural settings (e.g., home, community).
5. Community participation should be encouraged.

Providing more natural, normal, and functional learning experiences for the severely developmentally disabled necessitates active planning and systematic programming. Research interest in this area has just begun, and future work should provide the educator and administrator with answers to a number of questions, as well as strategies for effective programming.

Developmental Instruction

Curriculum development for the developmentally disabled typically follows a developmental model. The underlying assumption is that the normal sequence of development provides a logical ordering for educational events (Sailor and Guess, 1983). Research in child development supports this notion and has identified numerous developmental sequences that occur in nonhandicapped children, for example, the emergence of receptive language prior to expressive language (Fraser, Bellugi, and Brown, 1963) and the development of symbolic play prior to language (Nicolich, in press).

The developmental course of children with severe developmental disabilities has been described less frequently than that of nonhandicapped or mildly impaired children. Although the assumption is made by many authors that a hierarchy of abilities exists for the severely developmentally disabled learner, few data are currently available to support this hypothesis (Handleman et al., 1984). On the contrary, Guess and Baer (1973) found a limited functional relationship between receptive and expressive modalities and Handleman and colleagues (1984) found little support for a relationship between knowledge of concrete and pictorial representations of objects.

Disturbances of developmental rate and sequence are endemic among children with severe developmental disabilities. Thus, the assumption that teaching should proceed in accordance with the normative sequence may be based, at best, on clinical intuition (Handleman et al., 1984). Guess, Sailor, and Baer (1977) stated that although normative data suggest the presence of a sequence, its utility with severely handicapped children remains to be demonstrated empirically. Because of the particular nature of severe developmental disabilities, the application of developmental sequences based upon observations of nonhandicapped children must be investigated further.

SUMMARY

Curriculum planning for the developmentally disabled student is a complex process. Consideration of highly individual and idiosyncratic learning styles and coordination of input from parents and professionals are just a few of the intricacies. Even before planning can be initiated in the traditional curricular areas of academics and communication, careful attention must be directed to some very important building blocks of learning such as instructional control and basic skills.

The teacher of the developmentally disabled will need to spend considerable time ensuring that students are attending to instructional events and are motivated to learn. Very few IEPs and parent conferences are immune from discussions about a child's lack of interest and difficulty with sitting still and attending to classroom directions. Early attention to student motivation and vital foundation skills will ensure more durable performance and maintenance and facilitate the teaching of more sophisticated tasks. A methodology that includes techniques such as shaping and chaining is available for a systematic approach to instructional control and compliance training.

The severely developmentally disabled learner presents a special challenge to the teacher. Performance styles will probably be more idiosyncratic, and the need to establish basic skills will be heightened in contrast to other children. A continual sensitivity should be maintained to the difficulties that these students demonstrate with generalization. The teacher of the severely developmentally disabled child will also need to consider the special concerns for functional programming and appropriate sequencing of educational events.

Chapter 4

Curriculum Planning

Case Report: Jesse

The staffing on Jesse Kohl was called to order by the learning consultant. Also present at the meeting were Jesse's teacher and the child study supervisor. Staffings were routinely conducted in the district at least once a year for each student enrolled in special classes. These meetings were typically devoted to curriculum planning or special programming concerns. Jesse was 6 years old and beginning her second year in one of the district's self-contained classes.

The staffing was scheduled to discuss goal setting for the new school year. Jesse's progress in basic skills was very good, and she was ready for a shift in educational programming. Jesse's teacher described her success with instructional control tasks and shared with the group charts depicting steady acquisition of eye contact, sitting, and compliance with simple and complex instructional directions. The learning consultant confirmed the previous year's progress.

In spite of Jesse's good progress, Jesse's teacher also raised problems she was having in motivating Jesse to engage in new activities or tasks. She described the various techniques that were tried and the limited success that was achieved. For example, food, activities, and affection had all proved ineffective when attempts were made to introduce new material. The teacher then presented a self-charting procedure that was introduced in late May. Jesse was given responsibility for placing stars on a chart displayed in front of the class. The teacher described the delight Jesse displayed with this procedure and an increase in new interests and performance.

The supervisor inquired about Jesse's progress in readiness areas. Jesse's teacher indicated that recently an emphasis had been placed on discrimination learning and that Jesse seemed to be grasping basic identification of objects and shapes. She stated that programming would expand to include number, letter, and color identification when Jesse was ready. Jesse's teacher also indicated that some simple sorting and matching activities would be introduced shortly.

Jesse's social development was discussed next. The learning consultant reported an increase in social interactions both on the playground and in the lunchroom. Jesse was described as initiating more contacts with other children and being more tolerant of the interests of others. A situation was described in which a classmate no longer wanted to play the game Jesse had suggested and walked over to the swings. Jesse said "okay" and followed her friend. Jesse's teacher remarked that 3 months ago the same situation would have resulted in a tantrum and aggressiveness. The supervisor commented on how the after school play group they suggested last spring seemed to be providing Jesse with clear benefits.

The school's speech therapist joined the last part of the meeting to discuss Jesse's communication development. He summarized the end-of-year evaluation and reported gains in the consistent use of single words to describe events and make requests. Emerging use of two-word sentences was also described. The speech therapist recommended that Jesse continue to receive speech therapy twice a week and offered to continue his weekly meeting with the teacher to plan integrative activities.

Before concluding the meeting, the supervisor expressed his pleasure regarding Jesse's progress. He stated that too often staffings focus on the difficulties of the children and that many times their progress is minimized. Jesse's teacher thanked the group for their ongoing support and guidance.

Case Commentary. For many students establishing basic instructional control is an important prerequisite for other forms of learning. In Jesse's case her mastery of basic skills had laid the groundwork for more advanced programming. As discussed by the child study personnel, Jesse's lack of motivation and attention initially prevented the introduction of new tasks.

Curriculum planning for the developmentally disabled student is a complex endeavor. The educator is often faced with a wealth of resources and charged with the task of individualization. Many times the input from support professionals is needed to assist in initial goal setting and program monitoring. The activities of Jesse's team effectively facilitated curriculum planning in more advanced areas. As a result of Jesse's progress with instructional control tasks, attention began to be focused on academic readiness, communication, social skills, and prevocational activities.

INTRODUCTION

Curriculum planning for the developmentally disabled is an ongoing process that constantly undergoes expansion and revision and that should reflect the changing needs of the student. To be a successful planner, the educator is expected to keep current with educational research and theory, sort through a growing fund of materials, and remain sensitive to the individual needs of each student. To meet this challenge, the teacher of the developmentally disabled student will usually welcome assistance in the form of professional input or scholarly readings.

Chapter 3 presents a detailed discussion of the early steps of educational planning. The present chapter surveys curricular concerns in the areas of readiness, academics, communication, social skills, and life skills education. At every phase of planning educational experiences for the developmentally disabled student, one or more of these areas are typically considered. Depending on the nature of the handicapping condition or severity of the disability, some areas may be emphasized more than others.

The link between readiness and other areas of learning is an issue that has been widely discussed. For example, there have been suggestions that a hierarchical relationship exists between readiness activities and academic tasks, and some reports have indicated the lack of a functional relationship between these areas of curriculum. This controversy is one of the issues presented in this chapter to assist the educator in setting appropriate goals and in preparing successful educational experiences for the developmentally disabled student.

This chapter also presents important considerations for the severely developmentally disabled student. Curriculum planning for the child with severe or multiple handicaps is not as finely tuned as it is for those with mild or moderate handicapping conditions. The special educator is often left to develop self-made programs without the resources that are available to other teachers. The chapter includes material on resources that can lessen the challenge of programming for this special population of exceptional students.

READINESS

A commonly reported learning characteristic of developmentally disabled students is idiosyncratic and inconsistent response to sensory stimulation (Powers and Handleman, 1984; Schopler, 1978). Many students demonstrate difficulty with basic attending or the important information processing skills of discrimination and matching (Gersten, White, Falco, and Carnin, 1982). These deficits may interfere with more advanced academic or prevocational learning (Powers and Handleman, 1984).

Concern about a student's difficulty with readiness tasks is often accompanied by concern about overselective responding. Many developmentally disabled students demonstrate this pattern of responding, which may be a major contributor to information processing deficits (Cook, Anderson, and Rincover, 1982; Schneider and Salzberg, 1982). When a student responds in an overselective fashion, only a particular stimulus or selective set of stimuli are being attended to. For example, a child who consistently labels a saddle as a belt because of the fastening strap is not processing the full range of information. Effective strategies to overcome overselective responding, such as repeating material and stressing salient features, are being identified (Lovaas, Schreibman, Koegel, and Rehm, 1971; Rincover, 1978; Schneider and Salzberg, 1982).

Matching

The ability to match requires a student to note differences and similarities of objects, events, or other types of information. As a result of difficulties with matching, many developmentally disabled students are unable to place an object next to a similar one or put a picture on top of an identical photograph. Therefore, matching must be systematically taught at various increasing levels of complexity such as concrete objects, abstract representations, and with single and multidimensional items. An example of a program to teach matching is presented in Table 4–1.

Discrimination

Most academic, social, and communication tasks are dependent on the ability to discriminate. Discrimination requires an awareness of both similarities and differences of sensory input and the ability to match concepts, labels, or events with appropriate information. As with the skill of matching, many developmentally disabled students encounter difficulties with discrimination tasks and need direct instruction with concrete and pictorial representations of objects and with multiple pairs of items (Delprato, Pappalardo, and Holmes, 1984; Foxx, 1984; Miyashita, 1985). Table 4–2 presents a program designed to teach a student to discriminate common objects.

Other Information Processing Skills

In addition to being able to match and to discriminate sensory input, there are other information processing skills required for more ad-

Table 4–1.   Program for Teaching Matching

Target Behavior
Matching to sample

Operational Definition of Behavior
Given a choice of items and the S^D "Match," the child will place the stimulus object on or next to its match within 5 to 7 seconds.

Description of Program
Materials: Common objects
S^D: "Match"
Response: The child will place the stimulus object on or next to its match within 5 to 7 seconds.
Consequences: Reward correct response with appropriate reinforcement. If child does not respond or responds incorrectly, model correct behavior and prompt child to respond correctly.
Step 1: Present one item from the set. Present identical item as the stimulus and the S^D "Match." Model response, repeat S^D "Match," and present item to the child.
Step 2: Present two items from the set. Present one stimulus item, the S^D "Match," and model the response. Repeat S^D "Match," and present item to child (randomize positions).
Step 3: Present two items from the set. Present one stimulus item and S^D "Match" (*no model;* randomize).
Step 4: Present three items from the set. Present one stimulus item and S^D "Match."
Step 5: Present four items from the set. Present one stimulus item and S^D "Match."
Step 6: Present five items from the set. Present one stimulus item and S^D "Match."

Data
+ = correct response.
− = incorrect or prompted response.
Criterion: 85% on 2 consecutive days

Comments
This program may be used for object-to-object, object-to-picture, color, shape, size, and letter matching.

---

vanced learning that present difficulty to developmentally disabled students. For example, awareness, recognition, association, and memory tasks on both the auditory and visual level may be related to reading and mathematics activities. In addition, many perceptual skills have been considered readiness activities to academic learning. Table 4–3 outlines some of the information processing tasks that are targeted for instruction for many developmentally disabled students.

ACADEMIC SKILLS

The special educator is probably best prepared to teach basic academic skills. Teacher training programs, textbooks, and curriculum guides typically stress academic areas. Many preservice and in-

Table 4–2.   Program for Teaching Object Discrimination

Target Behavior
Object discrimination

Operational Definition of Behavior
Given the verbal S^D "(Name), touch _____," and two or three objects, the child will touch the correct object within 5 to 7 seconds.

Description of Program
Materials: Common environmental items
Establish good sitting and attending.
S^D: "(Name), touch _____." Present object with or without object distractors.
Consequence: Reward correct, unprompted response with appropriate reinforcement.
Correction: If child does not respond within the time limit or responds incorrectly, physically prompt child to touch the correct object.
Step 1: Position object and present S^D (no distractors).
Step 2: Position object in close proximity and one distractor at a distance of 18 in. and present S^D. Do not alter position (keep one on right and one on left).
Step 3: Position object in close proximity and one distractor at a distance of 9 in. and present S^D. Alter position of both from previous step (left-right).
Step 4: Keep distance between object and distractor object at 9 in. but randomly alternate positions for each trial and present S^D (left-right).
Step 5: Keep distance between object and distractor object equal and present S^D (no proximity prompt; no randomization of position).
Step 6: Keep distance between object and distractor object equal and present S^D (no proximity prompts; however, randomize position).
Step 7: Introduce third distractor at equal distance between object and two distractors and present S^D (randomize position).

Data
+ = correct response.
− = incorrect or physically prompted response.
Criterion: 85% for two consecutive sessions

Comments
For each session keep distractor constant; however, choose distractors from any previous sets, except for Set 1 (use Set 2). Build a review every three sets by posttesting sets by using Step 6 for two sessions at criterion and then Step 7 for two sessions at criterion. If child fails this step (25% or less), systematically introduce Steps 7a, b, and c by using proximity prompting as used in Steps 2 to 7.

service training activities include a focus on remedial mathematics or reading, and consultants in these areas are often retained by school districts. In addition, commercial materials devoted to academic instruction dominate catalogs and conference displays.

The teacher of the developmentally disabled student, however, needs to approach the wealth of resources for academic instruction with different selection criteria than do other teachers (Powers and Handleman, 1984). For example, goals, methods, and materials need to be more specific and systematic for these youngsters than for others. Sensitivity to idiosyncratic response patterns and difficulties with information processing frequently dictate special programming considerations. Table 4–4 includes some common goals for developmentally disabled learners in reading, mathematics, and writing.

Table 4–3.   Information Processing Skills

Modality	Skill
	Awareness
Auditory	Association
	Recognition
Visual	Discrimination
	Memory

Reading

Many developmentally disabled children have difficulty with reading. Poor reading skills are demonstrated by more exceptional children than any other learning problem and have been noted to be the most important single cause of school failure (Kirk and Gallagher, 1983). The developmentally disabled student typically encounters difficulty with basic word recognition or the more complex skill of comprehension. These problems could be related to difficulties with information processing skills such as discrimination and memory (Chalfant and Scheffelin, 1969).

The teacher of the developmentally disabled can usually find many resources for teaching reading. In addition to a growing availability of commercial materials, a choice of reading methods exists to assist individualization of instruction. The phonics method, for example, has offered teachers a traditional approach to beginning reading for many years, and a variety of modified alphabets such as the initial teaching alphabet (ITA) have been introduced from time to time. The language-experience approach is another method that extends reading into language arts by integrating listening, speaking, and writing skills. The basal reading series has also provided a highly comprehensive and structured approach to reading. These approaches, combined with a growing technology of programmed and computer assisted instruction, enable a teacher to successfully match performance styles with instructional method.

Mathematics

Although learning problems in mathematics have not received the same professional attention as reading (Wallace and Larsen, 1978), this area of learning also presents difficulty for many developmentally disabled students. The reasons why students encounter problems are many and range from lack of readiness, interest, and motivation to poor teaching (Wallace and McLoughlin, 1979).

Table 4–4.   Academic Goals

Reading	Writing	Mathematics
Vocabulary recognition	Use of utensil	Counting
Vocabulary comprehension	Random marking	Number identification
	Controlled marking	
	Tracing	Sequencing
Word attack	Copying	Concepts
Reading comprehension	Printing or writing	Computation

Mathematics difficulties can be found at all age levels and have also been attributed to deficits in visual memory and spatial relationships (Chalfant and Scheffelin, 1969).

The educator who is experiencing difficulty teaching mathematics to a developmentally disabled student will not find the same quality of remedial resources that are available for reading problems. Remedial mathematics has received less attention than other areas of corrective teaching and resources are limited (Wallace and McLoughlin, 1979). Although mathematics series and special programs exist, teachers often rely on teacher-made materials and various activities that can provide repetition and reinforcement of skills.

Writing

Writing is considered the most concrete of the academic skills and one that results in a permanent product. Many developmentally disabled students demonstrate writing deficits that ultimately interfere with various forms of written expression (Wallace and McLoughlin, 1979). Some students encounter difficulty with the mechanics of writing such as proper grasp of instrument or tracing, whereas others have problems with letter and word formation. Writing deficits have frequently been related to visual-motor integration problems (Lerner, 1976).

Creativity is probably the teacher's best tool for remediating writing problems. The fundamental teaching strategy of practice needs to be implemented in an interesting and motivating fashion. Variety and meaningful application become important programming considerations. Although commercial workbooks and series are available, ditto sheets, reams of paper, and other teacher-made materials often provide the needed practice.

COMMUNICATION

The ability to communicate is viewed by many educators and psychologists as being central to interpersonal relationships and academic learning. There has been a long-standing interest in the development of communication skills by exceptional children and growing concern for the communication disorders of developmentally disabled students. For many years psycholinguistic theory has contributed to the understanding of communication (Tager-Flushberg, 1985), and since Skinner's (1957) affirmation of the operant nature of language, considerable attention has been directed toward the application of behavioral principles to remediate communication deficits (Carr, E.G., 1985). The work of Ivar Lovaas and others in the late 1960s (Hollis and Sherman, 1967; Isaac, Thomas, and Goldiamond, 1960; Lovaas, Berberich, Perloff, and Schaefer, 1966) initiated interest in the speech, language, and communication development of severely developmentally disabled children (Bryer and Joyce, 1985; Schopler and Mesibov, 1985).

Discussions of the development of communication skills by developmentally disabled students focus on the acquisition of specific skills and consideration for certain issues. For example, assessing the integrity of sensory and neurological systems has been considered by many authors to be a prerequisite to instruction in verbal imitation and functional communication (Powers and Handleman, 1984). Also, increased attention has been directed toward the issues of spontaneity and alternative forms of communication.

Integrity of Peripheral Sensory Systems

Before initiating formal communication training for the developmentally disabled student, it is important to assess the integrity of sensory and neurological systems (Powers and Handleman, 1984; Wetherby and Koegel, 1982). Thoroughly investigating physiological conditions that influence behavior can provide useful information to clinicians. For example, diagnostic information about hearing, vision, and motor and speech mechanisms may assist the educator in the design of communication programs (Handleman, Arnold, Veniar, Kristoff, and Harris, 1982).

Audiologic, visual, neurological, and oral examinations of the developmentally disabled are often difficult to conduct and are complicated by the communication and social deficits of the children (Handleman et al., 1982; Powers and Handleman, 1984). The difficult-to-manage behavior of the severely developmentally disabled student may interfere with or prevent examination (Powers and Handleman, 1984). As a result of these difficulties, physicians might resort to sedating the child or parents might delay or avoid medical examinations in anticipation of their child's reaction. More suitable alternatives are discussed in Chapter 10.

Nonverbal and Verbal Imitation

After a student is under good instructional control and is reasonably motivated to learn, imitation training usually begins (Harris, 1975; Lovaas, 1981). The importance of imitation as a prerequisite to communication for developmentally disabled students is well documented (Baer, Peterson, and Sherman, 1967; Harris, 1975; Lovaas, 1981). As a starting point many authors suggest that gross motor imitation should precede vocal imitation even though the relationship between nonverbal and verbal imitation is not certain (Haring, N. G., 1982). Nonverbal imitation is reported to facilitate generalized imitative repertoires (Peterson, 1968) and to assist in shaping the imitation of mouth movements (Lovaas, 1981). In addition, nonverbal imitation is an important prerequisite to sign language and other manual forms of communication (Carr, E. G., 1981). Table 4–5 provides some examples of nonverbal imitation tasks.

There are various guidelines to consider for establishing verbal imitation with developmentally disabled learners. For example, recording the vocalizations that a preverbal child spontaneously emits provides useful information for targeting initial sounds. Lovaas and colleagues (1966) have suggested that those sounds that can be prompted manually (e.g., m, w, f, ŏ, ē, p, oo) should be attempted first, followed by sounds that have visual salience (p, b, m, w, f, th, ŏ, ē, ō). Imitation training is gradually expanded to include words and short phrases. Table 4–6 presents a sample program for teaching verbal imitation.

Functional Language

Once the rudiments of speech are established, communication training typically focuses on functional language (Cardosa-Martins, Mervis, and Mervis, 1985; Harris, 1975; Lovaas, 1981). Functional language extends beyond the mechanics of speech and includes an increased capacity to understand language and the ability to exchange information. Many developmentally disabled children who develop speech have difficulty with the interpersonal component of

Table 4–5. Nonverbal Imitation Tasks

Gross Motor Movements	Fine Motor Movements	Mouth Movements
Hand clap	Finger point	Tongue extension
Arm wave	Fist formation	Teeth tap
Head nod	Finger tap	Lip purse
Foot stamp	Foot twist	Mouth movement

communication (Powers and Handleman, 1984). There are also those students who demonstrate speech deficits and encounter greater difficulty with the more conceptual demands of language. Regardless of ability functional language training attempts to stress the utility of language for affecting the environment.

Initially, functional language programming is designed to establish or expand receptive and expressive identification of environmental objects and actions (Beisler and Tsai, 1983; Charlop, Shreibman, and Thibodeau, 1985; Litt and Schreibman, 1981). Next, attention typically focuses on increasing the complexity of language to include the use of questions (Sherman, 1965), prepositions (Lovaas, 1981), compound sentences (Stevens-Long and Rasmussen, 1974), and other grammatical forms. There is repeated confirmation of the acquisition of generative grammar by students with mild, moderate, and severe developmental disabilities (Bennet and Ling, 1972; Fygetakis and Gray, 1970; Garcia, Guess, and Byrnes, 1973). Table 4–7 presents a listing of functional language activities.

There are a number of issues to consider when designing a functional language curriculum for developmentally disabled learners. For example, although some authors advocate the use of developmental programming for these students, there are data suggesting that the developmental model may not always apply (Handleman, Powers, and Harris, 1984; Sternberg, 1982). Some students might be ready for picture identification even though they still experience difficulty with the identification of concrete objects. There is also concern for the lack of spontaneous responding demonstrated by some developmentally disabled students. Many severely developmentally disabled children acquire situationally specific responses and do not initiate verbal interactions. Programs designed to increase a student's spontaneity attempt to manipulate the environment to create a need for communication and reduce reliance on verbal prompts (Sosne, Handleman, and Harris, 1979).

Table 4-6.   Program for Teaching Vocal Imitation

Target Behavior
Vocal imitation: single sounds

Operational Definition of Behavior
The child will imitate a single sound within 3 to 5 seconds of S^D presentation.

Description of Program
Establish appropriate sitting and attending behaviors.
S^D: "(Name), say _____."
Response: The child will imitate a single sound accurately.
Consequence: Reward correct response with appropriate reinforcement. If child does not respond or responds incorrectly, provide prompt and social reinforcement only.
Step 1:   Present S^D and single sound from set. Child is to imitate modeled sound accurately within 10 seconds. Continue for 20 trials.
Step 2:   Same as Step 1 but decrease response time progressively until child can respond within 5 seconds. Continue for 20 trials.

Data
+ = correct program.
− = incorrect response.
Criterion: 85% correct response for two consecutive sessions

Comments
This program can also be used for imitation of words.

Alternative Forms of Communication

Consideration of the use of alternative forms of communication with developmentally disabled students has grown in recent years (Konstantareas, 1984; Wilbur, 1985). Sign language represents the most popular alternative to oral communication; however, communication boards and various electronic devices are being used with increased frequency (Powers and Handleman, 1984). Although the efficacy of sign language is still being discussed, there are numerous reports of the successful use of sign with developmentally disabled learners (Alpert, 1980; Bonvillian, Nelson, and Rhyne, 1981; Carr, E. G., 1982a). The decision to introduce sign language or another approach to communication as an alternative to speech or simultaneously with speech instruction is typically made only after a student's speech ability has been carefully assessed (Carr, E. G., 1982b).

SOCIAL SKILLS

Deficits in social skills are endemic among developmentally disabled learners (Davies and Rogers, 1985; Schloss and Schloss, 1985) and interrelated with other areas of functioning (Powers and Handleman, 1984). Avoidance of eye contact, interpersonal distance, desire to maintain environmental sameness, and various deficits in

Table 4–7.   Functional Language Activities

Social questions
Polar concepts
Yes or no responses
Expression of need
Function of objects or pictures
Description of objects or pictures
Requests
Greetings

adaptive behavior are displayed by many of these students and can interfere with cognitive and language development. Although the type and severity of social skill deficit may vary across the developmentally disabled population, social development is a major educational concern and an important curricular area.

There are a variety of factors that help to explain the social deficits of developmentally disabled children. Some students may have failed to learn certain social skills because of impaired language and cognitive abilities (Howlin, 1978) or a variety of developmental factors (Lovaas et al, 1979). Others may be having difficulty as the result of insufficient educational planning or experiences (Powers and Handleman, 1984). Regardless of the origin of the social skill deficit, there is a growing availability of resources to help teach skills of social interaction, social communication, and play and leisure activities.

Social Interaction

The development of interaction skills by developmentally disabled students reduces the dissonance with nonhandicapped persons and increases social integration (Powers and Handleman, 1984). It is often the unresponsiveness of these children that increases interpersonal distance. Regardless of cognitive functioning or communication ability, the child who laughs inappropriately or who climbs on furniture will quickly become the focus of attention. In addition, the extreme management problems of severely developmentally disabled children are largely responsible for their social isolation. Increased social participation is often related to improved social interaction.

Social interaction skills are varied and range from eye contact to a gesture of affection. An important prerequisite for successful community participation is the reduction of maladaptive and disruptive behaviors to increase social acceptance (Powers and Handleman, 1984). The student who is under good instructional control and is generally compliant with instructional demands is better prepared to respond to social cues that are often abstract. More advanced skills might include social approach behavior and social responsiveness (Foxx, 1977). Each of these fundamental interaction skills includes a variety of component behaviors such as determining proper distance, maintaining good posture, smiling, and listening.

Social Communication

Deficits in social communication often impede appropriate social interaction by developmentally disabled students (Powers and Handleman, 1984). Interfering skills include loudness, intonation, interruptions, speech latency, and rate of speech (Borstein, Back, McFall, Friman, and Lyons, 1980; Matson and Earnhart, 1981). These behaviors unfortunately become salient aspects of interactions that typically terminate the social encounter. Remediation of social communication deficits is fundamental to social comfort and competency.

The remediation of social communication deficits has received increased attention. For example, there have been various attempts to help developmentally disabled students modulate their voices (Borstein et al., 1980; Matson and Andrisak, 1982). Suggested techniques have included self-monitoring, direct feedback, and the reinforcement of appropriate volume. Matson and Andrisak (1982) also demonstrated the effectiveness of self-monitoring for reducing inappropriate communication behaviors such as insulting, arguing, or interrupting. In addition, these authors were successful in teaching developmentally disabled adults a variety of conversational skills such as introducing oneself, giving compliments, and talking politely.

Play and Leisure Activities

Many developmentally disabled students are unable to appropriately occupy themselves during unstructured times (Li, 1985; Murphy, Callias, and Carr, 1985; Wulff, 1985). Teaching children to play, to read a book, or to initiate interactions with others during noninstructional times challenges most educators and clinicians. For example, the severely developmentally disabled child will often choose a nonpurposeful or self-stimulatory behavior as a free-time activity. Some of the factors that contribute to these deficits include presence of interfering behaviors, lack of motivation, and dependency on various classroom cues.

Teaching the developmentally disabled student to adaptively use unstructured time is a complex task. Because motivation is fundamental to leisure-time activities, the educator must first become familiar with the individual student's interests and preferences (Mithaug and Hanawalt, 1978). Direct observation and parent interviews are two very effective methods for obtaining this important information. The reduction of those behaviors that interfere with performance is another important consideration (Powers and Handleman, 1984). Once a child has become more receptive and activities have been identified, the teaching of play and leisure activities can be facilitated by task analysis and shaping strategies (Keogh, Faw, Whitman, and Reid, 1984; Schleien, Wehman, and Kiernan, 1981), and by modeling and imitation.

LIFE SKILLS

As the comprehensive educational needs of the developmentally disabled are being considered, increased attention has been focused on independent and personal living skills (Adams, 1982; Powers and Handleman, 1984). Although disguised by many names throughout the years, life skills programming provides the bridge from traditional educational programming to functional everyday application. Daily living, self-help, and prevocational skills increase independence, self-sufficiency, and community participation. This careful balance of school, home, and community goals provides the developmentally disabled student with the most flexible, durable, and appropriate education. Table 4–8 provides a listing of common life skills activities.

Daily Living and Self-Help Skills

The independent functioning of developmentally disabled students is correlated with their ability to care for basic needs and participate in the community (Hull and Thompson, 1980; Smith and Belcher, 1985; Sutter, Mayeda, Call, Yanagi, and Lee, 1980). Although children with mild and moderate disabilities have benefitted for years from training in daily living and self-help areas, it is only recently that the severely developmentally disabled have been offered similar opportunities (Adams, 1982). The wider application of behavioral

Table 4-8.   Life Skills Activities

Prevocational	Daily Living
Matching	Toileting
Sorting	Grooming
Patterning	Cooking
Assembly	Gardening
Packaging	Dressing
Collating	Hygiene
Filing	Cleaning
Block printing	Setting table

strategies is probably responsible for this extension of programming to all students.

Daily living and self-help programming encompasses many skills. Probably the most widely discussed self-help skill is toileting (Azrin and Foxx, 1976; Largo and Stutzle, 1977). For health and psychological reasons toileting and other personal hygiene skills are important curricular considerations for all students. Eating, dressing, and grooming skills also represent major areas of programming (Diorio and Konarski, 1984). There are numerous accounts of developmentally disabled children learning table manners (Barton, Guess, Garcia, and Baer, 1970), proper use of utensils (Nelson, Cone, and Hanson, 1975), bathing skills (Treffrey, Martin, Samuels, and Watson, 1970), toothbrushing (Horner and Keilitz, 1975), and dressing (Azrin, Schaefer, and Wesolowski, 1976).

Prevocational Activities

Although the appropriateness of early vocational training is still being argued, many professionals agree that prevocational programming is important for all developmentally disabled students (Frederick, Buckley, Baldwin, Moore, and Stremel-Campbell, 1983). Once thought appropriate for the older student only, prevocational activities are now being included in the IEPs of young and old alike (Hill, 1982). It is not unusual to find prevocational goals set for the very young severely developmentally disabled child who needs the benefit of time to master learning. Preparing developmentally disabled students for the work world at an early age can often eliminate lost years of programming.

Reluctance by administrators to steal precious time from academic training is in part responsible for the limited attention given to prevocational programming in past years (Lynch and Singer, 1980). Combined with traditionally held low expectations for children with moderate and severe disabilities, curriculum development in this area has had a slow start (Hill, 1982). Recent years, however, have witnessed increased support and rapid growth in resources (Anderson-Inman and Deutchman, 1984; Foxx, McMorrow, and Mennemier, 1984; Wacker and Berg, 1984). For example, more agencies are developing prevocational programs, and there is greater dialogue between the schools and the community. As a result the younger child is exposed to prevocational and work-oriented activities for many years, and the older student is provided with community work sites and prepared for the work world by carefully arranged transitional experiences.

CURRICULUM RESOURCES FOR THE SEVERELY DEVELOPMENTALLY DISABLED

Curriculum planning for the severely developmentally disabled student is a complex task. Age of onset, presence of behavioral and communication disorders, and existence of multiple handicapping conditions are some of the factors that contribute to programming difficulty. A relatively short history of service delivery has also resulted in limited instructional support. The recent professional interest in the severely developmentally disabled student, however, has been responsible for a growing availability of resources. The following paragraphs include descriptions of a variety of materials that can help the teacher plan educational experiences for this special group of students.

Early Cognitive Instruction for the Moderately and Severely Handicapped (McCormack and Chalmers, 1978) is a two-volume series devoted to the design of instructional strategies for severely developmentally disabled students. The *Programming Guide* provides discussions on many topics related to assessing cognitive abilities and developing IEPs. Particular attention is placed on issues such as motivation, behavior management, and home programming. In the volume *Teaching Sequence* many strategies are presented for teaching basic cognitive skills. This volume includes step-by-step programs for matching, sorting, recognizing, identifying, and sequencing activities.

There are four short books in the *"How To" Series* (edited by Luce and Christian) that specifically address the needs of the severely developmentally disabled. *How to Create a Curriculum for Autistic and Other Handicapped Children* (Romanczyk and Lockshin, 1981) provides a very useful view of the administrative, legal, and educational issues involved in program development. The book contains many good examples and helpful guidelines for approaching tasks ranging from staffing to IEP preparation. *How to Teach Sign Language to Developmentally Disabled Children* (Carr, E. G., 1982b) is a valuable manual for teaching sign language. After a brief discussion of important considerations of alternative communication systems, E. G. Carr presents useful strategies for selecting appropriate signs and motivating students. *How to Teach Prevocational Skills to Severely Handicapped Persons* (Mithaug, 1981) is a timely presentation on prevocational training. This book provides the classroom teacher with guidance in selecting appropriate skills and sequencing instruction. *How to Integrate Autistic and Other Severely Handicapped Children into a Classroom* (Koegel, 1982) addresses the important programming issues of normalization and mainstreaming. The pages of this book provide informative discussions of topics such as increasing group size and the use of normal peer models.

Individualized Assessment and Treatment for Autistic and Developmentally Disabled Children is a two-volume series designed to help parents, teachers, and other professionals better understand the deficits and educational needs of severely developmentally disabled children. Volume 1, *Psychoeducational Profile* (Schopler and Reichler, 1980), describes a developmental approach to assessment. The psychoeducational profile (PEP) is an inventory of skills created to identify learning patterns in social, cognitive, and communication areas. Volume 2, *Teaching Strategies for Parents and Professionals,* (Schopler, Reichler, and Lansing, 1980), bridges assessment and programming by providing specific teaching techniques for remediating deficiencies as identified by the PEP. The strategies presented in this volume go beyond the PEP and are applicable to the general programming needs of these students.

Three books in the *Steps to Independence Series* are specifically helpful in curriculum planning for students with severe developmental disabilities. Although each manual is intended for parents, there are many useful guidelines for teachers as well. *Behavior Problems* (Baker, Brightman, Heifetz, and Murphy, 1976b) presents helpful strategies for dealing with the often troublesome behaviors of the children. Examples and diagrams throughout the book guide the reader through specific steps for promoting behavior change. *Early Self-Help Skills* (Baker, Brightman, Heifetz, and Murphy, 1976c) provides the reader with a systematic approach to teaching important life skills. Following directions; imitating actions; and eating, dressing, and grooming activities are some of the skills addressed in this book. *Play Skills* (Baker, Brightman, and Blacker, 1983) is equally informative in its presentation of strategies for teaching play skills.

This book is a needed contribution to an underrepresented area in the literature.

Teaching Developmentally Disabled Children: The Me Book (Lovaas, 1981), commonly called *The Me Book,* is a valuable addition to the libraries of parents and professionals. Lovaas has produced a book that carefully blends discussions on the nature and needs of the severely developmentally disabled with useful guidelines for programming. The scope of the book is comprehensive and includes discussions on readiness, early communication, basic self-help, and more advanced language. Of particular interest are the chapters on programming in community settings and building spontaneous behavior. The book also includes contributions from prominent authors in the field of developmental disabilities.

Teaching Makes a Difference (Donnellan, Gossage, LaVigna, Schuler, and Traphanen, 1977) is a well-organized manual for setting up classes and designing programs for severely developmentally disabled students. Whether concerned with creating a class for autistic children, conducting parent training, or implementing a discrete trial teaching format, this book provides useful considerations for professionals and students. There are some particularly informative chapters on basic classroom behaviors and discrimination learning. The book also includes appendixes on terminology and instructional materials.

SUMMARY

Designing a curriculum that addresses the various needs of the developmentally disabled is a difficult task. The highly individual and idiosyncratic learning styles of these students in many cases requires an interdisciplinary effort. Although Jesse Kohl's teacher in the case that opened this chapter was an effective educational planner, the input from the child study team contributed to the teacher's programming success. The task of educating the developmentally disabled is often facilitated by professional support and educational resources.

Once a student has mastered the basic skills, the teacher can begin the complex task of developing a comprehensive curriculum. As plans are made for the teaching of basic readiness skills and more sophisticated academic skills, the importance of proficiency in instructional control areas is heightened. If a student cannot sit still or attend to educational materials, little learning will occur. The teacher must be prepared to stimulate further knowledge while encouraging student motivation and attention.

The teacher of the developmentally disabled is usually well trained in curriculum development. Teacher training programs typically include methods courses in academics, communication, and social development. For example, the importance of reading instruction is usually stressed by a requirement for at least one course in remedial reading. This knowledge obtained from course work, combined with a wealth of commercial resources, provides the basic tools for designing individualized educational programs. Successful educational programming, however, must reflect an ongoing sensitivity to the individual needs of the student.

The teacher of the severely developmentally disabled is somewhat at a disadvantage. The generic teacher training programs do not usually include course work in severe developmental disabilities and there are very few specialty programs. In addition, the relatively restricted market has resulted in limited commercial resources. This teacher's best professional tools are commitment, experience, and a small but growing number of educational materials.

Chapter 5

Assessment of the Developmentally Disabled

Case Report: Risa

The elementary school child study team had gathered to discuss Risa Bates's 3-year evaluation. For the past 2 years Risa had attended an out-of-district program where she was placed in a class of neurologically impaired, communication handicapped children. The decision to place her in the private setting was based on her lack of progress in one of the district's self-contained classes. Risa was 8 years old at the time of the reevaluation, which was prompted by state mandate.

The purpose of the meeting was to integrate the findings of various evaluations that were conducted. The school psychologist, learning consultant, and speech pathologist had all completed testing and were prepared to discuss their findings. They all agreed that the assessment was extremely difficult because of Risa's communication difficulties and behavior problems. Each reported that modifications of testing practices were often necessary to obtain meaningful information. In many cases it was necessary for the classroom teacher to be present to motivate Risa and to interpret her responses.

The psychologist prefaced her comments by indicating that the results of testing should be viewed as only a baseline of current performance from which to measure future progress. She emphasized that because of testing difficulties and frequent modifications of test protocol, the results could not be interpreted as absolute measures of ability. An example of the intricacies of assessing Risa was provided during administration of the Stanford-Binet when Risa's lack of response to identifying the body parts of a doll prompted asking her to label her own body parts—a task that she performed successfully. The psychologist noted that without similar changes in procedure, information about Risa's abilities would not have been identified. In summary, she described Risa as continuing to function in the moderately retarded range of intelligence with communication and behavior difficulties.

The learning consultant also confirmed the tentative nature of his results and shared similar frustrations in testing. He described how useful the teacher's presence was during testing. On many occasions the teacher was able to redirect Risa's attention and motivate her to attempt difficult tasks. The learning consultant reported that the teacher was most useful in interpreting Risa's responses and making suggestions for alternative questions. He also stated that classroom observation provided him with useful information regarding Risa's abilities. In conclusion, he described Risa's difficulties with more abstract learning and the probable contribution of her inattentiveness to her deficits.

The results of the evaluation by the speech pathologist confirmed the reports of her colleagues and described the current status of Risa's communication difficulties. The speech pathologist indicated that she felt testing was greatly facilitated by the ongoing relationship she had with Risa during speech therapy. The evaluation was completed in a shorter time than was anticipated, and Risa was generally motivated throughout the sessions. She described how on occasion animal crackers were useful in prompting Risa's performance and how she used other techniques that have proved successful in the classroom.

The group agreed to recommend continued placement in the private program. Suggestions for short- and long-term programming were also generated. In light of the difficulties they all encountered during testing, the psychologist recommended that the team make more frequent visits during the upcoming year to help build and maintain rapport with Risa.

Case Commentary. Assessment of the developmentally disabled is an intricate task. The child study team's experience with Risa illustrated how factors such as communication deficits and behavior problems contribute to difficulties in testing. In fact, deviations from testing and classroom observations often provided the professionals with more valuable information than insisting on strict conformity with the rules would. All of the professionals who tested Risa described the tentative nature of their results and highlighted the importance of rapport building.

Clinicians and teachers need to approach the assessment of the developmentally disabled student with certain tools. A basic familiarity with the student is needed first to assist in test selection and modification of testing practices. A willingness to devote time to the assessment process, especially during rapport building, is also needed. In addition, the examiner must be open to using additional resources such as parents and teachers to facilitate responding and to using other assessment avenues beyond psychometric testing such as observation. Consideration of these important variables should result in useful evaluations and avoid frustrating situations in which little information is obtained and in which students are often described as "untestable."

INTRODUCTION

Educators and clinicians practicing in today's schools are faced with the complex task of assessing the developmentally disabled student (Powers and Handleman, 1984). The intricacy of diagnosis, the diversity of needs, and the variety of service options all contribute to the complexities of assessment. These factors require careful consideration by the professional, and in many cases specialized training may be needed to conduct successful assessments. Assessment of the severely developmentally disabled student, for example, often necessitates special considerations and alternative evaluation strategies.

Assessing the educational needs of developmentally disabled students provides the framework for comprehensive education. Creating a functional relationship between assessment and treatment facilitates educational planning and helps ensure individualized instruction. Also, ongoing evaluation can facilitate performance monitoring and encourage the continual fine tuning of programming. This meaningful relationship produces an assessment-teaching cycle that constantly remains sensitive to the needs of all students.

Although assessment practices are widely discussed, there are a variety of issues of particular concern to the developmentally disabled population. This chapter surveys issues such as the usefulness of testing and provides resources and guidelines for effective and successful assessment. A detailed discussion of the components of traditional and behavioral assessment and a model for comprehensive assessment are presented. Also, assessment considerations for the severely developmentally disabled are discussed and selected instruments critiqued.

PSYCHOEDUCATIONAL ASSESSMENT

Recent years have witnessed increased interest in interdisciplinary service delivery (Kirk and Gallagher, 1983). Input from various professionals is viewed as a necessary component of educational planning and programming. Medicine, psychology, social work, and speech are a few of the many professions currently contributing to educational decision making. The particular contribution of psychology to testing and evaluation practices, for example, has resulted in a united effort that is referred to as psychoeducational assessment.

Discussions of the psychoeducational assessment of developmentally disabled students typically include attention to both traditional testing practices and behavioral assessment strategies (Powers and Handleman, 1984). Although the merits and weaknesses of each approach have been argued, current practice tends to reflect a blending of traditional and behavioral strategies. For example, the results of psychological or educational testing are often combined with behavioral observations during testing or classroom activities. This combined effort produces information about a student's relative standing and individual performance.

The efficacy of testing in education has been widely discussed and has received more criticism than any other educational practice (Connelly, 1985; Galagan, 1985; Salvia and Ysseldyke, 1978). Testing practices have been considered ambiguous by some and imprecise by others (Swanson and Watson, 1982). Particular areas of concern include improper administration and inadequate standardization, and many clinicians are questioning the usefulness of testing for programming. In addition, many authors have reported a decline in the utility of traditional testing practices in the assessment process (Scott, 1980; Smith and Knoff, 1981).

Educators and psychologists frequently are called upon to assess developmentally disabled students. This assessment often includes the use of standardized tests. Requests for testing typically emanate from administrators, pediatricians, and other clinicians, and most states require standardized testing to determine eligibility for special services. Recent years, however, have witnessed a devaluing of the role of testing and an expansion of assessment practices to include behavioral strategies (Powers and Handleman, 1984). This redirection of educational practice has begun to emphasize the functional as opposed to the descriptive nature of assessment (Tucker, 1985).

Focusing assessment on the goals of planning and programming is much more compatible with the needs of the severely developmentally disabled than was traditional assessment (Powers and Handleman, 1984). Initially, when many students are described as "untestable," behavioral assessment strategies are valuable in determining skill deficits and in directing educational programming. As the student matures and behavior problems interfere less with test taking, formal testing can play an adjunctive role in assessment. For example, standardized testing can assist material selection and programming and can also provide a baseline measure from which to measure performance.

Elements of Traditional Assessment

Analysis of prominent positions on psychoeducational assessment reveals three major goals: (1) the observation and evaluation of behavioral repertoires during standardized testing, (2) the analysis of test data to provide a profile of strengths and weaknesses, and (3) the synthesis of findings to assist diagnosis and guide educational interventions (Powers and Handleman, 1984). These goals apply to the psychological and educational testing of developmentally disabled students and serve to encourage the clinician to integrate both behavioral and performance measures.

Although the sanctity of the test protocol is highly regarded, the maintenance of standardized procedures is often considered secondary in the assessment of the severely developmentally disabled (Powers and Handleman, 1984). The assessment of these students requires a somewhat different approach that deemphasizes comparisons and focuses on individual strengths and weaknesses. As a result modification of test practices may be necessary to combat interfering behaviors and limited test-taking experience. Although these deviations in procedure must be noted, they facilitate the gathering of important information about students who were once described as "untestable" (Alpern, 1967).

Behavioral Strategies

Behavioral assessment strategies, in isolation or as an adjunct to traditional practices, serve to objectify observations of behavior and facilitate the evaluation of students with moderate and severe developmental disabilities. The efficacy of behavioral assessment has been documented repeatedly for the developmentally disabled, and a respect for behavioral practices has resulted (Powers and Handleman, 1984). An emphasis is placed on present functioning as opposed to causes or past experience, and the specificity of behavioral assessment techniques greatly facilitates educational planning and programming.

Examination of various views of behavioral assessment (Hawkins, 1979; Hawkins and Dobes, 1975; Powers and Handleman, 1984) reveals several components. Initially, teachers, related professionals, and parents screen the student for global behavioral excesses and deficits. The anecdotal reports that are usually developed from this early screening serve to target specific areas of concern. Rank ordering of selected target behaviors next leads to the writing of operational definitions to guide the identification of both antecedents and consequences of behaviors. The results of this systematic data gathering prompt the design of educational interventions. Behavioral assessment strategies continue to monitor the effectiveness of the treatment plan to facilitate response maintenance, the generalization of learning, and the fine tuning of educational planning.

A MODEL FOR THE ASSESSMENT OF THE DEVELOPMENTALLY DISABLED

Efforts to combine traditional psychoeducational testing with behavioral assessment strategies have resulted in an assessment process that is more sensitive to the needs of the developmentally disabled (Salvia and Ysseldyke, 1978). Behavioral assessment complements traditional evaluative techniques and minimizes some of the limitations of testing (Powers and Handleman, 1984). This combined approach to assessment provides the comparative information that is often needed, as well as a valuable profile of individual strengths and weaknesses to guide educational programming. The intraindividual nature of behavioral techniques has increased the value of psychoeducational assessment for students with mild, moderate, and severe developmental disabilities. Table 5-1 presents a menu of tests and behavioral assessment strategies from which to tailor an individualized assessment plan.

Components of Psychoeducational Assessment

Maintaining the goal that assessment should guide effective programming and treatment creates a functional posture for the entire assessment process (Blankenship, 1985; Powers and Handleman, 1984; Swanson and Watson, 1982). Of the various assessment models that are proposed (Bateman, 1965; Deno, S. L., 1985; Germann and Tindal, 1985), those that include a testing-teaching cycle seem most compatible with the needs of the developmentally disabled. The following components, which stress evaluation for planning, have been useful when assessing many developmentally disabled students (Powers and Handleman, 1984).

Identification of Learning Deficits

Psychoeducational testing and behavioral assessment strategies can assist in identifying particular areas of learning difficulty. A dis-

Table 5–1.   Elements of Psychoeducational Assessment

Available Tests (Source)	Behavioral Strategies
Detroit Test of Learning Aptitude (Bobbs-Merrill)	Behavior definitions
Developmental Test of Visual-Motor Integration (Follett)	Behavioral objective
Frostig Developmental Test of Visual Perception (Consulting Psychologist Press)	Structured interviews
	Task analysis
Illinois Test of Psycholinguistic Abilities (University Park Press)	Measurement
Key Math Diagnostic Arithmetic Test (American Guidance)	Data collection
Motor Free Visual Perception Test (Academic Therapy)	Data evaluation
Nebraska Test of Learning Aptitude (Psychological Corporation)	
Peabody Individual Achievement Test (American Guidance)	
Peabody Picture Vocabulary Test - R (American Guidance)	
Slosson Intelligence Test (Slosson Educational Publications)	
Stanford-Binet Intelligence Scale (Houghton Mifflin)	
Wechsler Test Series (Psychological Corporation)	
Wide Range Achievement Test (American Guidance)	
Woodcock Reading Mastery Tests (American Guidance)	
Woodcock Johnson Psycho-educational Battery (American Guidance)	

crepancy between current functioning and expected performance is often a good clue that a learning problem exists. Further diagnostic assessment will usually uncover specific deficits or developmental imbalances.

Determination of Current Level of Achievement

Clinical observation, standardized tests, and informal measures can help to evaluate performance in various skill areas and can provide an index of general achievement. For example, testing usually can pinpoint areas of concern, and systematic observation can determine generalization and maintenance difficulties. In addition, informal assessment may provide information untapped by tests.

Assessment of Student Learning

Investigating the information-processing styles of individual students can help to identify learning deficits and assist educational programming. Initially, it is often useful to assess both the reception and expression of information on a global level. A more systematic analysis of learning modalities and motor functioning can then be conducted.

Analysis of Variables That Influence Learning

It is useful to consider the many possible correlates of learning problems in children. Motivational, environmental, and physiological factors all can influence learning, and the identification of these factors will increase greatly the value of assessment results. The findings of initial screenings can be confirmed easily by various professionals whose input can also assist treatment and educational programming.

Organization of Assessment Data

The accurate interpretation of assessment results depends on careful analysis. Consideration of test reliability and validity will heighten or minimize findings, and variables such as consistency of responding or motivation will affect the ultimate usefulness of the results. Also, organizing information according to student strengths and weaknesses across instruments will help to plan remediation experiences.

Creation of a Teaching Plan

The relationship between assessment and education is strengthened when the results of testing, observation, and other strategies direct planning and programming. A curriculum that addresses behavioral excesses, skill deficiencies, and contributing factors will effectively facilitate program individualization. In addition, a teaching methodology that reflects sensitivity to differences in learning styles will help to promote optimal performance and progress.

Provision for Ongoing Performance Monitoring

Ongoing evaluation fuels the assessment-teaching cycle. Continuous assessment and performance monitoring help to ensure effective goal setting and educational programming. The frequent evaluation of skill acquisition can also facilitate the most current needs assessment and a continual fine tuning of teaching strategies.

Guidelines for Psychoeducational Assessment

Because of the behavioral heterogeneity of developmentally disabled children, there are many issues to consider when attempting formalized assessment (Powers and Handleman, 1984). Formal assessment is distinguished from those ongoing evaluations that are conducted by familiar professionals in surroundings that are comfortable to the student. For example, it is important to consider the student's experience with other professionals. Although some reluctance with novel examiners should be expected, the developmentally disabled student might exhibit some hesitancy even with child study personnel who frequently visit the classroom. It is also useful to consider the student's comfort with other environments. Doctors' offices and hospitals are often frightening to all children. Also, the issue of generalization becomes an important consideration for the severely developmentally disabled child. Finally, the student's history with assessment procedures should be considered. Unusual equipment or unfamiliar techniques might be stressful for the developmentally disabled student.

The child's teacher can be a very influential person in the assessment process (Powers and Handleman, 1984; Swanson and Watson, 1982). The teacher can assist the referral by providing the examiner with valuable information concerning a student's communication ability, general compliance, and idiosyncratic response patterns (Handleman et al., 1982). Progress reports, records of behavioral observations, videotapes, and charts and graphs can be made available to the examiner before the evaluation. Also, preassessment visits to the examining room or office may be useful for the more fearful student. In addition, teaching a child a new response or how to wear certain equipment can be very helpful preparations.

The teacher can assist the actual assessment also. Having the child's teacher available to help motivate or manage the student or simply to interpret responses can sometimes make the difference between a successful and an unsuccessful session. That element of familiarity that a child's teacher can provide is often critical for the severely developmentally disabled child to prompt responding and facilitate generalization.

Although the amount of initial preparation time will vary from student to student, it is useful for the examiner to expect that some preparatory steps will be needed (Powers and Handleman, 1984). Typically, the more severe the developmental disability, the more time that will be necessary to help the student prepare for the assessment process. Once the examiner is ready to begin the actual assessment, consideration of the following guidelines should be useful.

Preparation for Formal Assessment Experiences

A detailed intake or referral record including a social and developmental history can help to set the stage for the assessment (Powers and Handleman, 1984). Table 5–2 presents some useful components of an intake record. Depending on the nature of the assessment, this record can be filled out by parents, teachers, or other professionals before the evaluation. Any questions that the examiner might have can be clarified in conferences or during preassessment visitations to the child's class. Classroom visits also provide a more comfortable ground for child-professional introductions and allow the examiner to gather valuable information from direct observation. These preassessment experiences better equip the professional to conduct a successful assessment.

Building rapport with the student is an important first step in the assessment process. Rapport building is especially critical during the first meeting and remains important in subsequent sessions. The amount of time needed to build a working relationship will depend on variables such as the nature of the handicapping condition, age, and the student's ability to tolerate novel situations (Powers and Handleman, 1984). Allowing a child to wander about the room or play with some toys can help place the student at ease. Brief conversations about personal interests also can help to reduce anxiety. Student comfort is an important prerequisite to a productive session, and much valuable information can be obtained during rapport-building activities.

Depending on the situation there are times when the child's parents can assist the assessment process. Initial participation by parents may help make the child more comfortable, and the parents can help identify preferred rewards and interpret responses. This involvement can also reduce the anxiety that many parents bring to the sessions, sometimes feeling that they too are being evaluated (Handleman and Powers, 1984). Nonetheless, parent presence can interfere with assessment, and it is important to be vigilant to both facilitative and disruptive effects. Parents, like teachers, are a valu-

Table 5-2.   Components of an Intake Record

1. Family demographics
2. Birth and developmental history
3. Educational and treatment history
4. Summary of interdisciplinary evaluations
5. Current status (communication, social, cognitive development)
6. Concerns
7. Release forms

able resource and frequently can make the difference between successful and unsuccessful sessions.

Selection of Appropriate Situations and Assessment Materials

There are many variables to consider when selecting appropriate instruments and designing effective assessment experiences for the developmentally disabled student. Formal and informal activities should be planned in light of student interests and initial sense of ability (Ho, Glanville, and Brave, 1980). Although chronological age will serve as an appropriate selection criteria for many students, developmental level is often a more valuable index for the severely developmentally disabled (Powers and Handleman, 1984).

Modifications of standardized tests may be necessary to accommodate multihandicapping conditions and idiosyncratic response patterns (Powers and Handleman, 1984). After a survey of tests not in need of adaptation, tests that are designed for particular handicapping conditions will be useful to consider. It is important for the examiner to assess the style of stimulus presentation and response format of the various instruments being considered. Although using alternative forms of stimulus presentation or accepting different response formats such as signs, gestures, or pointing deviates from protocol and must be noted, these adaptions often can provide important information. Reluctance to adapt traditional tests to the needs of the developmentally disabled can result in inadequate information or in termination of the evaluation.

Multiskill testing provides a comprehensive view of student strengths and weaknesses (Powers and Handleman, 1984). Using tests that measure a variety of skill areas gives the examiner a sense of relative abilities. Also, administering a variety of tests that assess similar areas can help confirm performance levels. A test battery that is sensitive to a broad range of functioning will result in the most complete student profile that is possible.

Assessment of the Student

Sensitivity to the learning styles of the developmentally disabled can contribute greatly to the success of the assessment session. For example, sitting quietly, maintaining eye contact, and attending to test materials are important test-taking behaviors. It may be necessary for the examiner to provide occasional prompts or initial training in these instructional control areas. In addition, frequent breaks and systematic encouragement may be necessary to maintain attention and responsiveness. The use of identified rewards and social approval will often serve to heighten and maintain student motivation. Carefully gauging the timing and tempo of the session will produce the optimal results (Powers and Handleman, 1984).

Assessing a student's experience with test taking is yet another challenge for the examiner. Many times students will respond incorrectly or not at all because they fail to understand the instructions or lack experience with a particular test format. A student who has difficulty generalizing learning, for example, will be at a disadvantage with traditional testing. For such a student the examiner must determine whether the child can be taught the required behavior or whether the response is beyond the child's ability (Powers and Handleman, 1984). Teaching to task can provide both valuable information about a student's learning style and test results that would not have been previously possible. All deviations from test practices must be noted in the final report to avoid misunderstandings and to increase usefulness to other clinicians.

CONSIDERATIONS FOR THE ASSESSMENT OF SEVERELY DEVELOPMENTALLY DISABLED STUDENTS

Assessing severely developmentally disabled children requires patience, creativity, flexibility, and clinical sensitivity (Parks, 1983; Powers and Handleman, 1984). Despite commitment and preparation by the examiner some children will not be amenable to formal evaluation. For these students the examiner must rely more heavily on behavioral observations in the classroom and other educational settings and on reports of third-party assessments conducted by parents and teachers. Visits to the child's home and other community settings can also provide valuable information about performance.

Ongoing performance monitoring is often the most valuable assessment strategy for severely developmentally disabled learners. The criterion-referenced nature of behavioral assessment techniques can reflect the changing needs of these students and promote the fine tuning of educational programming. For example, probing and behavior charting are two very useful techniques that can be used to assess a variety of skills and provide a visual record of student performance.

A probe is a quick test of behavior that can be conducted under a variety of conditions (Haring and Gentry, 1976). For example, a probe can assess learning in all curricular areas and can help determine if a behavior has been generalized or has been maintained. Behavior or skills to be sampled by probes can approximate the teaching task exactly or can be observed under different conditions. Also, probes should be sufficiently repeated to evaluate consistency of responding, and reinforcement for attending should be provided to motivate performance.

Charts and graphs visually present performance data and provide a permanent record of student progress. Charts that include a tally of correct responses, failures, and prompted behavior can provide the teacher will useful information about skill acquisition. Graphs depicting the frequency of a particular act or the duration of a disruptive behavior can present important data to the clinician quickly. These visual records of behavior provide valuable tools for monitoring teaching effectiveness and for ensuring accountability.

REVIEW OF SELECTED TESTS FOR THE SEVERELY DEVELOPMENTALLY DISABLED

Bayley Scales of Infant Development

The Bayley Scales (Bayley, 1969) assess functioning below the developmental level of 3 years. Although standardized on a population of nonhandicapped children, the Bayley Scales are useful for assessing severely developmentally disabled students (Powers and Handleman, 1984). Although the scales sample a wide range of behavior, an emphasis on motor functioning makes them appropriate for many nonverbal children.

Childhood Autism Rating Scale

The Childhood Autism Rating Scale (CARS) (Schopler, Reichler, DeVellis, and Daly, 1980) is designed to discriminate mildly and moderately autistic children from other developmentally disabled students. The child is observed and rated on each of 15 scales involving communication and social behavior. The CARS is a useful instrument for obtaining a descriptive profile of student behavior and for facilitating programming in social and communication areas.

Columbia Mental Maturity Scale

The Columbia Mental Maturity Scale (Burgemeister, Blum, and Lorge, 1972) provides a nonverbal measure of general ability. The scale includes simple perceptual classification tasks and some manipulation of symbolic concepts. This scale is particularly useful with severely developmentally disabled students (Powers and Handleman, 1984). Simple manipulative tasks and large stimulus materials make this instrument a good measure of nonverbal reasoning.

Developmental Profile II

The Developmental Profile II (Alpern, Boll, and Shearer, 1980) screens five abilities in children from birth through age 9 years. Information is obtained during an interview with a person who knows the student well. Because of the broad age range and concentration on areas such as self-help and communication, this instrument can provide useful descriptive information about severely developmentally disabled students.

Learning Accomplishment Profile

The Learning Accomplishment Profile (LAP) (Sanford, 1974) is an assessment device that allows teachers or parents to evaluate performance levels in six areas. The LAP was developed for children with developmental levels between 1 to 6 years and was designed to link assessment and instruction. Emphasis on the basic areas of co-ordination, self-help, and language development and the provision for teacher assessment make the LAP a useful inventory for severely developmentally disabled children.

McCarthy Scales of Children's Abilities

The McCarthy Scales of Children's Ability (McCarthy, 1972) was developed to assess intellectual functioning across a wide variety of areas. The 18 subtests range from Block Building and Puzzle Solving to Verbal Fluency and Conceptual Grouping. The variety of materials and the game-like quality of the tasks make the McCarthy Scales a viable instrument for the severely developmentally disabled.

TARC Assessment System

The TARC Assessment System (Sailor and Mix, 1975) is a behavioral assessment checklist designed to identify the current levels of functioning of severely developmentally disabled students. The TARC assesses the domains of self-help, motor ability, communication, and social skills and is designed to facilitate goal setting in these curricular areas. The TARC's reliance on direct behavioral observation provides a good bridge to assessment of educational programming.

Vineland Adaptive Behavior Scales

The Vineland Adaptive Behavior Scales (Sparrow, Balla, and Cicchetti, 1984) were designed to assess personal and social adaptive behavior from birth through 19 years of age. The questionnaire surveys the areas of communication, daily living, socialization, and motor skills and is administered during a structured interview. The Vineland's multi-item format can provide very useful information about the adaptive behavior of severely developmentally disabled children. Results obtained from the Vineland can assist diagnostic, educational, and research functions (Powers and Handleman, 1984).

Wisconsin Behavior Rating Scale

The Wisconsin Behavior Rating Scale (Song and Jones, 1980) was developed for children functioning below the developmental age of 3 years and uses a third-party informant. The scale contains 11 subtests ranging from motor abilities to socialization and life skills. The Wisconsin Behavior Rating Scale includes many items for severely developmentally disabled students and provides a good profile of adaptive behavior (Powers and Handleman, 1984).

SUMMARY

During the last decade assessment practices have assumed a major role in the diagnosis and treatment of developmentally disabled children. Once solely serving a very clinical function, today's practices are providing the foundation for educational programming. The combining of traditional psychoeducational testing and behavioral assessment strategies has created a more functional relationship between assessment and education. The evolution of an assessment-programming cycle continues to strengthen this link and to fine tune educational interventions.

The assessment of the developmentally disabled student is a complex process that requires consideration of various factors. In the case of Risa Bates's evaluation, the input from the interdisciplinary team was extremely valuable. The reports of the learning consultant, psychologist, and speech pathologist helped to confirm Risa's performance and crystalize areas of concern. Their findings led to a better understanding of Risa's abilities, and their recommendations and suggestions helped to modify current programming and to guide future planning.

The examiner of the developmentally disabled must bring to the assessment process personal training and experience and a willingness to modify practices to meet individual requirements. For example, the need for effective rapport building becomes heightened for these students, and the process of selecting appropriate instruments becomes analytic. In those cases in which test adaptations may be necessary, the examiner must feel comfortable in deviating from standard protocol and must be prepared to individually tailor assessment strategies.

Assessment of the severely developmentally disabled student presents additional challenges. Many of these students will not respond to traditional testing practices, and a reliance on those persons more familiar with the child will be needed. In these cases parents and teachers can serve as effective informants and active participants in the assessment process. In no other situation is the partnership between teacher, parent, and examiner more important.

Chapter 6

Children Live in Families

Case Report: The Torres Family

Maria and Carlos Torres had been married for 3 years when their first child, Miguel, was born. Carlos, a computer programmer for a small insurance corporation, and Maria, a nurse in the same organization, had joyfully planned for the birth of their child. With maternity benefits and an additional period of unpaid leave, Maria intended to remain at home with Miguel until he was a year old. At that time they expected that Maria's mother and Carlos's sister would provide some child care while Maria returned to work part-time.

In preparation for Miguel's arrival his parents had painted the nursery, bought shiny new furniture, and decorated with the gifts of stuffed animals, baseball gloves, and colorful pictures that came from all the family. Both Maria and Carlos felt ready to receive and love their first child.

Miguel's early months brought joy to everyone. He was a beautiful little boy with dark hair, dark eyes, and a quiet, undemanding disposition. He ate and slept well, seemed to need little attention, and would spend hours contentedly in his crib gazing off into space or staring at his hands. In fact, the first nibbling feelings of concern Maria felt were because her son seemed to need so little from her. Unless he was sick, Miguel almost never cried and rarely demanded his mother's company.

Miguel's motor development was on schedule. By the time he was a year old he had taken his first steps and used his chubby little hands to pull at and explore the many objects in his environment. In spite of this seemingly good progress Carlos and Maria felt a growing sense of concern because their boy still did not seem interested in them. He also did not babble very much and was often unresponsive when they called his name.

When Miguel was 18 months old, the Torreses raised their concerns with Miguel's pediatrician, who suggested they wait another few months and observe the boy's progress. Then, at 24 months, when Miguel still had not spoken his first word, seemed content to dwell within his own world, and had begun to spend long hours each day twirling the wheels on his toy truck it was evident to all concerned that something was seriously wrong with Miguel's development.

Extensive multidisciplinary evaluation at the local community mental health center eventually led to the diagnosis of infantile autism. The news was devastating to Carlos and Maria. Maria wept for several days, and Carlos, although he struggled to control his feelings and drag himself through each day at work, several times had to leave his desk in the middle of the day, retreat to the men's room, and cry. The couple felt as though all of their hopes and dreams had been shattered beyond repair. They could not believe that their shining, beautiful boy could be afflicted with so grave a condition. One night, about a week after they first learned the diagnosis, Maria and Carlos found themselves yelling at one another with a rage and frustration they had never before felt in their marriage. Suddenly, in the midst of their fight, they looked at one another and both began to weep. Their anger at each other dissolved as they clung together sharing their pain.

In the weeks that followed the Torreses began to reconstruct their lives. They had to rebuild their plans—accepting Miguel's handicap, doing everything they could to help the boy reach his potential, and creating a new set of dreams about their own futures. Maria's parents extended themselves to help the family. They insisted on taking Miguel to their home several evenings a week and every few months took their grandchild with them for a long weekend so that Maria and Carlos could have some free time without Miguel's insistent demands.

The Torreses also found an excellent behaviorally oriented classroom for very young autistic children and enrolled Miguel in that class shortly before his third birthday. Miguel's teacher was able to help the family develop home management programs, and the school's parent "rap group" provided both parents with a forum for sharing with other parents of handicapped children some of their feelings of disappointment, anger, and frustration. Although none of this cured Miguel, or made him the normal, healthy child the Torreses had dreamed of, it did enable them to integrate the boy fully into their lives, to meet his many needs as effectively as possible, and to still retain some sense of control over their own lives.

Case Commentary. Few experiences in the life of a parent are more painful than learning that one's child has a serious handicap. As seen in the case of Maria and Carlos Torres, parents build loving dreams for their children and react with intense pain, disappointment, and anger when those dreams are shattered. Although the Torreses felt grief, frustration, and other painful emotions, they were also able to take active stops to improve their difficult situation. Following an episode of explosive anger with one another they recognized their shared mutual pain and moved toward, rather than away from, one another in the effort to reduce their misery.

Their extended family was an important source of support for Maria and Carlos. Maria's parents did not abandon their handicapped grandchild; on the contrary, they moved quickly to become a central source of support. Concerned not only about Miguel but also about Maria and Carlos, they insisted upon having Miguel spend time in their home so that Maria and Carlos would have free time to meet personal needs. This kind of loving, generous support can be invaluable to a family with a handicapped child.

The other vital source of support for the Torres family came from Miguel's school. His teacher became a trainer for Maria and Carlos, helping them master the intricacies of behavioral intervention and providing consultation in home programming. It was also important to Maria and Carlos that the other parents at the school became a supportive extended network of mutual caring.

INTRODUCTION

The purpose of this chapter is to give the teacher an appreciation of the impact that a developmentally disabled child has upon the family. Although a teacher's primary responsibility is to the children in his or her class, it is difficult to meet that responsibility fully unless the teacher works cooperatively with the family. This is true for the teacher of any child, but most compellingly true for the child with a handicap. Research with developmentally disabled children has shown that these youngsters often have serious difficulty transferring skills learned at school to the wider world. Thus, it is essential that parents work closely with the school to help the child bridge the gap between school and home.

Although training parents in behavior modification techniques and helping them design home programs is an important component of the teacher's role in facilitating the school-home connection, a focus at that level of didactic training is not always sufficient to create a facilitative atmosphere. Parents of handicapped children are often dealing with painful, difficult emotions that preclude their being effective home trainers for their child. It is therefore essential that the teacher be sensitive to the experiences of parents, siblings, and other family members and use this understanding to create a context that will enable the parents to be receptive to input from the school. Although the teacher is not a therapist and should not try to bring about the kind of change in a family that might be attempted by a psychologist, social worker, or psychiatrist, the professional educator can, nonetheless, respond as a sensitive, informed, and caring individual in the face of a family's pain and dysfunction.

The pages that follow review the available research concerning the impact of a handicapped child on the child's mother, father, and siblings and the effect of the child's special needs on the marriage and the extended family. The chapter also considers the kinds of interventions that are appropriate for teachers and indications for referrals to other professionals for specialized help with family problems.

IMPACT ON PARENTS

Anyone who has visited a family who has a seriously self-injurious child, a profoundly withdrawn autistic youngster, or a brain damaged, severely impaired child who needs continual supervision has seen firsthand how the special needs of these youngsters can affect family life. Even the less intensely needy Down's syndrome child or other moderately impaired developmentally disabled child who poses no major management problems requires extensive family resources.

In spite of the exceptional stress encountered by the family of a developmentally disabled child it is important to note that there are few data suggesting that these families suffer from a greater degree of severe psychopathology than other families. To the contrary, Koegel and colleagues (Koegel, Schreibman, O'Neill, and Burke, 1983) found no differences between parents of autistic children and a normal comparison group who were administered the Minnesota Multiphasic Personality Inventory, a widely used test of psychopathology. Similar reports have been made by other experts in the field, including J. Carr (1975) and Gath (1978) in their work with parents of Down's syndrome children and DeMyer (1979) in her study of parents of children with autism.

Although these families do not suffer a greater than usual frequency of serious mental disorders, they do respond with measurable distress to the experience of raising a handicapped child and in many cases describe greater life discomfort than do other parents (Cummings, 1976; Cummings, Bayley, and Rie, 1966; Gath and Gumley, 1984). Mothers of mentally retarded children describe their family environment as less encouraging of intense relationships and personal growth in independence and recreation than do mothers of normal children (Margalit and Raviv, 1983). The stress appears to be greater for the parents of more-impaired children, including autistic children, than for the parents of less-handicapped children (Beckman, 1983; Holroyd and McArthur, 1976).

Effects on the Mother

Although both parents feel the effects of living with a handicapped child, the stress is typically greater for mothers than it is for fathers and greater for single mothers than for mothers in intact marriages (Beckman, 1983). DeMyer (1979), a psychiatrist, did a detailed study of the parents of autistic children in which she used questionnaires and lengthy interviews to learn about the lives of these families. She reported that the mothers in her study described more feelings of guilt, suffered more physical complaints and tension, and had more doubts about their ability to be effective parents than did fathers. These differences may be due in part to the fact that fathers typically play a less central role in direct child care than do mothers, and mothers may therefore have more physical demands placed upon them and find more of their definition of self tied up in the role of parent than do fathers.

Consistent with DeMyer's findings, Gath (1978) identified more symptoms of depression among the mothers of Down's syndrome infants than among the fathers. The mothers of the Down's syndrome children also described more feelings of depression than did a control group of mothers of normal children. Unlike DeMyer (1979), Gath (1978) did not find that the mothers of the Down's syndrome infants believed themselves to be any less competent in managing their child than did mothers in the control group. There are several possible explanations for this difference between the mothers of autistic and Down's syndrome children, including the fact that the Down's syndrome children were younger and probably posed fewer management problems than the autistic children. In fact, when Gath and Gumley (1984) contacted theses families 6 years later, the parents reported that their children now posed more demands than did the control subjects.

Effects on the Father

Although there has been much less research on fathers than mothers of developmentally disabled children, men too are subjected to significant stress in response to the special needs of their handicapped child. Because fathers typically provide less direct care for their children, they may have fewer opportunities to feel that they are doing something of immediate value (Cummings, 1976). Furthermore, as the primary wage earners in many families fathers tend to worry more than mothers about the financial burdens created by their child's handicap and to be especially concerned about how those obligations will be met when the parents reach retirement age (Lamb, 1983; Price-Bonham and Addison, 1978). This concern is well founded because there are a variety of extra expenses involved in raising a handicapped child (Buckle, 1984).

In addition to coping with their own sense of disappointment and loss, DeMyer (1979) found that fathers may react strongly to the experience of seeing their wives' pain and of being unable to protect someone they love from that kind of physical and emotional stress. Thus, fathers, although generally less stressed than mothers, do experience significant life effects during the course of raising a developmentally disabled child.

Role of the Teacher

Although the professional educator cannot hope to treat the depression, anger, anxiety, or other dysfunctional responses that parents may experience as they struggle to cope with their developmentally disabled child's demands, the teacher nonetheless can be sensitive to the presence of these responses and can recognize how these factors may affect the parent's life. For example, the teacher who attempts to pressure a depressed parent into doing home teaching programs may heighten the parent's feelings of guilt and failure and leave both parent and teacher frustrated and disappointed.

If teachers cannot treat these problems, do they have a role in helping the parent? The answer is yes. One strategy in these matters is initially to approach each family with the expectation that they will be receptive to doing home programming. For some parents learning procedures to cope with their difficult child's demands and hearing some sympathetic words of support from a caring teacher may make life considerably easier and thus contribute to a diminution of the sadness, anger, and other negative emotions that have burdened the parent's days. When this approach fails, it is then appropriate to seek consultation with the special services personnel in the child's school. The school psychologist or social worker may be in a good position to explore with the family some of the obstacles to the parent's effective cooperation. Although the teacher may not intervene directly, sensitivity to the parent's pain may be crucial in identifying the need for consultation.

EFFECTS ON THE MARRIAGE

Good marriages are not easy to create. It takes continuing effort, enough time for effective communication, and a profound emotional commitment to promote a satisfying relationship. The high frequency of contemporary divorce speaks eloquently of the difficulties of sustaining a good marriage. Given the complexities of maintaining and enhancing an effective marriage, it is not surprising that the presence of a handicapped child can make this task even harder (DeMyer and Goldberg, 1983; Gath, 1978).

Marriages That Suffer

In spite of the extensive demands created by the special needs of the developmentally disabled child, there is little evidence that the presence of a handicapped child is directly related to deterioration of a marriage (Koegel et al., 1983). Rather, there may be a more complex relationship: Some marriages are enhanced and others are weakened by the challenge of meeting the child's needs.

Gath (1978) found significantly more poor marriages among the parents of the Down's syndrome babies than among a control group. However, she noted that only the marriages that were weak or moderate in functioning before the baby was born were most likely to suffer. She also noted that some of the couples earned higher scores on a measure of marital satisfaction than did the control subjects and may have found their marriages strengthened by the process of mutually coping with stress. Furthermore, in a 6-year follow-up of families, Gath and Gumley (1984) found no greater deterioration in the marriages of couples who had children with Down's syndrome than in those of control couples. Similarly, DeMyer (1979) observed that although having an autistic child had an adverse impact on some marriages, it strengthened others.

Further support for the notion that a marriage can benefit as well as suffer from the impact of raising a handicapped child came from Lonsdale's report (1978) that 55 percent of the couples interviewed felt that the child's presence had adversely affected their marriage, 17 percent believed the marriage had improved, and 28 percent reported it had no impact.

Relationships Between Child Care and Marriage

Not much is known about which marriages will be enhanced and which will suffer in the face of this kind of stress. Very little research thus far has addressed this important problem. One variable that does appear to be correlated with marital satisfaction is the sharing of child care responsibilities. Boyle (1985) asked parents of developmentally disabled children to complete two questionnaires, one describing their satisfaction with the marriage and the other describing the distribution of responsibilities for the care of their handicapped child. Table 6–1 shows some of the questions Boyle used to evaluate the distribution of child care effort within the family. The results of his study suggested that families that had an equitable distribution of child care also had higher marital satisfaction, whereas those families with greater imbalance of child care involvement reported less satisfaction in their marriage. Although the mothers in both the high and low marital satisfaction groups were more involved than the fathers in caring for the child, the discrepancy was greater in the low marital satisfaction group.

Time Demands

Developmentally disabled children typically require substantial amounts of time and direct physical care. Time that the mother or father devotes to the child is time that cannot be spent in other ways, including strengthening the marital bond. Although all parents expect to devote considerable time to meeting the emotional and physical needs of an infant or toddler, with the mentally retarded or autistic child these same demands may continue for years beyond the point when most parents would expect to be largely free of the burden of basic physical care. This continual drain on parental resources has the potential to adversely affect the marriage.

Sexuality

One specific form of marital contact that may suffer when there is a handicapped child in the home is the sexual relationship. At least two sources of stress may be involved. One source comes from the fatiguing demands of physical care imposed by the child's special needs. A parent who is exhausted from being up all night caring for a screaming child, or a couple who cope with their child's refusal to sleep alone by taking the child into bed with them, will have little energy or opportunity for sexual activity.

A second source is concern about the risk of conceiving another handicapped child. For some parents this concern may be diminished with genetic counseling so that they are aware of the probability of bearing another disabled child and familiar with the option of amniocentesis or other medical testing to identify certain genetic and chromosomal defects. One limitation of genetic counseling is that current technology cannot detect many forms of developmental disabilities before birth. Additionally, not all couples would elect to use contraceptive methods to prevent conception or to have an abor-

Table 6–1.   Sample Items From Parent Involvement Questionnaire

To what extent are you and your spouse involved in
1. Dressing your child in the morning?
2. Preparing your child for school?
3. Helping your child eat at meals?
4. Toileting your child?
5. Playing with your child; engaging in physical activities with your child?
6. Working with your child on home programs?
7. Initiating communication with your child's school?
8. Initiating communication with your child's physician(s)?
9. Demonstrating affection toward your child?
10. Preparing your child for bed at night?

Note: Each item is scored on a 7-point scale from "Myself always" (1) to "My spouse always" (7).

tion if they knew the fetus to be impaired. Nonetheless, for some families having these alternatives may be important.

Role of the Teacher

Some of the activities educators view as useful for the developmentally disabled child, such as home programming and taking the child into the community for broad exposure to many activities, may be in the long-term best interests of the child and the parents, but they do serve to place an even greater immediate demand on parents by requiring substantial time commitments. Thus, parents who devote themselves with total effort to the child may do so at a substantial price to the marriage and family. This in turn could have a serious impact on the long-term family stability and therefore on the welfare of the handicapped child.

It is important for teachers to modulate their expectations of parents and to consider how their suggestions for the handicapped child will affect the family as a whole. Helping a couple find a baby-sitter, reminding them of the importance of keeping a balance within their family life, and generally supporting the view that the child is part of, but not the whole of, the family may contribute to the long-term welfare of everyone involved.

Understanding the complexities of mutual, shared accommodation in a family may be especially difficult for the young teacher who does not yet have a family and has had only limited experience with other person's families. These teachers may want to be especially careful to ensure that the suggestions they make for parents are feasible in light of the demands that exist within the home. Failure to offer realistic advice may substantially diminish a teacher's credibility as parents come to realize that the teacher does not understand their situation.

The best way to avoid blunders with families is probably to inquire carefully about what the parents would regard as helpful. What do they want from the teacher? What are their programming priorities? How much time do they have to spend with their child? Respecting the family's ability to make these judgments reduces the burden imposed upon the teacher while enhancing the parent's sense of control and of being respected in a collaborative relationship.

EFFECTS ON BROTHERS AND SISTERS

A number of researchers have wondered whether there is anything unusual, especially difficult, or possible beneficial about growing up in a family in which there is a handicapped child (Edmundson, 1985). In general the data have suggested that it is more stressful to be the sibling of a handicapped child than of one who is not impaired (Ferrari, 1982; Lavigne and Ryan, 1979; Tew and Laurence, 1973). Nonetheless, just as with mothers and fathers and their marital relationship, there are individual differences in response, and some siblings describe positive benefits from living with a handicapped brother or sister.

Sex and Birth Order

Two variables that can influence the impact of living with a handicapped sibling are sex and birth order. For example, several studies have suggested that the stress may be especially intense for older sisters (Cleveland and Miller, 1977; Gath, 1973, 1974; Grossman, F. K., 1972). One hypothesis to explain this increase in stress is that older girls are often found in the role of "parental child" (Minuchin, 1974); that is, they may be given considerable responsibility for caring for their handicapped sibling or for other brothers and sisters. Some girls might feel burdened and resentful of such demands and express this anger overtly; others might react with guilt when they find themselves angry at their parents or handicapped sibling and may therefore appear sad and self-critical.

Older sisters may not be the only group at special risk; younger brothers have also been identified as particularly vulnerable to stress when there is a handicapped child in the home (Breslau, 1982). Although there are no research data to fully explain this finding, it is worth noting that boys typically require more parental guidance in growing up than do girls and exhibit more behavior problems (Eme, 1979). It may be that when a boy is born into a family after a handicapped child, the parents must devote so many resources to the handicapped child that they cannot provide all the supervision and input the boy requires. Furthermore, the boy may find that the times when he acts up and becomes problematic are the times that he gains parental attention. Under these circumstances a coercive pattern of interaction may arise in which the boy acts up, receives parental attention, and is thereby reinforced for bad behavior. Under some circumstances even negative attention such as yelling can be reinforcing for a child.

Diminished Reinforcement

Regardless of sex or birth order all siblings of developmentally disabled children have a different pattern of interaction with their brother or sister than other children have with nonhandicapped siblings. The autistic or severely mentally retarded child may offer little in terms of affectionate response. Even the less severely impaired, more emotionally responsive Down's syndrome children can offer their siblings few opportunities for the kind of intimate sharing of secrets, adventures, and mutual support that characterizes many good sibling relationships. Neither do the siblings of handicapped children have the same opportunities to learn to negotiate, manage aggression, or modulate competition that other children can learn from dealing with their brothers and sisters.

In spite of the limitations inherent in their sibling role, most siblings of handicapped children, like most other children, do not exhibit serious adjustment problems. Furthermore, some of them have reported that growing up with a handicapped child in the house served to enhance their lives. Cleveland and Miller (1977) interviewed the grown siblings of mentally retarded adults and found that most were well adjusted and had a positive attitude toward their mentally retarded siblings. Sisters had more contact than brothers with their handicapped siblings. Those women who were older sisters reported the most burdensome childhood demands and were more likely than the other siblings to have sought professional counseling; they were also more likely to have selected a helping profession for their adult careers.

Role of the Teacher

One of the useful roles the teacher can play in relation to the sibling of a handicapped child is to help the parents ensure that the nonhandicapped child is appropriately aware of the meaning of the handicapping condition. Excluding siblings from discussions about their handicapped brother or sister can cause more stress than giving them accurate information (Kaslow and Cooper, 1978). However, McKeever (1983) found that siblings of handicapped children rarely asked questions. As a consequence, adults must assume the primary responsibility for ensuring there is an appropriate flow of information.

Parents are sometimes unaware of the developmental factors that affect a child's ability to understand different levels of information about the handicap. The teacher, as someone who is broadly experienced with children, may be able to help parents decide what information to share with siblings and in what terminology.

Developmental psychologists have shown that although a child may use the same words that adults do, the concepts may have very different meaning to the young person. Just as adults would sensitively adjust the level of information when talking to a child about death (Spinetta, 1974), adoption (Brodzinsky, Pappas, Singer, and Braff, 1981) or illness (Simeonsson, Buckley, and Monson, 1979), so must they consider the sibling's developmental level when talking about handicapping conditions. In addition, just as sex education is an ongoing process in which children understand more as they get older, so too should the siblings of developmentally disabled children be offered increasingly abstract information as they grow up.

It can be useful for siblings to be trained in basic behavioral procedures and encouraged to use these methods when they interact with their developmentally disabled brother or sister (Colletti and Harris, 1977; Schreibman, O'Neill, and Koegel, 1983). Such training must of course respect the child's developmental needs and never impose excessive responsibilities. Special sensitivity to the position of older sisters and younger brothers may be warranted in this regard.

Siblings may be good role models for their handicapped brothers or sisters when playing games, learning new skills, or engaging in simple communication. In this way they can feel involved and can receive a good dose of parental attention while not detracting from the time parents must spend with the developmentally disabled child. It therefore makes sense to consult with parents about designing home programs that incorporate siblings in pleasurable ways.

A home visit should never be made without taking time to acknowledge directly the other children who are in the home. Excessive task-orientation that results in ignoring the other children can leave them feeling excluded, unimportant, and rejected. Even a few minutes in conversation may leave siblings with the message that they are perceived as discrete persons who merit respect.

IMPACT ON THE EXTENDED FAMILY

As seen in the case of Miguel Torres and his family at the beginning of this chapter, grandparents and other members of the extended family can be a valuable resource for the handicapped child and the child's parents and siblings. On the other hand, as reflected in the many popular jokes about in-laws, relationships with a person's extended family are not unambivalent; the extended family cannot always be counted on as a source of support and caring.

Unfortunately, there are few research data that can help in understanding the reactions of the extended family to the handicapped child. It is not surprising that this is so—there is very little information about the psychological functioning of the extended family under any conditions. Thus, although grandparents are central people in many childhood experiences, there is little systematic psychological research on their roles and perceptions.

The little scientific data available on grandparents, coupled with individual recollections and experiences, suggests that these people are in a position to be very important to the developmentally disabled child and the child's family. Berns (1980) wrote both about the importance of being sensitive to the disappointment of expectations experienced by grandparents who have a handicapped grandchild and about the potentially useful role these elder family members can fill in providing support to parents and a sense of worth to the child. Rhoades (1975) described a workshop for helping grandparents better understand their grandchild's handicap and the role they might fill for that youngster.

The Grandparents' Perspective

A recently completed study with grandparents of autistic children (Harris, Handleman, and Palmer, 1985) explored the differences between how parents and grandparents view the autistic child and how they view their relationships with one another. The subjects were 19 mothers and their own 15 mothers and 11 fathers, and 14 fathers and their own 10 mothers and 7 fathers.

Each mother or father completed a 41-item questionnaire that had four sections: view of child, view of self, relationship to grandmother, and relationship to grandfather. The grandparents each completed a 32-item set of reciprocal questions that were worded from their point of view. Each item was scored on a seven-point scale from agree to disagree. Table 6–2 shows some sample items worded from the perspective of parent or grandparent.

The results of the study showed that when parents and grandparents disagreed, it was always the grandparents who took a more positive or optimistic view. For example, although the mothers and fathers reported that things had gotten worse in the family since the birth of an autistic child, the grandmothers disagreed. Similarly, the mothers felt that their autistic children were more demanding than necessary, indicated that they felt some discomfort when people asked what was wrong with their children, and expressed distress about their children's disability; the grandmothers did not agree with these views.

Research that has been done with grandparents of normal children has suggested that grandparents do not view themselves as responsible for their grandchildren's shortcomings or failures (Albrecht, 1954). The grandparent of a handicapped child may likewise feel less personal distress and sense of loss than the parents when confronted by the child's handicap. In addition, grandparents have less contact with the child and may not fully appreciate the impact of the child on the family. Grandparents also tend to idealize their role and therefore may be reluctant to acknowledge the negative aspects of their grandchildren's handicaps (Neugarten and Weinstein, 1964).

The study (Harris et al., 1985) also found that maternal grandparents visited the family more often than did paternal grandparents. This finding is consistent with Gath's (1978) identification of the maternal grandmother as an especially important source of family support. Interestingly, there was some evidence that paternal grandparents did not understand their son's experiences as well as maternal grandparents understood their daughter's lives.

Role of the Teacher

It is important for teachers to look for ways to involve the extended family. A school might organize a grandparents' day for families with special children and focus on helping grandparents understand their grandchildren's disabilities and the constructive role grandparents can play in the family. On an individual basis the teacher may want to be alert for ways to help parents encourage grandparents to become involved in meeting family needs. Of course, the teacher must be sensitive to the relationships within an individual

Table 6-2.   Sample Questionnaire Items for Parents and Grandparents

---

Parent's Perspective

1. My handicapped child is a full member of the family in every respect.
2. I feel closer to my handicapped child than to my other children.
3. The constant demands for care from my handicapped child have limited my growth and development.
4. I have had to give up important things because of my handicapped child.
5. My father would like to shelter me more from life's pain.
6. My mother understands the problems I have.

Grandparent's Perspective

1. My handicapped grandchild is more demanding of other people than is necessary.
2. In his or her own way my handicapped grandchild brings pleasure to the members of the family.
3. My son/daughter is usually too tired to enjoy life.
4. It is important for my son/daughter to get out of the house more without my handicapped grandchild.
5. Since my handicapped grandchild was born I have felt closer to my son/daughter.
6. I have openly discussed with my son/daughter how I feel about my handicapped grandchild.

---

family and must recognize those families in which this kind of involvement is not appropriate.

SUMMARY

Having a handicapped child in the home does not inevitably mean that a family will experience serious problems in their daily lives. As noted in this chapter there is no evidence of more frequent episodes of serious psychopathology among members of these families than among other families. Indeed, some parents report they feel they are stronger for the experience of raising a disabled child, some couples indicate their marriage has been enhanced by sharing the challenge of the child's needs, and some siblings regard themselves as better people for having learned to respond with compassion to their handicapped sibling.

Although neither the parents, nor the siblings, nor the members of the extended family will necessarily suffer in any sustained or major way from the complexities of adapting to a developmentally disabled child's special needs, research does indicate that these families experience more stress in life than do other families. Such stress can make a family's lives sadder and more difficult than the lives of other persons. It can also intrude on their willingness or ability to do home training with their child.

The special education teacher, in the role of consultant to the family, will find it helpful to be attuned to the special demands that are imposed upon the family by the developmentally disabled child's needs. When parents are feeling angry, sad, burdened, and so forth, it may be difficult for them to respond in a consistent and caring way to their child. Likewise, siblings who are perplexed about their brother's or sister's handicap, resentful of the time their parents spend with the developmentally disabled child, or excessively burdened by child care responsibilities may manifest their distress in ways that are uncomfortable for themselves and for the family as a whole. These reactions of family members may make it difficult for the teacher to fulfill the role of family consultant unless active steps are taken to help the family adapt to their stressful situation.

Although teachers are not psychotherapists and should not attempt the kinds of therapeutic interventions that are undertaken by psychologists, social workers, or psychiatrists, they can recognize the presence of maladaptive behavior patterns within the family and seek consultation with other professionals when they believe they have identified a family problem.

Chapter 7

Between Parents and Teachers

Case Report: A Parents' Group

Lauren Sheldon, a school psychologist, had worked for 7 years in an elementary school that included several special education classes along with a full complement of regular classes from kindergarten through sixth grade. A vigorous advocate of integrating children from the special classes as fully as possible in the mainstream, Lauren was aware also that the children in the special education classes needed services not usually required by other youngsters. In partial response to this need Lauren and Hal Fielding, teacher of the classroom for young children classified as trainable mentally retarded, had started a parent training group.

Tonight was the third in the series of meetings with the parents in Hal's class. Thus far attendance had been excellent, with all but one of the mothers and three of the seven fathers coming regularly. Schedule conflicts, baby-sitting problems, and in the case of one family a seeming hostility toward the school kept some parents away. Nonetheless, the majority of the families were represented, and everyone who came was enthusiastic. Although Lauren and Hal wished everyone could participate, they had learned over several years that they could not expect that level of response from all the families who had children at the school. In spite of that Hal and Lauren with their sympathetic, supportive styles had managed to recruit several initially reluctant families.

The topic for this evening was the use of positive reinforcement to reward children for good behavior. Lauren and Hal alternated providing primary leadership for the group and tonight was Hal's turn to make the introductory comments about the topic under discussion. He had presented a 10-minute talk about the concept of reinforcement, drawing many illustrations from the members of the group and encouraging them to join in with examples from their own children. At one point he asked the parents to jot down several items they believed their child would find reinforcing. He also stressed that the only way to know for sure if something is rewarding is to see what happens to the child's behavior. If a desired behavior increases after parents give hugs, chocolate pudding, or tickles, then the parents can know that they have found a useful reinforcer.

After his brief comments, which were framed in simple, nontechnical language, Hal and Lauren role-played being a parent and child. Lauren, who filled the role of child, was being taught by Hal how to put on her jacket. Hal modeled how a parent would use praise and tangible rewards to encourage a child to learn a complex self-care skill in simple steps. After that each parent was given an opportunity to try the techniques while the rest of the group watched and gave supportive feedback. As a result each parent had a chance to test the methods and begin to master them without the need to cope immediately with a child's demands.

The final portion of the evening was devoted to a discussion of the home programs that each family was conducting. Every family had one project they were doing on their own. These included several parents who were teaching their children to get dressed in the morning, one family who were coping with their son's very difficult and demanding temper tantrums, another family who were teaching their mentally retarded son to play simple games with his older sister, and one mother who was decreasing her son's resistance to going to bed at night. Thus the problems were varied, and as each parent listened to the others present their data and describe their experiences, there was a process of mutual learning.

Although the series of parent training meetings was only 10 weeks long, the process of consultation between parents and teacher would go on for as long as the parents' child was in Hal's class. Hal viewed this training as laying the groundwork for what would be a continuing experience in the next few years. He also knew that should he run into trouble working with a family he could call Lauren in as a consultant. Because the parents already knew and respected her from the group training, they were more likely to be responsive to her than if she were a stranger.

Case Commentary. There is widespread agreement among professionals who work with developmentally disabled children that close coordination between home and school is important in creating an optimal growth experience for the child. Children with cognitive impairments often need a very structured context in which to learn. Behavior modification procedures have shown themselves to be useful for creating that kind of facilitative learning environment. It is therefore to the advantage of all concerned that parents be skillful in using behavioral procedures to teach their children new skills or decrease behavior problems.

In the case report that opened this chapter a school psychologist and a special education teacher teamed up to provide parents of trainable mentally retarded children instruction in behavior modification skills. Ten weeks is not enough time to teach parents everything they need to know to be effective as behavior modifiers, but it is possible to convey the basic behavioral concepts and allow each participant to have some success with an initial home program. As Hal Fielding noted, that kind of training lays the groundwork for an ongoing consultative relationship between the teacher and the family.

INTRODUCTION

The purpose of the present chapter is to familiarize the teacher with the goals and techniques of parent training. It reviews some of the research that has been done on training parents to be teachers with their own children and provides a sample curriculum for those teachers who might wish to undertake parent training. It is assumed that the reader has a familiarity with behavior modification procedures or will gain a very competent working knowledge of those skills before attempting to teach them to someone else. Like any other aspect of teaching, parent training is best mastered under the supervision of an experienced colleague.

As noted in the preceding chapter it is important that parent training be done in a context that respects the needs of the family. A teacher who imposes this training on a resistant family will probably create a frustrating, potentially angering situation for all of the participants. Nonetheless, it is also important for the teacher to recognize the fundamental importance of these behavioral skills and to encourage every family to take advantage of the opportunity to receive the training.

Improved child management skills may contribute in an important way to decreasing some of the negative emotional experiences that are involved in raising a handicapped child. In particular, the training may increase the parents' sense of themselves as competent parents. In addition, changes in child behavior may significantly improve the atmosphere within the home by decreasing the child's demandingness and intrusion on the lives of other family members. Many parents of a handicapped child have commented that their improved ability to manage their child made it possible for their child finally to be a regular member of the family.

The pages that follow focus primarily upon the didactic needs of parents of developmentally disabled children. This emphasis is not intended to diminish the recognition of the family's need for support and affirmation but rather to emphasize that the didactic training is an integral component of any effective family intervention program. This training, coupled with a warm, sympathetic parent-teacher relationship, can meet a variety of the needs of many families of developmentally disabled children. Direct, person-to-person contact is probably more valuable to parents and teachers than numerous formal IEP conferences, newsletters, or note writing (Fuqua, Hegland, and Karas, 1985).

WHAT PARENTS CAN LEARN

There have been many case reports and a number of controlled empirical studies in the past two decades documenting that parents can learn to be behavior modifiers for their children. This work has show that mothers and fathers can intervene across a full range of home and family problems, including stubbornness, noncompliance, aggression, and dependency (Patterson, Chamberlain, and Reid, 1982) as well as the more debilitating handicaps of the developmentally disabled child (Harris, 1983; Howlin, 1981). Specific target behaviors that parents have treated include aggression and oppositional behavior (Dumas, 1984; Webster-Stratton, 1985), enuresis (Breit, Kaplan, Gauthier, and Weinhold, 1984), hyperactivity (Pollard, Ward, and Barkley, 1983), and reading deficits (Gang and Poche, 1982).

The accumulation of more than 20 years of research suggests that parents can learn essentially any behavior modification skill used by professionals in the treatment of children. Of course some parents may be so indifferent, intellectually handicapped, or emotionally distressed that they cannot or will not master the necessary skills. Nonetheless, the preponderance of parents do seem capable of learning to be effective in using the fundamentals of behavior modification.

Parents of the Developmentally Disabled

One of the most valuable applications of behavioral parent training has been with parents of developmentally disabled children. Beginning in the mid-1960s there were a series of studies showing that these parents, like others, can be effective change agents for their children. In 1966 Wetzel, Baker, Roney, and Martin described what they believed was the first demonstration of the outpatient training of parents of an autistic child to handle their child's autistic behavior. Shortly thereafter Risley (1968) made a systematic effort to train a mother of a developmentally disabled child to manage the girl's severely deviant behaviors. Other single subject studies by Moore and Bailey (1973) and Nordquist and Wahler (1973) expanded these efforts to help parents cope with a number of problem behaviors, including rituals, whining, and noncompliance, and to teach nonverbal and verbal imitation skills to their developmentally disabled children. Several early studies looked specifically at the parent's role in facilitating speech and language (Goldstein and Lanyon, 1971; MacDonald, Blott, Gordon, Spiegel, and Hartmann, 1974).

With the value and feasibility of training parents of developmentally disabled children well established (Lovaas et al., 1973; Schopler and Reichler, 1971), later research has focused more specifically on examining the relative value of home- versus clinic-based treatment (Koegel, Schreibman, Britten, Burke, and O'Neill, 1982), the enduring effects of home training (Clements, Evans, Jones, Osborne, and Upton, 1982; Harris, Wolchik, and Weitz, 1981; Holmes, Hemsley, Rickett, and Likierman, 1982; Howlin, 1981), and parental judgments of the efficacy of behavior therapy (Runco and Schreibman, 1983). In general this work has suggested not only that home-based treatment is superior to that in the clinic but also that it is difficult for parents of a handicapped child to sustain their efforts with their child over long periods of time. The problem of maintenance of parental effort is addressed later in this chapter and in Chapters 8 and 9 as well.

THE GOALS OF PARENT TRAINING

There are a number of skills that parents of developmentally disabled children should master by the time they complete a training program. First among these is an understanding of the "discrete trial procedure" (Koegel, Russo, and Rincover, 1977) as a way to present instructional material to the child. As discussed in Chapter 3, such an approach requires that the child be attending to the teacher, that a single, clear, discriminative stimulus be presented (e.g., "Look at me"), that a target behavior be selected and defined in operational terms, and that appropriate consequences be delivered promptly and contingent on the child's response. Parents should also understand the behavioral concept of punishment, know how and when to use punishment procedures, and understand various methods of data collection and simple assessment. Research has suggested that the curriculum presented in this chapter is effective at providing parents with these skills (Harris, 1983; Harris et al., 1981; Weitz, 1982).

In addition to these basic skills, parents should be able to analyze their ongoing programs and to identify and solve problems when they arise. The 10-week curriculum described in the following sections will not ensure mastery of these more complex skills by parents. Rather, such highly refined skills may be learned over the course of several years of a consultation relationship with the teacher. Over time the teacher can help parents troubleshoot programs and grow increasingly sophisticated in their ability to recognize and remediate difficulties as they arise. Intagliata and Doyle (1984) have also trained parents in interpersonal problem-solving skills to improve the parents' functioning as child advocates.

TRAINING IN GROUPS

Advantages of Group Training

Although some excellent parent training packages emphasize individual training (McClannahan et al., 1982), the curriculum described here was developed for small groups of parents. The same basic procedures have been used with groups of from two to six couples and the basic methods have been adapted for work with individuals and single families as well. One advantage to group training is efficient use of the trainer's time by reaching several families with the same basic information (Brightman, Baker, Clark, and Ambrose, 1982; Webster-Stratton, 1984).

In addition to being efficient, the group may act as a vehicle for social support and in that way have a facilitative effect that individual training might not provide. Many parents have commented that it was helpful to talk to other people facing the same problems. They have described having felt very isolated in their community where they may be the only family with a developmentally disabled child and having viewed themselves as "different" from the parents of nonhandicapped children around them. Coming together in a group with other parents can convey the message that they are not alone and that others are coping with the same difficult problems. Although a teacher may attempt to convey an empathic concern and understanding of a parent's difficulties, this can sometimes be done even more effectively by a peer who has shared the same pain. Thus, the parent training group, although primarily didactic, can also be a powerful source of support.

Disadvantages of Group Training

There can be drawbacks to group training. Problems are encountered sometimes when the needs of the parents are diverse. To take an extreme example, the parents of an adolescent Down's syndrome boy, a preschool autistic youngster, and a mildly retarded, middle childhood girl might have so little in common as to create minimal cohesion. Similarly, one family whose child is very high or low functioning compared to the rest of the group could produce considerable discomfort. It is best, therefore, to try to create groups that are reasonably homogeneous.

Another drawback to group training is that it does not allow much opportunity for dealing in depth with individual problems or for ensuring that the slower learning parent has enough attention. The best strategy therefore is a combination of group training to convey the basic facts coupled with an individual consultation model to provide ongoing help for families. The training model described in the case that opened this chapter is one in which the basic group training is followed by ongoing consultation with the teacher. Such consultation may be best done in the child's home where the consultant can observe the parents work with their child and understand whatever limits are imposed on programming by the realities of the living situation.

THE TRAINING SETTING

Although excellent training can probably be done in the most mediocre of physical conditions, it makes sense to offer parents a pleasant environment that is conducive to a relaxed but attentive attitude. A comfortable room with inviting chairs, good lighting, adequate temperature control, privacy, and freedom from distractions would be an appropriate setting. If there were also some place to heat a pot of coffee or tea and easy access to videotape equipment, that would be nearly ideal.

Offering parents coffee and cookies, although certainly not essential, does create an atmosphere of hospitality. When a teacher visits a child's home and is not offered a hot or cold beverage, it may reflect a certain reluctance on the part of the family to have a visitor. In the same fashion, the offer of a small snack contributes to a sense of welcome.

It is useful to have a couple of child-sized chairs and a small table to use as props in modeling teaching techniques. Some food reinforcers, data sheets, and pencils on the table are useful also. Because parents are encouraged to use trial-by-trial data collection procedures as part of their work with their children, these procedures should be modeled from the first session.

Arranging the chairs in a circle makes all the parents snugly part of the group rather than being scattered around the room. A small circle also makes it easier for the group leader to establish eye contact and ensure that everyone is focused on the group activities.

A small blackboard should be available to demonstrate how to graph data, to write down key words, and so forth. A videotape system with camera, monitor, and deck can be wonderful for providing feedback to parents on their teaching techniques, but this equipment is not essential.

SUPPLEMENTARY TEACHING MATERIALS

Some parents may find a book or two on the basics of behavioral child management useful supplements to the group meetings. Two good ones are *Behavior Problems* (Baker et al., 1976b) and *Early Self-Help Skills* (Baker et al., 1976c). Other books in this well-written and cheerfully illustrated series address more advanced self-help skills (Baker et al., 1976a, 1976d), speech and language (Baker, Brightman, Carroll, Heifetz, and Hinshaw, 1978a, 1978b) and independent living (Baker, Brightman, and Hinshaw, 1980). Some of these books are reviewed in more detail in Chapter 4.

In using books or other reading material the group leader should be sensitive to the possibility that some less well educated parents or people with learning disabilities may find even well-written books tough going. As a consequence, although parents should be encouraged to use the books, the books should be regarded as a supplement to direct instruction.

THE RETEACH FORMAT FOR PARENT TRAINING

A helpful format for organizing the individual teaching sessions of a parent group is the RETEACH model (Table 7–1). This format helps ensure that the group leaders touch the essential points of each meeting in a consistent fashion.

Table 7–1.   RETEACH Format for Parent Training

Review
Explain concept
Technique demonstration
Emphasize critical skills
Assess parent skills
Child progress
Homework

This format generally fits in a 90- to 120-minute time slot, depending on the number of parents in the group and the style of the group leaders. An effort should be made to keep fairly close control of the movement of the group, to be the focus for the parents' attention, and not to allow things to go far afield. Parents may understandably resent others who demand too much group time or raise intense personal issues; such digressions can therefore become harmful to group cohesion. Furthermore, this is not a "rap group" or a therapy group, and many teachers who feel quite comfortable leading a didactically oriented group wisely hesitate to allow the group to become too focused on emotional issues.

Review

Step 1 of the RETEACH model is a review of events from the past meeting. This is a brief, 5- to 10-minute period devoted to highlighting essential elements from the past weeks. For example, the group leaders repeat the meaning of the concept of reinforcement, make suggestions about ways to encourage the child to speak, review the steps involved in shaping a new behavior, and so forth.

Explain Concept

The second part of the meeting is devoted to a 10- to 15-minute explanation of the key concept being taught in the session. This might be the definition of reinforcement, punishment, shaping, chaining, and so forth. As illustrated in the work of Hal Fielding, this explanation is provided in simple, nontechnical terms, is related to the needs of the members of the group, and draws from the life experiences of the group members. The group leaders should offer a number of examples and encourage the parents to do likewise until it is clear that they understand the basic concept.

Technique Demonstration

After the concept is described, the techniques are then demonstrated for the parents. If the group has co-leaders, they typically adopt the roles of parent and child during this modeling procedure. This takes only 5 to 10 minutes and allows the group leaders to make concrete the material that has been discussed. It is helpful to take advantage of this opportunity to be funny, to point out mistakes (if they are made), and to maintain the session on a lighthearted note. Hudson (1982) pointed to modeling and role playing as valuable teaching techniques in parent training.

Emphasizing Critical Skills

After modeling of the procedures, the group leaders briefly emphasize the essential points of their performance. For example, if they were teaching reinforcement procedures, they would emphasize the need to respond quickly, to combine secondary reinforcement with primary reinforcement, and so forth.

Assess Parent Skills

The group leaders next ask each parent to practice the skill being taught while the rest of the group watches. If the group is large and there are two leaders, the group can be divided in half at this point to provide more time for individual feedback.

In assessing the parent's skill and giving feedback it is important to remember that the parents are being asked to learn a complex new skill and use it under public scrutiny. That can be very stressful for many people. It is helpful therefore to give a lot of praise, to focus on one specific skill at a time, and not to expect mastery of techniques in the first few sessions. It is also useful to identify those parents who seem most at ease and most adept and ask them to perform first in the feedback sessions. After they break the ice it is probably easier for other parents to follow. With six families this part of the meeting takes between 20 and 25 minutes, depending on the complexity of the skill.

Child Progress

The next phase of the meeting offers each family the opportunity to share with the group the progress their child is making on home programs. In the first two meetings this primarily involves helping each family select an appropriate target behavior, design a measurement system, present their baseline data, and plan an intervention. In the weeks after that the parents are encouraged to share their graphed data, describe their progress, and make any necessary changes in the program. Each family has approximately 5 minutes to make their presentation. The families are asked to listen carefully to each other's material and to offer suggestions as they wish.

Homework

Finally the meeting is closed by giving the parents their homework assignments for the coming week. This may include material to read, observations to make about their child, programs to develop for the coming week, and so forth.

CONTENT OF THE CURRICULUM

The authors wish to share with the reader the details of a parent training curriculum that has been used and refined over many years of practice. Although we have done a fair amount of research demonstrating the value of these training procedures, we recognize that not all the components of the package have been evaluated (Harris, 1983). We therefore urge you to feel free to make changes that make sense for the parents with whom you work or the setting in which you operate. We are offering you guidelines — not rules.

Most of our research and clinical work in parent training has focused on variations of a 10-week curriculum (Table 7–2). This curriculum includes the basics of both behavior modification techniques and of facilitating a child's speech and language development. When we eliminate the speech training component and do the training in a school setting where we know the teacher will have an ongoing consultation relationship with the parents, we condense the group training into six sessions.

Week 1

Our first session opens with introductions. We tell the parents about ourselves so that they will begin to feel some confidence in us as group leaders. Next we ask each parent to introduce himself or herself and say a bit about his or her child. After that we ask the parents to take a brief pretraining quiz about the fundamentals of behavior modification. The test will enable them, and us, to assess their progress at the end of training. Then we explain the goals of

Table 7-2. Outline of Parent Training Curriculum

Week 1   Introduction. Pretest. Goals. Concept of social learning theory. Operational definitions.
Week 2   Methods of data collection. Graphing. Concept of base line. Facilitating language development.
Week 3   Positive reinforcement.
Week 4   Establishing instructional control. Discrete trial format.
Week 5   Punishment. Ethical issues. Need for data-based justification.
Week 6   Shaping, chaining, prompting, and fading.
Week 7   Nonverbal imitation.
Week 8   Shaping speech.
Week 9   Formal and informal language instruction.
Week 10   Maintenance of change. Generalization of responding. Posttest. Consumer satisfaction ratings.

the course, describe the basic ideas that underlie social learning theory, and talk about how one defines behaviors in operational terms.

Before the end of the first session every family has selected an initial target behavior for their child and understands the kind of data they are going to collect to assess that behavior. Because we have not discussed the details of data collection, these instructions must be very explicit. For example, a family who wishes to teach their child to put his clothes in the hamper after he removes them might be told to give the command "Put your clothes in the hamper" each evening after the child undresses and record the number of times he complies. Similarly, parents who are concerned about their daughter's bedtime temper tantrums might be told to use a kitchen clock to time the total number of minutes that each tantrum lasts. We emphasize that parents are not to begin intervention but simply to collect baseline data for the next week.

Week 2

After the review period, the group leader presents a brief description of various methods of collecting data, including frequency counts and duration measures, and helps the parents understand when one method is preferable to the other. We draw upon the problems presented by the families the week before to highlight these ideas. The group leader also shows the parents how to graph data and demonstrates the technique with some of the baseline data. We also introduce the notion of examining behavior in terms of its antecedents and consequences in order to gain a full sense of the factors that may be affecting the child's actions. We also spend some time in this session discussing ways in which parents might facilitate their child's language development (see Chapter 8). Finally, each family presents their baseline data and leaves with an intervention plan in hand.

Week 3

As seen in the case illustration that opened this chapter, the third week of training is devoted to a presentation of the concept of reinforcement. Each family is asked to write down a short list of items they believe their child finds reinforcing. We then emphasize the importance of using an empirical definition of reinforcement and judging by the changes in the child's behavior whether the items that we believe to be reinforcing were in fact effective in increasing the target behavior.

Week 4

Many developmentally disabled children, especially autistic children or those with behavior problems, can benefit from learning to follow the commands to sit quietly and establish eye contact. We spend one session demonstrating techniques for teaching these skills. In the event that the child does not require this kind of training, the session can be devoted to the demonstration of basic self-help skills such as dressing or feeding. What is essential is that parents begin to master the discrete trial format of giving a command, waiting for a response, prompting as needed, and reinforcing appropriate behavior.

Week 5

This is the session in which we introduce the concept of punishment. The group leader describes the parallels between punishment and reinforcement and emphasizes the ethical issues that must be considered in the use of punishment. It is important in this regard to help parents discriminate between punishment as something done because of anger and something done to teach a child an appropriate behavior. We always demonstrate several punishment techniques, including time-out and overcorrection.

Some school districts may prohibit the discussion of the use of physical punishment even though the procedures are to be used by parents in the home. One obviously must honor such limitations. If the school does not preclude the discussion of physical punishment, the group leader may want to talk about the use of a mild physical punishment to enforce vital safety rules. Such techniques, even when not appropriate for use in the school, may be suitable for helping parents of some very young developmentally disabled children control dangerous behaviors at home.

The discussion of punishment offers an excellent opportunity to emphasize again the importance of data collection and the need to be accountable through data-based procedures when one uses behavior modification techniques.

Week 6

The sixth week is the one in which we introduce shaping, chaining, prompting, and fading as concepts. Self-help skills as well as basic attending behaviors such as eye contact and good sitting are appropriate target behaviors for illustrating these concepts. By this point in their training the parents should be growing increasingly independent in program design and development. We gradually begin to reduce our level of input and to encourage more active parental involvement.

Week 7

In the seventh week we teach the parents the skills they need to help their child master nonverbal imitation. The capacity to imitate nonverbal gestures is valuable to the child in being able to imitate the motor component of many activities. It may also strengthen the parents' awareness of their role as models for the child in learning new behaviors.

Week 8

For those children who are mute or have limited speech, the next step is to teach the parents how to shape sounds into words. This is a relatively complex skill for parents to master, and it demands a good understanding of all the preceding skills that have been taught, including the use of reinforcement, ability to prompt correctly, to fade prompts as necessary, and to build complex skills from simpler behaviors. Thus, this is an opportunity for the parents to polish the skills that have been developing over the past 2 months.

Week 9

During this next-to-last session we discuss the teaching of various forms of speech and the ways to provide informal as well as formal language instruction and stimulation.

Week 10

The final session is an opportunity to review the highlights of preceding weeks. We also introduce the concept of maintenance of change as well as emphasizing the need to create opportunities for the child to generalize responses to new settings, new people, and new objects. At the end of the session we give the parents a posttest and an anonymous consumer satisfaction rating sheet. We also ask them to share with us any direct feedback they wish to offer that might benefit groups to be held in future months.

Assuming that the group has been offered within a school-based context, this last session also should be an opportunity to discuss the teacher's role as a consultant to the parents in the months ahead.

MOVING TO A CONSULTATION MODEL

Although the initial parent training process is an important one, research has suggested that this form of concentrated, brief training is not sufficient to sustain parents in their efforts as teachers over the years (Baker, Heifetz, and Murphy, 1980; Harris, 1983; Holmes et al., 1982). A number of factors may contribute to the failure of parents to continue their work with their child, including not knowing how to solve difficulties in programming, lack of reinforcement because of limited change in the child, time demands from other aspects of the parents' lives, and the myriad of emotional factors that were discussed in Chapter 6.

Some families need more support than others. Research with mothers whose children demonstrate conduct disorders, aggression, or oppositional behavior has suggested that parent training is less successful if the mothers are socioeconomically disadvantaged or experience significant negative life stress (Baker and McCurry, 1984; Dumas, 1984; Webster-Stratton, 1985) as compared to other mothers in training. Dumas (1984) also suggested that those mother-child dyads that are characterized by a high level of aversive interaction are less likely to be successful than those with a lower level of aversive behaviors. In addition, Wahler (1980) presented data indicating that those lower socioeconomic mothers who led relatively isolated, "insular" lives were less likely to continue to use behavioral procedures effectively over time than those mothers who had a more effective social network.

Because mothers of developmentally disabled children may be more socially isolated than other mothers (Breiner and Young, 1985), they may be at special risk in terms of the likelihood of sustaining their teaching efforts over time. Economically disadvantaged or single parents with a developmentally disabled youngster may require the most intensive support in this regard (Kornblatt and Heinrich, 1985). Furthermore, there may be some families in which the child's needs for physical care or parental limitations preclude the parents' assumption of a teaching role (MacMillan and Turnbull, 1983).

The availability of an ongoing consultation relationship with a teacher may contribute in an important way to parents' efforts to work with their child over the years. When we contacted a group of parents of developmentally disabled children whom we had trained in behavior modification techniques 4 to 7 years earlier, we found that among the parents whose children were now enrolled in schools that had an active parent training and support component, 72 percent of the mothers and 50 percent of the fathers were still using the behavioral techniques. In contrast, among the parents whose children were attending less supportive programs only 46 percent of the mothers and 28 percent of the fathers continued to use behavioral procedures. Such a finding points to the importance of a continuing active involvement between parent and school over time. The next chapter discusses in more detail the teacher's role as consultant.

SUMMARY

Most parents of developmentally disabled children can probably benefit from a sound knowledge of behavioral procedures for child management. Mentally retarded and autistic children have more difficulty learning complex skills and may pose more management problems than other children. The systematic, detailed method of teaching that is inherent in a behavioral approach lends itself well to meeting the needs of these youngsters. In addition, problems in generalization and maintenance of responding make it important that the developmentally disabled child experience consistency between home and school.

The RETEACH format for conducting training sessions suggests that each session include a *Review* of important information from the past week, *Explanation* of the concept being taught, demonstration of the *Technique* under discussion, *Emphasis* on critical skills, *Assessment* of parents' skills, *Child* progress report, and *Homework* assignment.

We have described a data-based, 10-week parent training curriculum designed to teach parents the basics of behavior modification.

The curriculum stresses the essential skills of the discrete trial format, including knowing how to give commands, prompt responses, reinforce or punish behavior, and pace the presentation of material. After parents have mastered these essentials, they can continue to learn more sophisticated techniques through ongoing consultation with their child's teacher.

Chapter 8

Creative Home Programming

Case Report: The Van Allen Family

Andrew White, a special education teacher for 7 years, felt with increasing intensity each passing year how much he valued his work and how central "his kids" were to him. Andy's class included eight moderately retarded youngsters, six with Down's syndrome, one with a seizure disorder, and another who had suffered serious brain damage from a bout of illness in infancy. Because of his experience and expertise, Andy had offers from other schools that paid somewhat more than the center where he worked, but there were special features about his current job that he valued more than a few dollars. One of these features was the freedom to do home visits and work closely with the parents of his kids. Some school systems assigned that responsibility to other staff personnel, and Andy felt that was probably a mistake. He really knew the children in his class and felt most able to advise their parents about management problems and skill training.

A snowy, gray, late November afternoon found Andy on the freeway driving from the center to the home of Josh van Allen, one of the most perplexing children in his class. Josh's parents had asked Andy for a consultation because of serious problems with their son's behavior at home. As Mrs. van Allen told Andy, all day in school Josh was in an intensive behavioral program with seven other children and two adults. When he came home at 3 P.M., it was as though a little tornado had broken loose in the house. He flung himself around the house, bumping into people and furniture, pushing past his 4-year-old sister, and caring little for the reprimands of his parents. The van Allens wondered if Josh were getting too much structure in school and needed to blow off steam when he came home or if he could learn to control himself.

When Andy arrived at the van Allen home, he saw instantly why they were concerned. The house was in a state of uproar as Josh ran from room to room trailing a roll of toilet paper that he was gleefully throwing about in handfuls. His little sister sat to the side and watched in wide-eyed amazement. When Josh finally spotted his teacher, he stopped very nearly in midair. When Andy told Josh, "Stand still and look at me," Josh's laughter ceased and he assumed a more sober expression as he looked at this teacher. Then Andy said, "Good boy, Josh, you stood still and looked at me." Andy asked Josh to get one of his toys and show it to his sister. For a few minutes sister and brother played together, but soon Josh was off wandering about the house, and this time Andy let him go. It was more important to talk to the van Allens than to try to control Josh's behavior at that moment.

Andy and the van Allens went to the kitchen to have a cup of coffee and talk about Josh's problem. Andy told the van Allens he was pretty sure Josh did not need to blow off quite so much steam, that some rough-and-tumble outdoor play was important for every kid, but that Josh's problem was probably more one of not knowing how to fill his time. Andy had had similar problems with Josh in the classroom the first 2 months of the school year and now had several programs in effect to teach Josh how to occupy his time more effectively. Andy suggested that it might be a help to the van Allen family if Josh learned to play some simple games by himself and with his sister. Reinforcing him for appropriate play would probably be a more effective intervention in the long run than punishing his wildness, although some kind of time-out might have to be applied for the out-of-control running.

After an hour consultation the van Allens and Andy had developed the first stage of their behavioral intervention. They agreed that for the next week the van Allens would keep a baseline of Josh's "wild" behavior. Every 10 minutes, when a kitchen timer rang, they would make a note of whether he were being wild. At the end of a week of baseline two programs were to be put into effect. One was a time-out procedure requiring Josh to go to his room for 2 minutes each time he was wild. The other program involved teaching Josh two new games. One, to be played with his little sister, consisted of a simple picture-matching game. The other involved teaching Josh to play alone with a shape-sorting box. Each activity was to be taught for two 15-minute sessions a day. Josh's parents knew they would have to be actively involved initially in reinforcing Josh for every small step, but they had planned how they would fade their involvement toward a goal of verbal praise every 5 to 10 minutes to reward continued quiet playing and small food snacks after 20 to 30 minutes of independent play. They also made plans to introduce new toys and to keep the activities stimulating for Josh.

Case Commentary. The problems of the van Allen family are similar to those confronting many parents and teachers of developmentally disabled children. The van Allens were warm and caring people who had started to feel overwhelmed by their son's "bad" behavior. Left alone their sense of failure might have grown, creating increasingly negative interactions among the members of the family and stirring doubts for Mr. and Mrs. van Allen about keeping Josh at home.

Fortunately, Andy White's skillful behavioral consultation gave the van Allens some new tools for coping. The program was attractive in many ways: It involved Josh's sister as well as the boy, it focused on independence skills that would be important for Josh over the long haul, and it left Mr. and Mrs. van Allen feeling like the competent parents they were—not bad for a 60-minute consultation!

Although Andy was an experienced teacher with a backlog of 7 years of similar work, there was nothing he did in his consultation with the van Allens that could not be done by other teachers who understand the principles of behavior management and who think about children and families in the interactional terms discussed in this book.

INTRODUCTION

The present chapter focuses on helping the teacher provide creative consultation when parents seek help for problems in the home. To accomplish this goal the teacher-consultant needs to know various styles of teaching and problem solving potentially available to parents, the special needs of the individual family, and how to help the family adapt general solutions to their specific needs.

The chapter first describes the CONSULTED model for consultation with parents of developmentally disabled children. This model provides a general outline of consultation procedures for all kinds of problems that parents might raise about their child. Next, the chapter examines home programming in two broad domains: communications skills and daily living activities. Within the category of communication skills fall such considerations as creating a stimulating language environment, teaching speech, and using nonverbal communication. Daily living activities encompass such diverse routines as play and social skills, self-help skills, recreational activities, and other routines of family life.

The focus is not on teaching parents specific behavioral skills such as how to reinforce, use a discrete trial format, and so forth but upon how these behavioral skills can be used to build communication or daily living skills. Examples of specific activities found useful are included. It is assumed that parents already have mastered the rudiments of behavioral techniques or that such training will be integrated into the consultation process. In the case of the van Allen family, the teacher already had provided basic training for the parents and was consulting with them about the application of skills already in their repertoire. He also provided some direct modeling of procedures that were new to the van Allens.

A MODEL FOR CONSULTATION

The teacher-consultant has a complex role to fill when joining with a family to help them solve a problem concerning their developmentally disabled child. We have organized the steps we use in this process into a model we call CONSULTED (see Table 8–1).

Confer

The first essential step in the consultation process is to confer with the family concerning what they see as the problem and what kind of help they would like. It is important from the very first to ensure that the teacher-consultant is aware of what the family wants and not imposing outside objectives on them. For example, a child's hyperactive behavior at school might be disruptive to the class but might not be as much of a source of distress to the parents as the child's not falling asleep at night. The most effective consultants listen to the parents and respect their ultimate responsibility for home programming.

Observe

Following the initial conference with the parents it is often helpful to observe the problem behavior. This allows an opportunity to evaluate antecedents and consequences, to assess environmental factors that may affect treatment, and to identify other problems that may cause, follow from, or co-occur with the problem described by the parents. Much of this observation can be conducted by well-trained parents, but consultants will have a better firsthand sense of the issues if they spend some time engaged in personal observation.

Name Problems

Once a preliminary set of observations is completed, the teacher-consultant and parents can explicitly name the problems they observed and generate appropriate behavioral definitions for data collection and treatment planning. The process of observation often

Table 8–1.   The CONSULTED Model for Intervention

Confer
Observe
Name problems
Set priorities
Utilize resources
Label obstacles
Try intervention
Evaluate outcome
Determine next step

leads to a more refined definition than was possible during the initial consultation phase. For example, a broad parental complaint of out-of-control running may turn out to be under the inadvertent control of parental reprimands.

Set Priorities

Parents may have a number of different target behaviors they would like to address and the teacher-consultant may identify others during the observation period. Everything cannot be done at once, and some behaviors are of higher priority than others. These priorities may be set on the basis of objective danger to the child, long-term goals, and parental preference. For example, self-injurious behavior is so clearly dangerous that it ranks high in most lists of treatment planning. An irritating sound made by the child might set everyone else on edge and thus become a high priority target behavior.

One of the most important aspects of setting priorities is being sensitive to the needs of parents. What matters most to the teacher-consultant may have less significance for the parent. Our experience has been that it is important to attend closely to the priorities set by parents. As the people who live with a child, and who will be carrying out the program, they should have the biggest voice in this decision making. This is not to say that there should not be an open exchange of views between parent and consultant. The parent has typically asked for consultation because of a respect for the teacher's opinion, and that opinion can be voiced freely. But, after the full exchange of views, if a parent wishes to proceed in a different order than the consultant, we believe that is the parent's responsibility and right.

Utilize Resources

Throughout the observation phase and during the ensuing discussions the teacher-consultant should be making an ongoing assessment of the family, environmental, and school resources that can be brought to bear on this problem. Will both parents be able to carry out the program? Can a sibling lend a hand? Should a baby-sitter be trained? Will the program be jointly initiated in home and school? Will it be done in one setting and then the other? Do the physical resources exist for things such as a time-out space? Are new or different toys required as stimulus objects? Do parents need additional training in behavioral procedures?

A family who lives in a small apartment with several young children might hesitate to follow the suggestion to use an extinction process on bedtime tantrums for fear of arousing the anger of their neighbors. Similarly, if a father cannot stand to hear his son cry, the mother may have to be the first parent to initiate a time-out program and support her husband in ignoring the crying behavior. The assessment of available resources can lead to creative programs that respect the needs of the individual family.

Label Obstacles

The teacher-consultant should be aware from the onset of treatment of possible obstacles to success. For example, if in-laws who live upstairs are likely to disagree with the treatment program designed by the parents, steps may be needed to deal with the issues raised by the older generation. Likewise, if there are questions about the child's developmental readiness to master a particular skill, the program may have to be monitored with special care to ensure that it is not creating a failure experience for the child. Similarly, issues between the parents about the priorities they wish to establish for their handicapped child or for the family may intrude upon their ability to follow through with treatment. Depending upon the nature of these obstacles, the consultant may label them explicitly for the parents or may simply note them for future reference as a possible basis for referral to other professionals if the consultation process encounters too many failures.

Try Intervention

Once the groundwork is laid, the teacher-consultant steps aside to allow the family to proceed with the intervention phase. Aside—but not out of the picture, because the consultant must remain available for troubleshooting and reinforcing success and as a resource for the parents' questions.

Evaluate Outcome

Based on the reports of the parents, data collected, and possibly personal observation, the teacher-consultant and the parents evaluate the outcome of the intervention. This evaluation should be done frequently, certainly at least once a week. It need not be an extended meeting but can consist of a telephone call or a note discussing the current status of the program.

Determine Next Step

After evaluating the current status of the treatment program the parents and consultant will want to decide what to do next. If the treatment has been a complete success, they may decide to go on to the next item on their list of priority problems. If the treatment is working, but not yet complete, they will probably leave the procedures in place or make minor modifications. If the treatment was a failure, they may modify the intervention, reevaluate the problem to identify weaknesses in the current assessment, consider whether the problem merits additional resources, and then decide either to pursue the problem or shift to a new item on the priority list.

This process of determining the next step can develop into a new CONSULTED cycle with reentry to the conference step.

COMMUNICATION SKILLS

In helping parents provide appropriate verbal stimulation for their developmentally disabled child it is useful to know something about the language environment of handicapped children in general. What do persons say when they talk to mentally retarded or autistic children? Is it different from the way they talk to other children? Are the language needs of the developmentally disabled child different from those of other children?

Parents as Language Models

In general research comparing the parents of mentally retarded or autistic children with the parents of normal children or youngsters with dysphasia (a failure to use or understand language) has suggested that the speech of parents of developmentally disabled children does not differ in major ways form the parents of other children of the same language ability (Cantwell, Baker, and Rutter, 1977; Frank, Allen, Stein, and Meyers, 1976; Wolchik, 1983).

The knowledge that a child is language impaired does of course affect how adults attempt to communicate with that youngster. When Lord and her colleagues (Lord, Merrin, Vest, and Kelly, 1983) compared the behavior of preschool teachers with a socially unresponsive 4-year-old autistic boy and his nonhandicapped twin brother, they found that language to the autistic boy was simpler, more concrete, and accompanied by more gestures than was the conversation with his brother. In this respect it resembled the speech the teachers might have addressed to a younger child.

Reciprocity Between Parent and Child

Any examination of how parents talk to children must take into account that adults are only part of the equation. A child's language environment is not created by the parents alone; the child is a potent factor in the mutual interchange that shapes the language behavior of each participant. It is known, for example, that the parents of young, normal children as well as the parents of handicapped children match the complexity of their speech to that of the child (Buckhalt, Rutherford, and Goldberg, 1978; Cramblit and Siegel, 1977; Lederberg, 1980).

Studies that have examined the language interactions of mentally retarded children and their mothers (Cunningham, Reuler, Blackwell, and Deck, 1981; Gutmann and Rondal, 1979) have suggested that mentally retarded children are less socially active and less responsive to their mothers than are normal children. The mothers of the mentally retarded youngsters tended to be more actively directive with their child, made fewer initiations for interaction, and were less positively responsive to their child's compliant behavior than the mothers of the normal children (Cunningham et al., 1981). Such a pattern creates a danger of a repetitive cycle with the reduced responsiveness of the child failing to provide sufficient feedback to the mother who in turn fails to initiate sufficient interaction with the child.

The Feedback Loop

It may be that deficits in the mentally retarded or autistic child's communication skills impair the normally sensitive language feedback mechanism between parents and children. Mahoney (1975), in discussing this problem of a potentially defective feedback loop for communication, noted that part of the problem may lie in the child's deficient nonverbal as well as verbal skills. The child's inability to provide nonverbal cues may make it difficult for adult models to modulate their own behavior because of an inability to "read" the child.

Cheseldine and McConkey (1979) noted that "mentally handicapped children apparently need more than an adequate linguistic input" (p. 618). They argued that in some cases parents of the mentally retarded child may have lower expectations than parents of normal youngsters and so may fail to advance their language modeling rapidly enough for the child. They noted that those parents in their research who became more effective language teachers decreased their mean length of utterance, used fewer words, and tended to increase statements and decrease questions.

Do Parents Need Special Training?

The research on communication between developmentally disabled children and their parents has at least two messages. One is that these parents talk to their children in essentially the same fashion as parents of other children matched for language age. The second is that there may be a breakdown in the feedback loop between parents and children such that the parents do not receive sufficient cues to tell them they should be increasing their language demands on their children. This in turn might slow a child's language development. Thus, even though the mothers and fathers of developmentally disabled children resemble other parents in their conversational skills with their children, they may not be providing an optimal learning environment for their handicapped children.

As a result of this defective feedback loop developmentally disabled children may present extraordinary problems that normal verbal interactions cannot solve. Howlin and her co-workers (1973) suggested that the low frequency of appropriate speech by autistic children may reflect a lack of active encouragement to speak, insufficient reinforcement for speech, insufficient correction of errors and prompting of correct responses, or a combination of these that results in a failure to give the children feedback about their linguistic performance. Such a hypothesis may be correct. Nevertheless, because the parents of developmentally disabled children resemble other parents in how they talk to their handicapped children, it is also likely that these children require instructional techniques far beyond the intuition of most parents to provide. It is not necessary to conclude that there is anything pathological or inherently deficient about the language environment of the developmentally disabled child to argue that the youngster requires something very special in order to learn language.

The Language Environment

Appropriate language stimulation may be a nearly universal need of developmentally disabled children. The teacher-consultant will often be called upon to assess the home environment and make suggestions to parents about ways to increase such stimulation within the context of the family's daily life.

Assessment is the first step of intervention. Helping families change the way they talk to their children is not an exception to that principle. Therefore, the first steps in a language stimulation consultation would be to confer with the parents about their goals and to observe the parents and child with a special emphasis upon their communicative patterns. As shown in Table 8–2, such an assessment addresses itself to questions about the quality of the language interaction between the adults and the child. Do the parents actively encourage speech or do they make things easy by giving the child desired items before the child asks? Do the parents speak to the child frequently, in simple, redundant language that relates to the child's immediate needs and interests? Are the parents' expectations about the child's current abilities too high? Too low? Posing these kinds of questions enables the teacher-consultant to identify potential points of entry into the family's communication system.

Arranging the Physical Environment

In our own work with families we try to alert parents to ways in which they can actively manipulate the physical environment to create a need for speech from the child (Sosne et al., 1979). For example, we urge that the child be denied free access to desirable items. Although this might sound harsh, it makes good instructional sense when it is done in a way that respects the child's frustration tolerance.

In accordance with the principle of expecting language a youngster is required to verbalize, manually sign, or otherwise communicate to receive a toy, special food, or other wished-for events such as being tossed in the air or tickled. The precise modality of communication is chosen on the basis of the child's skills. Although the child's communication may be minimal, it is nonetheless an early

Table 8-2.   Assessing the Language Environment

Arranging Stimulus Conditions

1. Do parents ensure that interesting items are in clear view so that the child will be attracted to them?
2. Do parents place desired items beyond the reach of the child so that the child will have to initiate communication to obtain the object?
3. Do parents take advantage of routine child care events to stimulate language and encourage speech?

Assessing Parental Expectations

1. Are parental expectations of the child's language skills too high? Too low?
2. Do parents consistently demand some form of communication at a level compatible with the child's skills?

Assessing Adult Models

1. Do parents speak in simple, redundant terms, using brief sentences?
2. Do parents talk about events within the child's immediate experience so that the child has the opportunity to relate words to concrete events in the environment?
3. Do bilingual parents use a single language in all communication with the child?

Encouraging the Child's Attempts

1. Do parents reinforce all communicative attempts on the part of the child?
2. Is reinforcement for language rapid and specific?
3. Is reinforcement tied to the response whenever possible?
4. Do the parents build upon the child's efforts by repeating the child's words and expanding them?
5. Do parents establish eye contact and then wait a few seconds to give the child a chance to respond before they offer a prompt?

---

lesson in the notion that language can manipulate the environment. If parents find it difficult to deny their child pleasurable experiences when the child fails to communicate at an appropriate level, it may be helpful to point out that what appears to be kindness can work against the child's best interests and that as long as the expectations for performance are set at an appropriate level, denial will actually be minimal.

Reinforcing Communication

It is important to ensure that parents are reinforcing the child's efforts to communicate. The most optimal reinforcement is probably that which is intrinsic to the communication. Williams, Koegel, and Egel (1981) demonstrated that autistic children learn to follow commands more quickly when the reinforcer is tied to the response than when it is not. For example, when a child was asked to pick up a box and found a candy beneath the box, this response was acquired more quickly than when candy was placed in the child's mouth after the child picked up a box.

It is likely that the same holds true for the acquisition of language. For example, if a child asks for juice and receives the desired beverage, the link between language and reward is a direct one. Sometimes, however, the connection will be intrinsically less direct, such as when a child is learning to talk about remote events (e.g., "What did you have for breakfast?"). In these cases verbal praise, tokens, points, food, or other reinforcers may have to be used to strengthen the desired verbal behavior. In any event adults should be encouraged to respond to the child's language attempts with praise, affection, and other reinforcing behaviors.

Our own experience has been that parents rapidly can become skillful at labeling and rewarding verbal behavior. For example, Tables 8–3 and 8–4 provide brief excerpts of parent-child language exchanges between a preschool autistic boy and his parents before and after an intensive 10-week parent training course. After training, the parents talk in shorter bursts and reward the boy with considerable enthusiasm for his speech attempts. Communication is much simpler and clearer after training than it was before.

Prolonging the Verbal Exchange

In addition to withholding desired items as discussed previously, it is possible to create circumstances that require more extended speech by the child. For example, if a child asks for juice, the child might be given a pitcher, but no glass. Hence, the child would next have to ask for a glass and thus the verbal exchange would be drawn out. Other examples would be giving the child a puzzle without the pieces or a shape box without the shapes. In each instance the child must engage in more speech to complete the task. Obviously, the child's frustration tolerance must be kept in mind. This process should not be an odious one; done in moderation it can be quite effective.

Maintaining Appropriate Expectations

Sosne and his colleagues (1979) also urged that the demands made upon the child be gradually but definitely increased. Although it may be acceptable initially for the child to say "co" for cookie, there comes a time when "want cookie," "want cookie please," and "Mommy, I want a cookie please" are appropriate levels of response. As each new skill is mastered it should be integrated into the child's routine. When a child has learned colors, for example, the parent would now expect "want red crayon" rather than "want crayon." If a

Table 8–3.   Pretraining Communication

F(ather): Wanna comb your hair? Comb your hair.

M(other): Ah, isn't he cute? Tommy.

F: Comb your hair.

M: Isn't he cute? What do you want to name him?

C(hild): Eh, eh.

M: Let's name him Dumbo. There's Dumbo, Tommy. You wanna comb Dumbo's hair? Ain't that nice?

F: Comb, you gonna comb his hair? Huh, you gonna comb his hair? Huh?

M: Comb Dumbo's hair. Oh boy, what's this? Tommy, look at this.

C: Ball.

M: Ball, very good. What's that? What's this, Tommy? Look at this, Tommy. Remember these: Wha, don't you have some of these at home? What are those, huh?

C: Eh.

M: Hmmm? Here's a horn. Whoo, whoo, whoo, whoo.

F: Okay, cool breeze. Okay, cool breeze. You got glasses on?

C: Doooody.

F: Yeah, yeah. I see, come on.

M: Yeah, I see you, man. Oh.

F: Put that back. Are you going to clean up the school? You gonna clean up Rutgers? Heh? Heh? What's that, Tommy? Tommy, what's that? You got anything? Money. Look and see, anything in there? Anything in there?

M: Tommy, you wanna another doll, babe? Oh.

F: That's right, put it back. Put it away.

---

child has learned numbers and asks "candy please," the child should be required to say "two candies please."

An intervention as simple as asking parents to record samples of their child's speech may increase language. Waters and Siegel (1982) asked parents of toddlers with Down's syndrome to write down words their children said and found a subsequent increase in the children's vocalizations.

When a Child Does Not Speak

Even if a child cannot speak, there are things parents can do to stimulate language development. As discussed in Chapter 3 naturalistic teaching strategies can be used to create a learning context. For example, the techniques used by Ivancic and his colleagues (Ivancic, Reid, Iwata, Faw, and Page, 1981) to encourage staff personnel to talk more to children in an institutional setting can be applied in the home as well. As was done in that study, parents should be encouraged to talk to children while they are dressing, bathing, and

Table 8–4.   Posttraining Communication

F: Pear, say pear. What's that?

C: Gape.

F: Grape, right.

M: All right!

F: Grapes, right, man. What's that?

C: Apple.

F: Apple. All right!

M: Very good.

F: All right!

M: All right!

F: What's that?

C: Nanow.

F: Nana, right. Banana.

M: Right. Hey, you did the whole thing. That's very good.

F: Right. Big man. What's next?

M: OK.

F: What's next, what's next?

C: Da ma.

M: Hmmm?

C: (unintelligible)

M: You gotta turn it over. Who is that?

C: (unintelligible)

M: Tommy, that's right.

M and F: (laughter)

M: That's Tommy.

---

feeding them. Such talk can include imitation of sounds made by the child, modeling simple speech, reinforcing communicative attempts by the child, and encouraging the child's efforts to speak.

Some mute children may never speak or may be very much delayed in the acquisition of speech. Clearly, these youngsters require alternative modes of communication to reduce their frustration and encourage them to interact with other people. E. G. Carr (1982a) has written at some length about the use of sign language with mentally retarded and autistic people. He has cautioned that although some of the literature has been encouraging in that subjects learned to use signs, other studies have failed to demonstrate progress in teaching even simple signs.

When the teacher-consultant encourages parents to try signs, it is important to use appropriate caution and to assess progress on a regular basis. A useful strategy in this regard might be to initiate signing in school and transfer the skill to home once it is shown to be feasible. This caution aside, the data do suggest that at least in some cases, parents can become skillful in using sign language to communicate with their developmentally disabled child (Casey, 1978).

Schepis and her colleagues (Schepis, Reid, Fitzgerald, Faw, van del Pon, and Welty, 1982) trained institutional staff members to facilitate the use of sign language by nonverbal mentally retarded and autistic youth in a residential setting. The techniques used by these staff members, including arranging the environment to encourage the youngsters to sign to gain access to the items they wanted, providing manual prompts, reinforcing signing, and giving brief mini-training sessions throughout the day are all readily adaptable to home use. These techniques essentially parallel those used with the speaking child—only the modality varies. Thus, parents should be encouraged to place objects where the child will have to request them, to provide necessary help in positioning hands to form the signs, and in lavishly rewarding attempts to sign.

In addition to manual signs developmentally disabled children can learn to use pictures to communicate. Lancioni (1983) taught low functioning autistic children to select cards depicting various activities such as throwing a ball and to carry out the activities described. In our own work we have suggested to parents that they provide their nonverbal child with photographs of preferred items or with cutouts from package labels that the child can use to match the object the child wants. A child can learn to present a picture of a cookie or juice to request the item or to match the cutout from the puffed rice box to that box on the shelf to designate a desired breakfast food.

In Sum

These strategies for creating a demand for language can certainly be used in the classroom, but they are nowhere so comfortable and integral a part of daily living as for the child at home. It is therefore important for parents to be well trained in these methods for facilitating language. They must also be aware of the child's current level of ability so they can pitch their demands to an appropriate level. Such awareness requires close coordination between home and school.

DAILY LIVING ACTIVITIES

There are many reasons to teach daily living activities within the home. Considered from the perspective of the child this is the natural environment in which the practice of these activities takes on real meaning. Teaching a mentally retarded child to put on pajamas at school is certainly possible, but it is much less functional than that same training conducted in the child's bedroom as part of a nighttime routine. As discussed in Chapter 3 many of these youngsters have serious problems in generalization of responding and find the transfer of skills from school to home baffling. Training on the scene reduces this complexity.

Skills in daily living are essential to the young person's eventual move from the family home to a supervised apartment, group home, or other community-based living arrangement. Even more than some of the academic information taught in school, these skills of independence may predict the quality of life that lies ahead for the developmentally disabled person. Put in concrete terms, the parents who wipe their children's bottoms after bowel movements rather than teaching the children to do it for themselves are doing those children a serious disservice.

From a parent's viewpoint there are several important reasons to focus on daily living skills within the home. One of the most important is that the more skills for independence the child has, the less the child will have to rely upon others to provide basic care. This removes a burden from the parents. In addition, if a developmentally disabled child can participate in family chores, recreational activities, and daily routines, that child can become more fully a member of the family and provide the rest of the family greater flexibility in pursuing activities they enjoy. The case of the van Allen family demonstrated how this training can integrate other children in the family into the learning process.

Play Is Important Work

Everyone recognizes how important play is to the normal child's mastery of the environment. The manipulation of objects, pleasure of fantasy, and interaction with other children in collective projects all offer children opportunities for learning a great deal about themselves and the world. For many mentally retarded and autistic children this learning comes more slowly, and with difficulty. As seen in Chapter 4 some of these children do not seem to know how to occupy themselves at play and may be so active or distractible that they do not focus on their toys. Autistic children in particular have considerable difficulty in the acquisition of symbolic play (Doherty and Rosenfeld, 1984; Riguet, Taylor, Benaroya, and Klein, 1981).

Parents of handicapped children may regret the failure of their children to occupy themselves at play both because of the learning opportunities lost and because it leaves the children with one less constructive way to occupy themselves. In response to this problem, it is helpful to suggest programs aimed at facilitating play behavior.

When a younger sibling is present, games that involve both children may be helpful because this reduces the number of activities the parents are supervising, increases the pleasure the children derive from each other, and provides the handicapped child with a competent role model. Several studies have supported the notion that normal peer models can facilitate the acquisition of skills by developmentally disabled children (Egel, Richman, and Koegel, 1981; Strain, 1983). In addition, as Twardosz and her co-workers demonstrated (Twardosz, Nordquist, Simon, and Botkin, 1983), teaching children group affection skills such as patting one another on the back, hugging, and so forth can increase an isolated developmentally disabled child's integration into the group. Furthermore, Odom, Deklyen, and Jenkins (1984) found no negative impact on normal preschoolers in a classroom with handicapped children.

Independent Play

As seen in the case of Josh van Allen some developmentally disabled children have considerable difficulty focusing on play activities and remaining with the task long enough to master its complexities. For these children a program that emphasizes reinforcing sustained periods of independent play and correct manipulation of objects may be in order. A hazard to avoid in these instances is that of mistaking repetitive (but quiet) self-stimulation for play. Therefore, the duration of the activity must be considered in the context of the quality of the behavior. Flapping a puzzle piece in front of the eyes for 30 minutes—even if it is self-sufficient, sustained, and includes holding a toy—is not play.

Eason and her colleagues (1982) taught mentally retarded and autistic children to play with toys such as a shape box, jack-in-the-box, Mr. Potato Head, puzzle, blocks, Legos, and Etch-a-Sketch by rewarding them with praise and food for increasing durations of appropriate play behavior. In response to treatment the children increased their play behaviors and decreased inappropriate self-stimulation. Such findings support the notion that giving developmentally dis-

abled people interesting things to do will decrease their rates of un-
desirable behaviors. One of the attractive features about the procedures used by Eason and colleagues (1982) was that they did not
have to punish self-stimulation to decrease it—rather, they rewarded
appropriate play.

Social Play

One way to increase social play among developmentally disabled
children is to teach the children and their siblings to play together
(Powell, Salzberg, Rule, Levy, and Itzkowitz, 1983). Although a study
by Powell and colleagues (1983) showed that simply asking parents
to "get the children to play together" did little to increase play between the siblings, concrete and specific suggestions were very helpful. For example, after parents attended a 3-hour workshop and were
given written instructions, there was a striking increase in parental
prompts and praise for play behavior and the children's interactive
play increased.

The research by Powell and colleagues (1983) suggests that if the
teacher-consultant wants to help a family increase interactive play
among siblings, the parents should be encouraged to select toys that
facilitate social interaction such as a ball, a simple board game,
blocks, dress-up clothes, and so forth. Blocks, vehicles, and water
play materials have been shown to facilitate play between handicapped preschoolers and their nonimpaired peers (Stoneman, Cantrell, and Hoover-Dempsey, 1983). Parents also need to learn to recognize and reinforce appropriate social interactions such as sharing,
assisting, or organizing play and to prompt these behaviors when
they do not occur. Feedback from the families in the study by Powell
and colleagues (1983) indicated that parents regarded these skills as
easily acquired, and the data suggested that they quickly became
skillful enough to make an impact on their children's social play behavior. Research at the Douglass Developmental Disabilities Center
has indicated the importance of gradually fading adult supervision
if the teacher-consultant or parent wishes to sustain independent social play by developmentally disabled children (Romanczyk, Diament, Goren, Trunell, and Harris, 1975).

Social play can increase language as well as provide leisure time
activities. Bates and Renzaglia (1982) taught a profoundly retarded
adolescent to play a simple board game that required him to name
pictures in order to advance around the board. The youngster
learned 14 new verbal labels while playing a game. Such an activity
could be developed for children at different levels by varying the

complexity of the tasks each person has to complete to advance on the board.

Household Chores and Family Routines

It is sometimes difficult for parents of handicapped children to impose the same kinds of demands and expectations upon the handicapped child as they hold for their other children. For example, they may expect their other children to do chores around the house, learn to care for their clothing and their room, and become contributing members of the family. The handicapped child, to the child's marked disadvantage, and to the resentment of the other siblings, may be exempted from such demands.

We encourage parents to involve their developmentally disabled children in family routines from early childhood. Removing utensils from the table, putting the paper napkins in the trash, carrying the cereal box to the table, picking up toys, and so forth, are skills that eventually can be mastered by all but the most disabled children. These small units form building blocks for more complex skills such as shopping for groceries (Aeschleman and Schladenhauffen, 1984; Nietupski, Welch, and Wacker, 1983) or doing the laundry (Thompson, Braam, and Fuqua, 1982). Although it may take years to master the whole sequence, children who learn to bathe themselves, set the table without supervision, or dust the living room furniture will have that skill available to them for the rest of their lives. Ten minutes a day of teaching a child to do a chore adds up to 70 minutes each week and 60 hours each year. A lot of learning can take place in 60 hours.

Recreational Activities

Every Christmas at the Douglass Developmental Disabilities Center there is a visit from Santa Claus. Many of the children, especially the little ones, seem quite indifferent to the fellow with the white beard. New parents sometimes wonder why the center goes through this routine when it has so little apparent impact on the children. In the same fashion, parents are urged to send small treats for a classroom party when their child has a birthday. In the early years the children seem to pay little attention to the event, perhaps eating the cupcake, perhaps smearing it on the table or dipping it in the apple juice. If the children don't understand that birthdays are special, why bother?

Over the years it has been seen again and again that what might have appeared to be a futile routine becomes transformed into an anticipated pleasure as the children learn to expect and enjoy these recreational activities. The parties take on meaning through repeated exposure. If the preschoolers do not comprehend the meaning of birthday, the older children learn to wait with great pleasure for their turn at being the birthday child. They have learned that pleasure through experience.

It is important for children to be integrated into family recreational routines whenever possible. For example, if a family enjoys jogging, taking walks, or playing ball, there should be a concerted effort to teach the handicapped child some minimal skills to participate in the activities. As was the case with household chores the developmentally disabled child may take much longer to master these skills than the other siblings require, but that need not preclude deriving pleasure from the small units of accomplishment along the way.

Arguing for including the child in family recreational activities does not mean that the handicapped child need be part of everything the family does. In most families individual members have separate activities. The presence of a developmentally disabled child should not preclude those individual pursuits. Indeed, it may be all the more essential to ensure that the other siblings can freely pursue their interests and not feel obligated to have their brother or sister tag along. For example, if a sibling were performing in a school play and feared her autistic brother might have a tantrum during the performance, it would be very appropriate that he not attend the show. Everyone needs special times to shine in the eyes of parents and friends.

In general, parents should be urged to identify a few family recreational activities that can readily accommodate a wide range of skills. For example, a family might go roller-skating or hiking or visit a zoo, children's restaurant, or amusement park and find wide latitude in acceptable behavior and level of performance necessary for self-enjoyment. Special scouting and Y programs may also provide good leisure experiences.

Increases in basic leisure skills will lead to increases in social interaction (Jeffree and Cheseldine, 1984). Repeated exposure is probably essential to teaching handicapped children to be appropriate in a public setting, to enjoy themselves, and to be comfortable. It can be suggested to parents that they go for brief periods of time, have very discrete goals, and gradually increase the length and complexity of these activities.

In the Good Old Summer Time

Recreational activities offer a useful focus for filling vacation time. Parents can form small vacation groups to take their children to various events during school vacation. For example, two or three families might get together and take their children to a zoo, pool, or playground. Traveling together they have social support in case one of the children is troublesome, know they can count on one another for such simple but important things as helping out when they need to use the restroom, and can enjoy one another's company while providing stimulation to the children. Siblings in these family groups can enjoy one another as well as their handicapped brother or sister. Even one or two of these activities a week can provide a break for parents, offer structure to the week, and keep the children sufficiently stimulated so that they are easier to live with the rest of the time.

Many parents say that establishing a schedule for vacation days makes life simpler than just leaving events to move at their own pace. Certainly, this will vary with the individual child, but many developmentally disabled children do seem to welcome a predictable schedule. For example, after breakfast a parent might spend 15 minutes on an independent dressing program for the child, followed by free outdoor play for 30 minutes, 20 minutes of play with a parent, another 30 minutes alone, and so forth through the morning with a snack time included. After lunch there might be a trip to the community pool for several hours, a midafternoon quiet time, individual play, and meal preparation followed by dinner and a family activity before bedtime. Although such a schedule may seem somewhat confining at first glance, many parents report that their children are better behaved and therefore less tiring than when they are left to their own devices.

SUMMARY

Classroom teachers of developmentally disabled children may be uniquely qualified to provide home consultation to parents. The teacher, as an expert in child development, works with the child 5 or 6 hours a day, 5 days a week, for many months. This intense contact offers plenty of opportunity to try various educational techniques and learn what works best for each child. Many, although not all, of the problems encountered by parents have probably been seen by the teacher as well. Thus, when a teacher offers advice, it can be founded upon a substantial data base.

The CONSULTED (Confer, Observe, Name problems, Set priorities, Utilize resources, Label obstacles, Try intervention, Evaluate outcome, Determine next step) model for consultation with families is one way to ensure a systematic approach to working with families.

Two areas of home programming that can be especially fruitful are communication patterns and daily living skills. Although parents of developmentally disabled children are not very different as language models than parents of other children of the same language age, many handicapped children seem to need an exceptional level of stimulation to make optimal progress. Parents of mentally retarded and autistic children cannot rely upon the cues from their children as the sole guide to communication. The children may be deficient in nonverbal and verbal cues and thus not convey accurate messages to adults. As a consequence parents must self-consciously create an atmosphere that stimulates the use of speech or other language.

Daily living skills are essential to a handicapped child's long-term adaptation. The tiny building blocks that parents establish in childhood when they teach a child to pull a zipper, play with a simple toy, put the glasses in the dishwasher, and so forth will ultimately form prolonged sequences of self-help skills that can maximize the disabled adult's independence.

Although this chapter could not describe all possible home programs to meet the needs of parents, it is hoped that the reader will be guided by the principles offered and the examples provided and will feel free to generate a great many innovative solutions with parents. As discussed in Chapter 6, this problem-solving process is a joint partnership to which the teacher-consultant and parents bring their special expertise.

Chapter 9

Life Cycle of the Family

Case Report: Coming of Age

At 19 years of age Danny Harrell was an amiable, gentle natured young man whose even temper and friendly smile made him popular with the staff of his program for mentally retarded adolescents. Classified as suffering from Down's syndrome, Danny showed the visible stigmata of that disorder, including his almond-shaped eyes, small mouth, and protruding tongue. Heart surgery in early childhood had corrected a serious heart defect. Educationally, Danny was in the high trainable range and was in a prevocational classroom at his regional high school.

Danny was in his last year of the prevocational program and was being considered for placement in a vocational class for the following fall. Although he had made excellent educational progress over the years and clearly had benefitted from his school years, Danny's parents were increasingly concerned about their son's future. Danny had been born to them relatively late in their lives; his father was now 62 and his mother 54. Within a few years Mr. Harrell expected to retire and Mrs. Harrell, who had had a heart attack the previous fall, was finding herself preoccupied with the question of what would happen to Danny if she or her husband died. As she commented to her physician, she knew both of them would probably die before Danny—it was a question of when, not whether. Because she could not live forever, she needed to know that Danny would be cared for after she died.

Danny was the Harrell's second child. They had an older daughter, Kimberly, who was a senior at the state college, majoring in physics and planning to teach science when she graduated. Although Kimberly told her parents that she loved Danny and wanted him to live with her, the Harrells had serious reservations about that solution. It bothered them to think of Kimberly carrying the burden of her brother's care for many years into the future and perhaps having to adjust her own plans for a family to meet Danny's needs. It was reassuring for them to know that Kimberly would always be there to provide Danny with a sense of family and loving concern, but they felt that both children would be better off if Danny could lead a life separately from his sister's.

The Harrells had begun the process of searching for alternative living arrangements for their son. Although they had been aware of the possibility of institutional placement at one of the state's residential schools, they were relieved to find a number of alternatives to these institutions for a person like Danny who required little in terms of special medical care and who posed no major management problems. Primary among the possibilities for Danny were a group home as his first placement and perhaps later, as he acquired more skill for independent living, a supervised apartment.

Knowing about these attractive living arrangements made things easier for the Harrells, but it did not eliminate their distress and sadness in watching their son leave home. Some of this was the sadness any parent feels on seeing a child launched into the wider world. Some of it was the pain of being forced to confront once again the realization of Danny's handicap and how it affected his life and theirs. The Harrells always felt some underlying sadness about Danny's disability, and the decision to place him in a group home intensified that sorrow once more. Some of the pain came too from the realization that they were making this decision for Danny because they were growing older and their own lives now had very real limits.

Case Commentary. As an adolescent about to enter early adulthood, Danny Harrell's maturation posed important challenges to him and to his family. Danny was confronted by the problem of learning how to separate from his parents and live in a small group with other mentally retarded persons. He had to learn new routines and rules, adapt to the idiosyncrasies of the people with whom he lived, and understand that his parents and sister continued to love him even though he was no longer at home. Danny's good nature and relatively well-developed self-care skills eased the transition for him, but it nonetheless was one of the most demanding tasks of his adolescence.

The challenge was no less demanding for his parents. Mr. and Mrs. Harrell loved their son deeply, and his leaving felt as though a part of them were being pulled away. Although they were intellectually committed to the idea that this living arrangement was in Danny's best interests, it was nonetheless a difficult change. The move was made all the more difficult because it signified to the Harrells their own increasing age. Accepting the fact that they, like all other persons, were truly mortal and would not go on forever was very difficult. The gap between what a person understands with words and how a person understands with feelings made the process a slow, sad, and difficult one.

Once the Harrells and Danny made their adaptation to Danny's move, life improved for everyone. Danny enjoyed the companionship and activities of the group home and felt himself very grown-up living beyond his parents' home. Mr. and Mrs. Harrell had more freedom to travel and found that with Danny gone they had more opportunities to spend time with each other and renew the meaning of their marriage. Kimberly, although initially disappointed, felt some sense of relief that her parents did not expect her to care for Danny in her own home. Thus, 6 months after the move everyone in the family could say with conviction that it had been the right choice. But during the phase of transition it had been a difficult and painful process that demanded effort from the entire family.

INTRODUCTION

In recent years psychologists, sociologists, and social workers have made extensive use of the concept of the family life cycle to describe the important life transitions that persons pass through as members of a family (Carter and McGoldrick, 1980; Figley and McCubbin, 1983; McCubbin and Figley, 1983). Table 9–1 summarizes some of the major transitional events that most families encounter as they move through life.

When two young people meet and marry they encounter the first of the transitions they must face as a unit: the passage from being children in their families of origin to being partners in a new marriage. Although many tend to view the early months of marriage as a time of romantic glow and contentment, there are major developmental challenges that face a couple as they adapt to living together and separating from their families of birth. The couple must learn to work together to solve problems, to accommodate each other's needs in ways that maximize their mutual satisfaction, and to establish a new relationship with their parents. Their success or failure at these kinds of tasks will significantly influence their readiness to move on to new family and personal developmental tasks.

Once the marital unit has stabilized, the couple may elect to take on a new transitional task: having children. Again, although persons may view rearing children in somewhat idealized terms as a new source of gratification in their lives, having children also places significant demands on a couple to meet the needs of the new family members while still finding satisfaction within the marriage.

Table 9–1.   Life Cycle Events

Marriage	Learning to be intimate
Birth of child	Expanding to include others
Child starts school	Involvement of wider community
Child enters adolescence	Intensification of separation
Child leaves home	Parents' renewal of marriage
Retirement	Facing issues of aging
Old age	Facing death, being alone

Demands for change continue throughout the life cycle of the family. There are adaptations when children start school, when they enter adolescence, and when they leave home to go to college, take jobs, or marry. Families must also adapt to the aging of parents, the death of a spouse, and so forth. These events go in an endless cycle: When a young couple marry and start a family of their own they also have an impact on the functioning of their own families of origin. Similarly, a couple who are dealing with the adolescence of their own children may also be struggling to meet the needs of aging parents from their families of origin.

It is useful for the professional who works with families of the developmentally disabled to be aware of the normal impact of major transitional events on the family. Such awareness makes it possible to understand how the needs of the handicapped person may influence normal transitional processes in the family as well as how the family's normal transitions affect the handicapped person. The lives of all the family members are woven tightly together: A single individual in the family cannot be understood without an appreciation of the family as a whole. Thus, considering the family as a mutually interacting unit may serve to broaden the teacher's perspective on the responses that parents and siblings have to the needs of a developmentally disabled person.

The purpose of this chapter is to consider how the needs of developmentally disabled persons and their families change throughout the family life cycle. It reviews this process from birth through adulthood of the handicapped person and considers the role that teachers and other professionals can play in helping families cope with difficult and demanding life changes.

BIRTH AND INFANCY

Most persons have hopes and dreams about what their children will be like—children to take to ball games, teach the way to sew a straight seam, show the wonders of oceans and mountains, guide through the complexities of growing up. Regardless of whether parents hope their child will take over the family business, go to college, or in some other way fulfill their dreams, they all want a child who is healthy and capable. Given this backdrop of gratifying dreams there are few things in life more painful for parents than accepting the fact of their child's developmental disability. Table 9-2 summarizes some of the transitional issues encountered by every family of young children and highlights additional or different issues that may arise for the parents of a developmentally disabled child.

Learning the Diagnosis

Parents of children who have Down's syndrome or some other form of disability with conspicuous physical characteristics will be confronted by their child's handicap shortly after birth. For the parents of an autistic child or one whose mental retardation is not accompanied by obvious physical indicators, the knowledge of the handicapping condition may follow months later and be even more painful when it is evident that the child's behavior or ability to learn is significantly different from that of other children (Bernheimer, Young, and Winton, 1983). In either case it is a jarring experience and one that runs counter to the parents' dreams for their child's future. Although life for the parent of a developmentally disabled child will always have its sad times, there may be no single event as wrenchingly difficult as learning that the child has a serious, lifelong disability (Featherstone, 1980; Wikler, 1981).

Unhappily, professionals can make the intrinsically difficult process of learning the diagnosis even more difficult because of a lack of sensitivity in conveying the news. This inability to respond to the parents' emotional needs in a time of stress may well reflect the professional's discomfort at having to convey painful information, but it is nonetheless a grave failure in responsibility when a professional does not take the time to help parents assimilate the knowledge of their child's diagnosis.

Although teachers will rarely if ever be called upon to convey initial diagnostic information, those who work with very young children may very well be involved in helping parents understand the meaning of the diagnosis and the long-term implications for their child. Because physicians sometimes do this job poorly, there may be a considerable demand on teachers to fill in the gaps in the information that parents have been given about their child. It is therefore important for teachers to be aware of how parents experience the di-

Table 9-2. Families of the Developmentally Disabled Transitional Challenges—Marriage, Birth, Preschool Years

Phase	Normative	Added or Different
Marriage	Adaptation to spouse's routines, values, etc. Development of negotiation skills Separation from family of origin Pursuit of vocational goals	None
Birth and infancy	Adjustment of routine to include child Adaptation to changes in marital relationship Negotiation on philosophy of child care with spouse Negotiation on extended family involvement with child	Acceptance of diagnosis Meeting medical needs Resolving issues of blame, anger Dealing with sorrow

agnostic process and how to help them understand their child's disability.

Parents' Views of the Diagnostic Process

Talking with parents of developmentally disabled children will reveal that many of them are angry or disapproving of the way they were first informed of their children's handicaps. For example, Gath (1978) found that only 27 percent of the parents of babies with Down's syndrome were satisfied with the way they were told, and 40 percent were definitely not satisfied, and 33 percent felt that nothing could have altered the impact of the news.

In a series of studies of mothers of babies with Down's syndrome or spina bifida in Scotland, Murdoch (1983, 1984a, 1984b) found that only slightly more than half the mothers in each group felt their physician did a good job of informing them of the baby's diagnosis. In addition, one third of the mothers of Down's syndrome babies and more than half the mothers of spina bifida babies felt they were given no opportunity to ask questions or express their feelings. Murdoch further noted the lack of continued services for parents after they took their babies home from the hospital and the failure to provide parents with appropriate prognostic information or to help them make plans for the babies' needs. These kinds of failures can contribute in significant ways to the anger parents express about the diagnostic process.

Abramson, Gravink, Abramson, and Sommers (1977) examined questionnaires completed by more than 200 families of mentally retarded children. Only 18 percent of these families felt the early advice they received about their children was helpful; 51 percent were very dissatisfied, dissatisfied or uncertain about the advice they got. Because 94 percent of these families had turned first to their physicians, this degree of unhappiness with the quality of help reflects a serious need for physicians to better understand developmental disabilities. Interestingly, the respondents in this survey reported more satisfaction with the early intervention centers than with the diagnostic process.

One facilitative factor in informing parents appears to be immediacy of sharing information; it is important that parents be told about the diagnosis as soon as possible. Gath (1978) found that all but one of the families who had a child with Down's syndrome who were satisfied with the way they were told about the diagnosis had been told in the first week after the child's birth. McMichael (1971) reported similar findings for parents whose children suffered from physical handicaps. Research by Cunningham, Morgan, and McGucken (1984) indicated that parents value being told about their child's handicap promptly, directly, honestly, in the company of their spouse, and with help in finding appropriate resources.

Teacher's Role

Shea (1984) wrote about the importance of helping parents understand the facts of their child's disorder, aiding them in coping with their feelings, and helping them make plans for their child's treatment. To the extent that such services have been provided by an effective diagnostic team, the teacher will be able to carry through with well-grounded educational plans. However, if other professionals have neglected their responsibilities to help parents accomplish these initial goals, the teacher may find it necessary to fill in the gaps. In doing this work the educator will have to be sensitive to the frustration and anger parents may have experienced in their previous dealings with the professional community. Some parents may be very reluctant to open up until they are certain that the teacher is going to be receptive to them.

Chronic Sorrow

The experience of mourning a child's handicap is not something that happens once and then is completed for the rest of a parent's life. Rather, there are episodes of sadness stirred by important developmental events in the child's life that reawaken a sense of grief. The term that has been used to describe this process of episodic mourning is *chronic sorrow* (Olshanksy, 1962; Wikler, 1981).

Wikler (1981) pointed to the time of the child's diagnosis as one of the most powerful episodes of sorrow that the family will face. Learning that their child is handicapped imposes the demand for major transitions in a family's life. They must turn away from their dreams for the child's future as college graduate, sports hero, or valued companion and adapt to a future with more limited vocational horizons and possibly with a continuing need for supervised care. They must also make adjustments in their family's life-style to meet the special needs of a handicapped child.

In spite of the powerful impact of this initial transitional event, Wikler (1981) indicated that a number of other difficult life cycle transitions await the family of the developmentally disabled child and each of these has the potential to trigger renewed feelings of grief and loss. Thus, the age when a child would normally begin to walk, talk, enter kindergarten, and so forth are all potentially stressful times that may precipitate strong emotional responses in parents. Chronic sorrow does not end in childhood but goes on to include such events as the age of high school graduation, the child's twenty-first birthday, and the time when the child might have married and had children. All of these normal developmental events may underline for parent the discrepancy between their child's actual development and the dreams they once had of their child's future. Although birthdays and other life marker events are only symbols, they are psychologically potent events that have a powerful impact on parents.

Given the nature of chronic sorrow it is important that teachers not expect parents to "get over" their child's handicap. They also should not be surprised when well-functioning parents, leading an effective life with many sources of satisfaction and pride, suddenly begin to weep when talking about their developmentally disabled child. The sadness is always hovering beneath the surface. A parent learns to live with it and to gain pleasure from other aspects of life, but the sadness never disappears completely from the lives of most parents.

Normative Needs

Although the focus of discussion is on the special needs of developmentally disabled children, the experiences of families of very young developmentally disabled children cannot be fully appreciated without understanding that in many ways the needs of these youngsters do not differ dramatically from those of their nonhandicapped age peers. As a consequence the lives of their parents may not differ in basic routine from those of other parents (Carr, J., 1975; Gath, 1978; Waisbren, 1980).

Reasonably mature parents expect to spend several years providing basic physical care for their children. They know there will be diapers to change, faces to wash, curious hands to be redirected from a vase of flowers to a colorful toy, sleepless nights spent walking a sick infant, and so forth. As caring adults they agree to the terms of that contract when they assume the responsibilities and potential pleasures of parenthood.

These basic needs for love, physical care, and attention to safety and health are as valid for the developmentally disabled child as for any other child. In that sense the task of being the parent of a developmentally disabled infant or toddler does not differ dramatically from that of other parents. Although handicapped children learn more slowly and in some cases may present more serious management problems, they are nonetheless little people who require a level of intensive care typical of all children. It is not until the child reaches school age that some of the major discrepancies between the developmentally disabled and normal child become increasingly conspicuous. With these changes there emerge a new set of demands on parents and another series of transitional challenges to be met.

It is important for the teacher who works with parents of very young developmentally disabled children to remember the ways in which these children resemble all other children as well as the ways in which they differ. Such a perspective can sometimes be helpful to parents who need to understand that not all of the burdens of child care are related to the child's handicap. Raising a child, any child, is hard work.

EARLY AND MIDDLE CHILDHOOD

The normal child's entry into kindergarten is one of a series of graded separations between parents and child that occur in the life cycle of the family. When the school system becomes part of the child's life, there is a broadening of social and interpersonal horizons and an opportunity for the child to establish relationships beyond the home. Although most parents are pleased to see their child go off to school, there may also be some feelings of regret that the preschool years have ended.

For the parents of a developmentally disabled child this transitional event may be more stressful than for other parents because it serves as a vivid reminder that their child is different from others. When other children walk to school or take a big yellow school bus, their child will be picked up at the door in a special van. When other children on the block all go to the same school, their child may be bussed miles to a special class with children whom they do not know. When other children are learning to read and understand numbers, their child is still struggling to master basic self-help skills. Thus, although it is a blessing to have their child enrolled in a good school and receiving an appropriate education, it is also a reminder of the ways in which their child differs from others.

Table 9–3 summarizes some of the major family transitional events that occur during the children's school years. This table also identifies some of the additional or special stresses that confront parents of developmentally disabled children.

Impact on Parents' Development

The developmentally disabled child's need for continuing supervision and physical care at an age when most children are assuming increasing independence has an impact on the adult development of parents. For example, many women look forward to the time when their children enter middle childhood as an opportunity to return to work, to become more involved in community activities, or in other ways to pursue their own interests. The mother of a developmentally disabled child may find this personal development more difficult to achieve because her child continues to need more of her time and attention than do normally developing age peers.

The mother may also find herself increasingly isolated from other mothers (Birenbaum, 1971). When developmentally disabled children are very young, they may be relatively inconspicuous among their age peers, but as they grow older the gap in terms of social, play, and intellectual skills becomes increasingly obvious. For example, a 10-year-old boy with Down's syndrome may not be welcome among a group of normal preschool children, even if his interests are compatible with theirs, nor would he fit comfortably among most groups of normal 10-year-olds. His mother, likewise, will find that she has little in common with either set of mothers and thus come to see herself as different and separate.

The school-aged developmentally disabled child's special needs affect the father's development as well as the mother's. For example, the child's special educational needs may necessitate that the family

**Table 9-3.   Families of the Developmentally Disabled
Transitional Challenges–The School Years**

Phase	Normative	Added or Different
Kindergarten	Child's increased independence	Continued dependence
	Separation between parent and child	
	Increased influence of other people	Acceptance of special school placement
		Use of special child management methods
School years	Growing independence	Continued dependence
	Personal development of parents	Constraints on parents' growth
	Development of sibling relationships	Extra burdens on siblings
		Growing gap with peers

remain in a particular town that has the necessary schools or medical facilities, and the father may therefore be forced to turn down
promotions that would require a move. Similarly, the father may
have to pass up out-of-town business trips to stay home and provide
child care. As a consequence he may find that his professional development is limited and that one basic source of personal growth and
satisfaction is at least partially denied. The same would hold true
for a working woman, just as a man who had primary child care responsibilities might experience the constraints felt by many
mothers.

Impact on Siblings' Development

The developmentally disabled child's needs will affect siblings as
well as parents. As noted in Chapter 6 there are special stresses involved in growing up as the brother or sister of a handicapped child.
Although this does not always manifest itself in maladaptive ways,
and may sometimes have positive consequences, there are nonetheless special demands on the sibling of a school-aged mentally retarded or autistic child. As seen in the case of Danny Harrell and his
sister Kimberly, siblings may feel deep love and responsibility for
their handicapped brother or sister and also feel a conflict about the
extent to which they should make that sibling a part of their own
adult lives.

Brothers and sisters may have to forego some childhood experiences because their handicapped sibling cannot participate or would
disrupt the activity to everyone's displeasure. They may receive less

attention from their parents because of the extra demands created by the handicapped child's special needs. Brothers and sisters may also find they have to assume child care responsibilities and provide extra help for their parents. Perhaps more difficult for some siblings, they must learn to deal with the reactions of their friends to their brother's or sister's handicap. Although many children learn to deal with this problem with grace, and may voice the opinion that they would not want a friend who did not accept their brother or sister, there is nonetheless an additional source of pressure on them as they grow up. Teasing, unkind comments, and ignorant responses are very much a part of the world of childhood; as a consequence the brothers or sisters of a handicapped child are inevitably going to encounter unpleasant interactions concerning their sibling.

The consequence of all of these added demands is that the relationship between handicapped children and siblings will not be the same as other sibling relationships. Although there may be substantial love, concern, and a form of companionship, the sibling relationship will offer the normal brother or sister many fewer of the opportunities to learn social skills, negotiation skills, or fair fighting and will provide little intimate exchange and support.

ADOLESCENCE AND ADULTHOOD

There are few times in the life of a family as tumultuous as the children's adolescence (Kidwell, Fischer, Dunham, and Baranowski, 1983). The separation process between children and adults reaches a peak of intensity as both parties struggle to define themselves in new ways in relation to one another. It is one of the most demanding normal transitions in the family's life cycle (Ackerman, 1980), and parents commonly describe this time as one of the least satisfying periods of their life in a family (Burr, 1970). Table 9-4 indicates some of the primary transitional issues confronted by most families with adolescent children and includes special issues encountered by the family of the developmentally disabled teenager or adult.

If the maturation process goes well, the adolescent children are able to enter adulthood, establish themselves in intimate relationships beyond their family of origin, and begin to create their own families. Their parents in turn have the opportunity to renew their marriage and to enjoy a degree of independence and freedom they may not have known since their first child was born. If the process does not go well, there can be painful and enduring consequences for the entire family as their lives remain either so intertwined that

**Table 9–4.   Families of the Developmentally Disabled
Transitional Challenges—Adolescence and Adulthood**

Phase	Normative	Added or Different
Adolescence	Intensive separation, individuation struggle	Continued dependence, must encourage separation
	Increased marital stress Need of aging grandparents for attention from parents	Increase in emotional and physical fatigue
Adulthood	Child's transition to own nuclear family	Continued dependence
	Renewal of marital relationship	Renewal of marriage more difficult
	Acceptance of life achievements	Risk of burnout
	Illness of self or spouse	
	Death of spouse	Need to plan for child's care after parents' death

they cannot lead separate lives or so remote that they cannot derive pleasure and support from one another as a unit. Thus, the transitional experiences that occur during adolescence are very important and very demanding.

The Developmentally Disabled and Their Parents

For the family of a developmentally disabled child the special demands of child rearing do not end with the closing of childhood. In fact, the demands may grow more intense because of decreases in formal support services such as schools, recreational programs, and respite care (DeMyer and Goldberg, 1983). Bristol and Schopler (1983) found that older autistic children as a group created more stress for their families than younger autistic children. Many long years of providing basic physical care, insufficient community resources, lack of emotional and social support, and neglect of their own needs for personal growth may place the parents of older developmentally disabled persons at risk for burnout (Marcus, 1984; Sullivan, 1979). Although, as Bristol and Schopler (1983) reported, most parents do not burn out and are functioning well, many are also weary of the unrelenting needs of their children.

Developmentally disabled children may make few moves toward their own independence, and as a consequence the family may not be impelled toward what can be a vital developmental experience for the parents as well as the children. Parents must face the important problems of how to deal with their adolescent child's continuing needs for supervision, potential out-of-home placement, and separation, as well as their own feelings of emotional and physical fatigue, their wishes for increased freedom, and the knowledge of their own eventual deaths with all that implies for the care of their child.

As noted earlier, the mourning process does not end when the developmentally disabled person is a child. Wikler, Wasow, and Hatfield (1981) found that the young person's twenty-first birthday was second only to the time of initial diagnosis as a source of stress in parents' lives. Although developmentally disabled young persons continue to grow and change in positive ways as they get older (Mesibov, 1983), they are also grossly different from their peers. Parents who may have held on to illusions of change as their child was growing up are forced to surrender these ideas as they are confronted by the child's marked vocational and interpersonal limits. For the adolescent or young adult there is little question about the prognosis—whether poor or good the evidence is available and the future clearly defined.

Out-of-Home Placements

There are no absolute rules concerning the best living arrangements for an adolescent or adult developmentally disabled person. Each family has its own view about what constitutes an optimal arrangement, and each family has its own financial, personal, and advocacy resources for meeting the needs of their child. Under some circumstances keeping a child at home may be very appropriate, whereas in other conditions a group home, supervised apartment, foster home, or residential facility may be the most desirable setting.

It is important for the parents, and to the extent possible the young person, to make the choice that is best for them. Such freedom depends on both the availability of suitable community resources and the ability of the family to make decisions in their joint best interests.

Sometimes transitional issues within the family can hamper the freedom to make appropriate changes. For example, some families have insisted on keeping their young adult at home even when it appeared that this was not the best decision for the adult child. Close examination of the family as a whole may reveal that the child is functioning as an emotional buffer between the parents, giving them a common focus without demanding that there be any real intimacy between them. Were the child to leave home they might be confronted by the emptiness of their marriage or their need to expand their personal development.

Prolonged, unnecessary dependency can be detrimental to parents and child alike. For the child there is a denial of the opportunity to become increasingly independent and be established as fully as possible in the community prior to the parents' death or incapacitation in old age. For the parents there is a lack of opportunity to grow beyond their roles as parents and enhance their marriage.

Many families of developmentally disabled young persons who have kept their child at home regard late adolescence or early adulthood as an appropriate time to seek alternative placements. As seen in the case of the Harrell family this choice can be determined by many factors, including the needs of the young person, the health of the parents, and the parents' concerns for their child's long-term adjustment after they die. Chapter 10 looks more closely at some of the factors that lead to a residential placement.

Placements for the Elderly

Although this book is written for teachers and the focus is on the needs of children and their families, no view of the family life cycle would be complete without considering the needs of the elderly developmentally disabled. Even a teacher who never works with older clients should be aware that concerns about their child's adulthood and old age will loom large for the parents of many adolescents and young adults (Kotsopoulos and Matathia, 1980).

With the death of their parents it is almost inevitable that the adult developmentally disabled person will enter some form of out-of-home placement, although a small number do live with siblings (Janicki and MacEachron, 1984). Most of the noninstitutionalized developmentally disabled live in foster care or community residences such as group homes. It has been suggested that the expansion of foster care for older mentally retarded persons may offer a valuable placement alternative for these individuals (Sherman, Frenkel, and Newman, 1984). Middle-aged and elderly mentally retarded people who live in foster care homes are usually accepted by the community and able to use community resources; they also have the benefits of a homelike atmosphere (Sherman et al., 1984).

As seen in the case of the Harrell family, knowing that high-quality community resources are available can contribute in a substantial way to easing a parent's decision about an out-of-home placement.

SUMMARY

The basic unit of human social organization is the family. The family is the unit that has primary responsibility for the initial socialization of the child as well as providing for the child's safety and emotional development. People who live in families go through a series of transitions together, and these transitions follow general patterns within a society. Thus, in contemporary Western society young persons leave their parents' homes and join together to form a new nuclear family. Although they remain part of their families of origin, they typically invest more of their time, energy, and emotional commitment in establishing their own nuclear family, meeting a series of developmental challenges as they create an intimate marital relationship, adapt to the needs of children, and help the children through childhood and into adolescent separation. Each of these events poses its own set of demands, and the successful meeting of each challenge brings its own satisfactions.

The family of the developmentally disabled child must respond to these same fundamental transitions, but the precise nature of their life cycle experiences is determined in part by their response to the special needs of their handicapped child. The professional who provides services to these families should therefore understand not only the normative experiences involved in the family life cycle but also the special circumstances created by the child's handicapping condition.

Understanding the concept of the family life cycle also requires an appreciation of the multilayered interactions that occur within families. In a family each member affects the others, and vice versa, in a continuous fashion that often makes it difficult to disentangle an interaction and say that one event directly caused another. It is more useful to think about patterns of events and about the mutual impact on one another than to think in terms of linear, straight-line cause and effects transactions.

This chapter briefly examines the life cycle experiences of the family when the developmentally disabled child is very young, during the school years, and during adolescence and adulthood. It also highlights the notion of chronic sorrow to describe the continuing, episodic grief that parents experience when their child passes certain developmental landmarks such as the age of starting kindergarten, learning to drive a car, or celebrating a twenty-first birthday. These symbolic events may trigger sadness in the parents of a developmentally disabled child.

An understanding of the transitional events in the functioning of a family may enable a teacher to respond with greater sensitivity to a parent's needs and may help the teacher and the parent appreciate the normative, nonpathological nature of some of the distress that everyone must experience as a part of life.

Chapter 10

Life in the Community

Case Report: Allison Anders

Ilona Kay hurried to put away her books and papers at the end of the school day. She had an appointment in 20 minutes with Mr. and Mrs. Anders and their daughter, Allison, at the office of Dr. Judson Davids, Allison's pediatrician. Having worked with Dr. Davids twice before, she was delighted that Allison's parents had chosen a pediatrician who was very sensitive to the special needs of the developmentally disabled child. As she hurried from her classroom Ilona tucked into her briefcase the rather extensive file of data she had collected on the frequency and duration of Allison's increasingly troublesome and aggressive tantrums as well as a record of Allison's self-injury over the past year. Although it was the aggressive tantrums that created the crisis leading to the need for a medical consultation, the self-injury had been a worrisome behavior for several years.

The decision to seek a medical consultation about Allison's behavior had been reached about 3 weeks earlier when Allison had several especially bad days during which she bit her younger sister and one of the children in class and badly bruised her own forehead by banging her head against her knee. A variety of behavioral interventions had been tried to deal both with her self-injury and her aggression in the 2 years that Allison had been in Ilona Kay's classroom. Twice outside experts who were authorities in the management of problem behaviors were called in for suggestions. Unfortunately, none of the very careful behavioral programs that were in use at home and at school had been sufficient by themselves to calm Allison's behavior, and her parents and teacher were worried that the tantrums coupled with her history of head banging had reached the point where she could not be managed well in any setting. They were consulting Judson Davids to determine whether medication might be helpful for Allison.

A gentle, patient man, Judson Davids examined Allison carefully, noting the bruising at her temples and on her forehead from her repeated head banging. He also had a sample of Allison's tantrums when she lashed out at him as he drew the blood he needed to minimize the risk of harmful side effects from medication he might prescribe. After the examination was completed and Dr. Davids had reviewed the records from the school and home with care, he suggested they try a medication that had been shown in several good research studies to be of benefit to some children with behavior like Allison's.

Dr. Davids was emphatic about two things when he wrote the prescription. One was the importance of regular visits to him and careful observation at home and school to look for any dangerous or unpleasant side effects from the medication. He described in detail the kinds of problems they should be alert for in supervising Allison, noting that because she could not talk they would have to be all the more vigilant to ensure that she was not experiencing any bad effects from the medication.

The second thing Judson Davids stressed was that he would only continue to prescribe the drug as long as there were data showing that it was in fact effective for Allison. He appreciated the baseline data that Allison's parents and teacher had collected, commenting on how rare it was that he received that kind of support. Then he indicated that it would be essential that they continue to keep track of the problem behaviors on a regular basis to ensure that Allison was continuing to benefit from the treatment. He expected to take Allison off the medication periodically to assess her behavior and determine whether she continued to need medication.

Case Commentary. Allison Anders exhibited serious, dangerous behaviors that placed her and those around her at risk. They were the kinds of behaviors that sometimes make it difficult for parents to keep a child at home or for a school to be willing to keep a child in class. It is not uncommon for children who are aggressive or self-injurious or both to end up in residential settings, sometimes badly overmedicated so that they are too lethargic to move, or restrained with mechanical restraints so they cannot hurt themselves or other persons. Excessive medication, physical restraints, or life in a highly segregated treatment facility are very limited solutions to a life-threatening problem.

Fortunately for Allison, her parents, her teacher, and her physician were broadly informed about the needs of the developmentally disabled and were able to try a number of less restrictive alternatives before they turned to such solutions as residential care or mechanical restraints. The intensive behavior modification programs that had been used for the past several years had in fact had a significant impact on Allison's behavior. Her rate of self-injury was lower than it had been when she started school, and her aggression was also reduced. Nonetheless, in spite of some creative programming, the behaviors persisted, and as Allison grew older and stronger the danger to herself and others increased.

The decision to use medication and the ongoing monitoring of its effects by all of the adults who were concerned with Allison provide a good example of how drugs can be used while placing a child at as little physical risk as necessary. The behavioral data collected on Allison's tantrums and self-injury would allow objective decisions about whether the drug was helping and thus ensure that she did not end up taking medication for years because of someone's subjective hunch that "maybe she was a little better than before."

INTRODUCTION

Teachers of developmentally disabled children are often called upon to provide parents with information about resources that extend beyond the bounds of the classroom. For example, parents are concerned about how to find a physician who will have both the expertise and the willingness to care for their child, or parents ask how to prepare their child for a visit to a physician or a dentist in order to reduce the stress for all concerned. They also worry about providing for their child's long-term financial welfare through wills, trusts, social security payments, and so forth. Parents also may seek information about community resources such as respite care, parent support groups, or parent-run advocacy groups to promote the welfare of children and adults with developmental disabilities.

Although the teacher cannot be expected to have the legal or medical expertise to answer a parent's questions directly, a teacher can fill the valuable function of helping parents find appropriate resources within the community. Thus, while it would be very inappropriate for a teacher to suggest that a child be given a specific drug or that a parent use one method of financial planning versus another, it is highly appropriate for a teacher to identify people within the community who can offer families the various kinds of professional support they require. Similarly, the teacher can work with a parent to design a behavioral program to prepare a child for an essential medical procedure or audiological examination.

The present chapter provides an overview of various community resources and ways to help parents make efficient use of these resources. It may be helpful for the teacher to remember that medical facilities, school systems, advocacy organizations, and other community resources are themselves systems that have a mutual impact upon one another. Parents or teachers who are trying to obtain services or bring about changes in community resources will want to be sensitive to how various community organizations view the school, the developmentally disabled person, and so forth. Failure to do so can sometimes heighten antagonism between various organizations and reduce the likelihood that parents will obtain the services they seek.

This is not an argument against the notion that parents should take an assertive stand to obtain the services they need for their child—to the contrary parents are potentially the child's best and most committed advocates. However, being assertive does not necessarily mean being belligerent or aggressive or ignoring the organization's structure in a way that leaves important people feeling they have been bypassed or ignored. The advocate must also be aware that power does not always reside exclusively within the formal organizational structure. Many young professionals can testify to the unfortunate error of failing to appreciate the power of secretarial staff in a well-run office. Thus, dealing effectively with organizations demands an appreciation of their formal and informal structures.

MEDICAL CARE

Historically, the interactions between educators and physicians concerning the welfare of developmentally disabled children have not been wholly satisfying to either party. Indeed, this appears to be an excellent example of two service delivery systems that tend to operate relatively independently from each other and to have poorly developed mechanisms for sharing information. The victims of this systemic failure are the children and their parents.

Gaps in the Physician's Knowledge Base

Several studies have examined the question of how well informed pediatricians and family practitioners are concerning the educational needs of developmentally disabled children. In general this work suggests that even physicians who specialize in the treatment of infants and children are not as knowledgeable as might be wished about the special needs of developmentally disabled youngsters.

Singh and Winton (1984) found that although physicians were aware of a responsibility to provide counseling for parents of developmentally disabled children, most of them knew relatively little about available resources. Support for that finding comes from several other studies. For example, one survey of physicians in Texas

found that only 64 percent of them were aware of PL 94–142 (Mc-
Donald, Carlson, Palmer, and Slay, 1983). That lack of basic knowledge would make it difficult for physicians to encourage parents to
know and demand their child's educational rights.

Another survey of primary care physicians in Arizona revealed
that only 50 percent of the pediatricians and 28 percent of the family
practitioners provided routine screening for developmental problems
(Fischler and Tancer, 1984). An unfortunate 10 to 25 percent of the
physicians continued to wait for children to "outgrow" their problems. One positive finding was that physicians in practice for 10
years or less were more likely to make early referrals for speech and
hearing evaluations than were those who had been in practice
longer. This may reflect a greater sensitivity to issues of early identification among physicians being trained more recently than
among those trained in years past.

These findings as a whole suggest the importance of ensuring
that physicians are properly informed about the nature and treatment of developmental disabilities. The teacher should not assume
that a physician's failure to respond to the needs of a developmentally disabled child reflects indifference on the practitioner's part.
Rather it may indicate a lack of knowledge about precisely what are
the best interests of the child and what resources are available to
meet the need. Educators will sometimes find themselves in the position of having to educate medical colleagues. It is important for
teachers to recognize that their special expertise in the area of educating the developmentally disabled child far exceeds that of the
physician. Educators may therefore be called upon tactfully to share
knowledge while still respecting the boundaries that exist between
medicine and education.

The Use of Medication in the Classroom

One of the issues that might benefit most from communication between educator and physician is the use of medication for children.
Teachers often view themselves as ill-informed about the medication
needs of the children in their class (Gadow, 1982). They describe
problems with not knowing the effects and side effects of the medication, the appropriate use of the drug, its use at home, or changes in
the drug regimen that might affect the child's behavior. The teachers surveyed by Gadow (1982) also complained that physicians often
failed to assess the child's needs adequately or to monitor the effects
of the medication once the drug was prescribed. They expressed a
need for ongoing systematic evaluation of drug effects on the child

and were concerned that a lack of effective communication between teachers and physicians precluded this exchange of information.

These concerns are shared by physicians as well. Brulle, Barton, and Foskett (1983) surveyed physicians concerning the exchange of information with schools and parents. They found that although all the respondents valued the idea of the exchange of information, very little information was actually transmitted. Although the majority of physicians said they got information about children before they instituted treatment, only 33 percent felt the information was objective. Similarly, 62 percent of the medical doctors said they got some information from the schools about the effects of medication, but only 10 percent felt this information was objective. Thus, it appears that there is considerable dissatisfaction on both sides concerning the exchange of essential information between the physician and the teacher.

In response to these concerns Gadow (1982) offered several suggestions to both teachers and physicians. One recommendation was that teachers learn more about the specific medications being given to the children in their class. Such information can be obtained in part from the *Physician's Desk Reference,* an annual review of prescription drugs, and in part from asking questions of the physician who prescribes the drugs. Gadow (1982) also suggested that some formal training in drug therapy might be an appropriate part of the special education teacher training curriculum.

To know what drugs a child is currently taking, the school might ask parents to complete a medication form at the beginning of each school year (Gadow, 1982). An effort should also be made to include the physician in the staffing conference for the child. As seen in the case of Allison Anders involving the physician may require active effort on the part of the teacher to make an office visit with parents and child and be part of that evaluation rather than to have the teacher's input filtered through the parents to the physician and then have the physician's recommendations come through the parents to the teacher. This suggestion is not intended as a negative reflection on the concerns or skills of parents. Rather, it is an acceptance of the fact that parents may not always be able to anticipate the questions a teacher would ask if present and thus they come away from the meeting with incomplete information. For some families, if the parents are particularly anxious or stressed during the visit, the teacher can be a source of support to the parents and provide helpful information to the physician.

A teacher in the kind of a behaviorally based classroom described in this book should have little problem providing the physician with complete and detailed records concerning the child's problem behaviors, attempted treatments, and response to medication. One of the strong points of the behaviorally based classroom is the data-based approach to intervention. As seen in the case of Allison Anders this kind of preparation prior to a meeting with a physician concerning medication can make the task easier for all concerned. Even when physicians do not initiate a request for records, they will probably be delighted to be offered systematic information about the child's progress. In fact, skepticism might be warranted if a physician ignored those kinds of carefully collected behavioral records.

Figure 10–1 illustrates the data Maria Arnold, the head teacher at the Douglass Developmental Disabilities Center, collected to examine changes in handplay for one boy who was being treated with medication. Notice that in the weeks before medication was used, this boy had an average of 6.2 episodes of handplay each school day. When the medication was introduced, handplay fell sharply to a mean of 1.6 and remained at low levels for the rest of the school year.

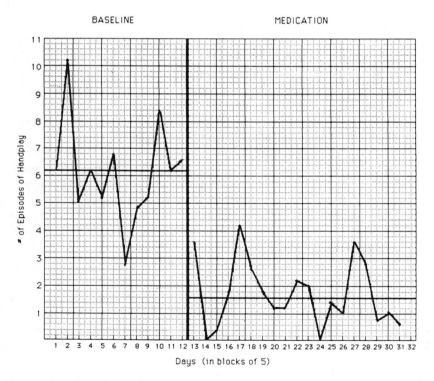

Figure 10–1. Changes in an autistic boy's frequency of stereotypic handplay in the classroom with the use of medication.

Preparing a Child for an Evaluation

Parents, physicians, dentists, or audiologists sometimes ask teachers to help them prepare a child for an important diagnostic procedure. Developmentally disabled children may be frightened by the examining equipment, have difficulty understanding instructions for a test procedure, or be unable to respond to the reassurances that comfort other children. Many of them have undergone a number of stressful and painful medical procedures in the past and therefore have come to expect the worst when they enter a physician's office. Unfortunately, many test procedures require the child's cooperation for an optimal assessment; although a specific procedure may not be painful, previous conditioning to medical settings will make it difficult to even keep the child in the situation, much less obtain a cooperative response. Happily, it has been found that gradually exposing the child to the procedure and the equipment can make the actual examination easier, thereby ensuring that the examiner has an optimal opportunity to obtain the needed diagnostic information and the child does not suffer needless trauma (Dahlquist, Gil, Kalfus, Blount, and Boyd, 1984).

For example, when one child needed to learn to wear a headset to participate in a hearing test, he was helped to adapt to having the apparatus placed on his ears. The procedures were the same as might be used with any shaping program in that he was rewarded for gradually increasing periods of appropriate behavior. Likewise, children have been taught to tolerate wearing electrodes and sitting quietly during an electroencephalographic examination. These procedures may take a few minutes every day for several weeks. Such a schedule is relatively easy to provide in a school, whereas if it were done in the medical facility it could demand hours of travel simply to bring the child to the setting. Nonetheless, once the child has mastered the skill at school, the teacher or parent may want to run one or more training sessions at the medical facility to ensure that there is sufficient transfer of learning from the school.

Whenever possible the teacher should accompany the parents and child for the actual procedure. Because the teacher is an expert at interpreting the child's needs and is probably less stressed than the parent in that particular situation, the teacher can both aid the examining professional and be an advocate for the child as necessary. This level of involvement requires a school that is flexible about allowing teachers to be involved beyond the classroom and teachers who do not view their job as narrowly bounded by the four walls of a classroom.

ALTERNATIVE LIVING ARRANGEMENTS

When younger children pose special problems in terms of behavior management or medical needs, when special problems such as illness exist within a family, or when the child reaches late adolescence or early adulthood, an out-of-home placement may be desirable. It is therefore important for a teacher to be familiar with out-of-home living arrangements for the developmentally disabled.

Out-of-Home Placements

A number of studies have explored what factors influence a family's decision to seek out-of-home placement. Sherman and Cocozza (1984) reviewed some of that work and concluded that the developmentally disabled person's characteristics are not the only factor in decision making; the family also responds to the stress they are experiencing, and the social support and community resources they have available to them. Tausig (1985) found that the age of the developmentally disabled person influenced the factors that lead to the decision to seek residential placement. Among people less than 21 years old behavior problems were the most important variable, whereas for older individuals disruption of family relations and burden of care were the most salient factors.

Not surprisingly, younger children are more likely to be kept at home than older ones. Wynne and Rogers (1985) noted that the average age of initial placement is rising and that parents are more likely to keep younger children at home today than in years past. They speculated that this may be due to improved community-based resources and a reluctance on the part of institutions to accept very young children.

Parents' affective response to the suggestion that a child be placed in an out-of-home setting is an important predictor of the likelihood of the placement actually being made (Wynne and Rogers, 1985). Those parents who decide to keep their child at home are likely to respond to the placement suggestion with anger, resentment, or generalized opposition, whereas those parents who decide to place their child show more evidence of depression or denial of any affective response to the suggestion. Thus, professionals should be closely attuned to a parent's initial response, because this seems to have long-term implications about the decision to place a child.

The variable of family support can be very important in keeping a younger child at home. German and Maisto (1982) found that mothers who elected to keep their children at home felt they had more support from their parents and extended family and had more baby-sitting services than did mothers who sought residential placement. Mothers who kept children at home were also more likely to be married, to have only one retarded child, and not to view that child as posing behavior problems.

The decision to place a child in a residential setting is rarely reversed. Seltzer and Krauss (1984) surveyed the current placements of children who had been placed in residential settings in the 1970s. The majority remained in institutions, and of those who were released, very few had returned to live with their parents. Among the children who did return home the need for medical support was much lower than among those who remained in out-of-home placements.

The Teacher's Role

When a family reaches the decision to seek residential placement it is important that they receive effective and supportive assistance in exploring the out-of-home alternatives. Although some teachers may tend to place a negative value on putting children in residential settings and thus be reluctant to help in the process, the longer a teacher works with families, the more likely the teacher is to realize how difficult the choice is for parents. The decision to seek residential care is typically reached very reluctantly and after much thought. In general it is not the educator's role to second-guess parents who have gone through that wrenchingly difficult decision-making process.

Staff members at the Douglass Center try to facilitate the out-of-home placement process by having the child's teacher accompany the family when they visit potential placements. An experienced and objective perspective often can enable the teacher to identify important features of the placement that might not be evident to the parents. In addition the teacher can share important information with the staff of the new facility and thus speed the placement decision.

RESPITE CARE AND LEISURE ACTIVITIES

As noted in earlier chapters of this book, living with a developmentally disabled child can be a draining, demanding, sometimes disheartening experience that can leave some parents feeling depressed

(DeMyer, 1979; Featherstone, 1980) or so emotionally and physically exhausted that they are burned out (Marcus, 1984). Even when parents' feelings are not that intense, they still need periodic relief from child care, whether that be provided through their informal family support network or a more formal community-based respite care system (Bristol and Schopler, 1983; Pueschel and Bernier, 1984) and well-developed program of leisure time activities.

Respite Care

Many families prefer to keep their developmentally disabled children at home as long as they can, and they do an excellent job so long as they have appropriate services in the community. A suitable school placement may be the single most important component of the resource network parents require to keep their child with them. Appropriate training in child management; availability of medical, dental, and other professional resources; and a supportive family network are also important. In addition, the existence of suitable respite care increasingly is being recognized as helping many parents sustain their efforts with their child for a longer time, with a greater sense of optimism than would be possible without such support.

Most of the studies that have examined parental reactions to respite care have indicated a very positive response (Joyce, Singer, and Isralowitz, 1983; Ptacek et al., 1982). One survey of 32 families using in-home respite care found that 53 percent of the parents felt the respite services enabled them to relate better to their children, 53 percent believed their family was getting along better, 68 percent said family stress was reduced, 76 percent indicated that they could do some things such as travel that they had not been able to do before, and 30 percent felt they could not keep their child at home without respite care (Joyce et al., 1983). These findings suggest that respite services may keep some children out of residential settings as well as improving the general quality of life for the family.

Although there are a variety of models for the delivery of respite services, including having the child stay with a respite care family or in an institutional or group home setting or having the respite care worker go to the child's home (Russell, 1984), some preliminary data have suggested that many families prefer the in-home model in which there is only minimal disruption of the child's routine (Upshur, 1982a, 1982b).

Although respite care services are an invaluable component of a total family support package, one limitation that Upshur (1982b) noted in current respite services is that some of the programs lack provisions for persons with autism or severe behavioral or emotional problems or serious medical problems. These limitations may exclude some of the families who most urgently need the respite care services. Teachers will want to be familiar with the resources that are available in their own community; if these services fail to meet the needs of the severely developmentally disabled, parents and teachers alike may be called upon to be advocates for a more broadly based program.

Leisure Activities

Many find that their pleasantest hours are spent in some kind of leisure activity, whether it be gardening, rock climbing, reading, soaring, fishing, or playing computer games. Persons are often willing to spend a great deal of time and money taking lessons to master the necessary skills to be good at a leisure activity for the sheer pleasure it brings them. The developmentally disabled individual likewise can derive pleasure and a sense of mastery from learning and practicing leisure-time skills. Wehman (1983) suggested that the handicapped person's needs for leisure activities may be even greater than other persons' because the developmentally disabled so often lead relatively barren and drab lives with an excess of unstructured free time. In addition, community-based leisure-time activities can provide considerable support to families by giving the handicapped individual a supervised and appropriate activity outside the home.

Although developmentally disabled persons may have plenty of time available for leisure activities, they typically lack the necessary skills to enjoy this time. It is therefore important that a structured program be provided with careful attention to teaching the behaviors required to enjoy a particular activity. Wehman (1983) argued that with appropriate modification in equipment, rules, and instructional sequences the developmentally disabled person can learn to enjoy many of the same leisure activities as the rest of the community. He pointed to bowling, basketball, pool, card games, cooking, photography, and fishing as examples of suitable activities for the handicapped. There is considerable empirical support for the argument that many of these skills indeed can be learned by autistic or mentally retarded people (Lagomarcino, Reid, Ivancic, and Faw, 1984; Schleien, Certo, and Muccino, 1984).

Many communities are still relatively deficient in recreational programs for the developmentally disabled, and if teachers cannot identify appropriate resources in their own area, this may be another domain in which advocacy efforts will prove important in establishing suitable programs.

LEGAL NEED OF FAMILIES

As noted in Chapter 9 the parents of adolescent and adult developmentally disabled people are likely to be especially concerned about providing for their children's long-term financial welfare (Apolloni, 1984; Frolik, 1983; Kotsopoulos and Matathia, 1980). Such issues are not confined, however, to older age groups. Many parents of very young developmentally disabled people also want to ensure that the terms of their wills are in the best interests of their handicapped children. Although concerns about death will be less salient for most families of young children than for families of adolescents and adults, every parent should have a current and adequate will. The teacher will therefore find it useful to be conversant with some basic legal terminology and able to direct parents toward legal resources in the community.

As Frolik (1983) pointed out, the parents of developmentally disabled children have three different areas in which they can respond to the legal needs of their children. The first of these he described as the parents' role as advocate on behalf of the child. The second role is that of guardianship in which the parents assume legal responsibility for the management of the child or the child's property or both. The third, by virtue of the terms of their wills, is distribution of the parents' funds in a way that best meets the child's needs.

The Parent as Advocate

Developmentally disabled adolescents and adults often must interact with a variety of state and federal agencies to receive the services they need (Frolik, 1983). Dealing with a government bureaucracy can be difficult for any one of us; for the developmentally disabled it may be a nearly impossible chore. Parents therefore can be of vital continuing help to their children by assisting them in negotiating the rules and regulations of service providers as well as by keeping abreast of the latest major court decisions that might impact on their children. Parents who are no longer able to act as advocates for their child will want to ensure that someone else fills this essential role (Frolik, 1983).

The Parent as Guardian

When developmentally disabled persons reach legal age, they will become legally responsible as adults unless parents or the state make an active effort to demonstrate the need for guardianship. Therefore parents who believe that their child needs continuing protection must take legal steps to become the young adult's guardian. Not all developmentally disabled persons will require guardians; some higher functioning persons may be able to make appropriate decisions for themselves so long as a parent or other concerned individual fills the role of advocate and advisor. However, for many of the children described in this book there is a clear need for a guardian. Although the exact role and requirements for guardianship vary from state to state, every state does make provision for someone— whether parent, relative, or member of the community—to act on behalf of the developmentally disabled person. When no one else is willing or able to assume the responsibility, the court will direct a representative of the appropriate state agency to assume the role of guardian. Frolik (1983) has provided an extended discussion of the various types of guardianship arrangements that are possible depending upon the degree of competence of the disabled person.

Estate Planning

If parents of a developmentally disabled child want to ensure that they provide the best protection for their child, they will need to consider carefully the terms of their will. One of the critical issues involved is ensuring that the funds are appropriately managed for the child and that the inheritance does not disqualify the child from federal or state benefits that are based on a person's total assets. This should not be viewed as a reflection of greed. If parents leave a modest sum of money to a severely disabled child, this may be sufficient to ensure that the child has a few of life's small pleasures over many years; whereas if those funds are used by the state to pay for 6 months of residential care, the child will then be left impoverished for the rest of the child's life and will be unable to buy some of the special little things that might make life pleasanter.

Apolloni (1984) noted that if a parent leaves money directly to the handicapped child and has a guardian appointed to manage the funds for the child, this may not provide optimal protection because there may be a loss of eligibility for public assistance. Although some parents have considered the solution of leaving their property to another person with the expectation that the third person will take care of the needs of the handicapped child, this assumption does not carry any legal power. Unlike a trust that obligates the trustee to act correctly, an informal arrangement does not carry legal force and therefore might be subject to abuse. Any informal arrangement therefore demands considerable confidence in the person who is to manage the funds.

An alternative to leaving the money directly to the child, or leaving it to someone else who is informally expected to act for the child, is the establishment of a trust (Apolloni, 1984; Frolik, 1983). A prime advantage of a trust is that it does not intrude upon receipt of Social Security payments or other public benefits while still ensuring that the money is dedicated to the needs of the child. Many families may find this an optimal solution. Nonetheless, one limitation to a trust is that it does require the willingness of someone to administer the trust and file all necessary documents. Although large trust funds may be well managed by banks or other financial institutions, the fees charged make this a less attractive solution for small trusts. Families wishing to establish small trusts therefore must rely upon loving relatives or friends, or else, as has been done in some states, join with other parents to support an organization that will manage trusts for developmentally disabled people.

The specific details of estate planning vary from state to state and will change from year to year as various pieces of legislation come and go. It is therefore of considerable importance that parents consult with an attorney who is familiar with the current law as it applies to the needs of the developmentally disabled when writing a will. Teachers can help parents by identifying legal advocacy and referral agencies within the state and by helping parents become aware of the need to make formal, legal provisions for their child.

THE ROLE OF THE SCHOOL

Although the kinds of community resources described in this chapter are not typically based in school settings, schools have an important role to fill in ensuring that parents become aware of these resources and know how to use them. One of the methods developed for facilitating the communication of this information at the Douglass Center is regularly scheduled parent-teacher meetings. These meetings, held once every 6 weeks in the evening, involve 30 minutes spent in the classroom with the teacher and the other parents in the child's class followed by a 45- to 60-minute talk for the entire parent and teacher group on a topic of mutual interest. Speakers have included parents, physicians, attorneys, psychologists, teachers, nutritionists, camp directors, and psychiatrists. Table 10-1 illustrates some of the diverse topics that have been presented.

SUMMARY

Although a teacher's primary responsibilities are within the classroom, it would be difficult to meet the needs of developmentally disabled children if they confined their efforts to the four walls of a school building. As seen in previous chapters effective teaching often requires considerable involvement with parents, providing didactic training in behavioral child management techniques as well as offering support and understanding for the difficulties that arise in the life of the family. The present chapter stresses another role of the teacher: that of family consultant for community resources.

One of the community systems that teachers deal with frequently is the medical profession. Many developmentally disabled children have special medical problems; some are taking medication for the management of behavior or the control of seizure activity. These problems often manifest themselves in the classroom and therefore become a concern of the teacher as well as the parent. There is an unfortunate tendency for physicians to be relatively ill informed about the special needs and characteristics of developmentally disabled children and for teachers to know little about the effects of medication. There is also a history of relatively poor communication between educators and physicians. Along with educating themselves about the use of drugs, special education teachers may therefore be called upon to tactfully educate medical colleagues about developmental disabilities and to ensure that appropriate data are collected in the classroom to assist the physician in making vital decisions about the child's medical treatment.

Teachers also have a valuable role to play in helping parents become familiar with out-of-home placement alternatives when such a move is appropriate for the child and family. The decision to place a child in a residential setting may reflect the special management or medical needs of the child, medical or other problems in the family, or the increasing age of the developmentally disabled young person. Although the decision to move a developmentally disabled child to an out-of-home placement is never easy, the teacher can help facilitate the process for parents by helping them locate and evaluate potential placements.

Table 10–1.   Guest Speaker Topics

First aid for children with special needs
Getting what you need from your child study team
Can nutrition affect behavior?
Genetic counseling for parents of handicapped children
Meeting the needs of your adolescent child
Sexuality and the disabled young person
Current research findings on fragile-X syndrome
Group homes for the developmentally disabled
How to communicate with your physician
Issues throughout the family life cycle with a handicapped child

Yet another useful role for the teacher involves helping parents become aware of their child's legal needs and how best to meet these needs. Three different roles for the parent were defined by Frolik (1983). These include the role of the parent as advocate for the child, parent as guardian for the adult child, and the parent's responsibility to ensure that the parent's will makes suitable provisions for the welfare of the developmentally disabled child. Although parents may leave property directly to the child to be managed by a guardian, or to a relative or friend with the informal agreement that the funds are for the child, many families find the establishment of a trust may be the most suitable way to provide for the young person's long-term welfare without intruding upon the child's eligibility for public assistance.

The teacher as a consultant about community resources can help parents identify their existing needs and the appropriate programs to meet those needs. When the available resources do not meet the family's needs, the teacher may want to help families contact local or national advocacy groups that can help parents organize to bring about changes in the service delivery system. Teachers may also help parents become aware of the best ways to negotiate with service providers to obtain optimal services for the child.

References

Abramson, P.R., Gravink, M.J., Abramson, L.M., and Sommers, D. (1977) Early diagnosis and intervention of retardation: A survey of parental reactions concerning the quality of services rendered. *Mental Retardation, 15,* 28–31.

Ackerman, N.J. (1980). The family with adolescents. In E.A. Carter and M. McGoldrick (Eds.), *The family life cycle: A framework for family therapy* (pp. 147–169). New York: Gardner Press.

Adams, G.L. (1982). Independent living skills. In L. Steinberg and G.L. Adams (Eds.), *Educating severely and profoundly handicapped students* (pp. 243–268). Rockville, MD: Aspen.

Adams, G.L., Sternberg, L., and Taylor, R.L. (1982). Social skills training. In L. Steinberg and G.L. Adams (Eds.), *Educating severely and profoundly handicapped students* (pp. 97–132). Rockville, MD: Aspen.

Adubato, S.A., Adams, M.K., and Budd, K.S. (1981). Teaching a parent to train a spouse in child management techniques. *Journal of Applied Behavior Analysis, 14,* 193–205.

Aeschleman, S.R., and Schladenhauffen, J. (1984). Acquisition, generalization and maintenance of grocery shopping skills by severely mentally retarded adolescents. *Applied Research in Mental Retardation, 5,* 245–258.

Albrecht, R. (1954). The parental responsibilities of grandparents. *Marriage and Family Living, 16,* 201–204.

Alpern, G.D. (1967). Measurement of "untestable" autistic children. *Journal of Abnormal Psychology, 72,* 478–496.

Alpern, G.D., Boll, T.J., and Shearer, M.A. (1980). *Developmental profile II.* Aspen, CO: Psychological Developmental Publications.

Alpert, C. (1980). Procedures for determining the optimal nonspeech mode with the autistic child. In R.L. Schiefelbusch (Ed.), *Nonspeech language and language and communication* (pp. 23–59). Baltimore: University Park Press.

Altman, K., and Krupshaw, R. (1982). Increasing eye contact by head-holding. *Analysis and Intervention in Developmental Disabilities, 2,* 319–328.

Anderson-Inman, L., and Deutchman, L. (1984). Neatness counts: Effects of direct instruction and self-monitoring on the transfer of neat-paper skills to nontraining settings. *Analysis and Intervention in Developmental Disabilities, 4,* 137–155.

Apolloni, T. (1984). Who'll help my disabled child when I'm gone? *Academic Therapy, 20,* 109–114.

Armstrong v. Kline, 476 F. Supp. 583 (E.D. Pa. 1979).

Azrin, N.H., and Foxx, R.M. (1976). *Toilet training in less than a day.* New York: Pocket Books.

Azrin, N.H., Schaefer, R.M., and Wesolowski, M.D. (1976). A rapid method of teaching profoundly retarded persons to dress by a reinforcement guidance method. *Mental Retardation, 14,* 29–33.

Baer, D.M., and Guess, D. (1971). Receptive training of adjectival inflections in mental retardates. *Journal of Applied Behavior Analysis, 4,* 129–139.

Baer, D.M., Peterson, R., and Sherman, J. (1967). The development of imitation by reinforcing behavioral similarity to a model. *Journal of the Experimental Analysis of Behavior, 10,* 405–416.

Baker, B.L., Brightman, A.J., and Blacher, J.B. (1983). *Play skills.* Champaign, IL: Research Press.

Baker, B.L., Brightman, A.J., Carroll, N.B., Heifetz, B.B., and Hinshaw, S.P. (1978a). *Speech and language: Level 1.* Champaign, IL: Research Press.

Baker, B.L., Brightman, A.J., Carroll, N.B., Heifetz, B.B., and Hinshaw, S.P. (1978b). *Speech and language: Level 2.* Champaign, IL: Research Press.

Baker, B.L., Brightman, A.J., Heifetz, L.J., and Murphy, D.M. (1976a). *Advanced self-help skills.* Champaign, IL: Research Press.

Baker, B.L., Brightman, A.J., Heifetz, L.J., and Murphy, D.M. (1976b). *Behavior problems.* Champaign, IL: Research Press.

Baker, B.L., Brightman, A.J., Heifetz, L.J., and Murphy, D.M. (1976c) *Early self-help skills.* Champaign, IL: Research Press.

Baker, B.L., Brightman, A.J., Heiftez, L.J., and Murphy, D.M. (1976d). *Intermediate self-help skills.* Champaign, IL: Research Press.

Baker, B.L., Brightman, A.J., and Hinshaw, S.P. (1980). *Toward independent living.* Champaign, IL: Research Press.

Baker, B.L., Brightman, A.J., Heifetz, L.J., and Murphy, D.M. (1980) Behavioral training for parents of mentally retarded children: One-year follow-up. *American Journal of Mental Deficiency, 85,* 31–38.

Baker, B.L., and McCurry, M.C. (1984). School-based parent training: An alternative for parents predicted to demonstrate low teaching proficiency following group training. *Education and Training of the Mentally Retarded, 19,* 261–267.

Barton, E.S., Guess, D., Garcia, E., and Baer, D. (1970). Improvements of retardates' mealtime behaviors by timeout procedures using the multiple baseline technique. *Journal of Applied Behavior Analysis, 3,* 77–84.

Bateman, B., (1965). An educator's view of a diagnostic approach to learning disorders. In J. Hellmuth (Ed.), *Learning disorders* (Vol. 1, pp. 102–145). Seattle: Special Child Publications.

Bates, P., and Renzaglia, A. (1982). Language instruction with a profoundly retarded adolescent: The use of a table game in the acquisition of verbal labeling skills. *Education and Treatment of Children, 5,* 13–22.

Battle v. Commonwealth, 79–2158, 79–2188–90, 79–2568–70 (3rd Cir., July 18, 1980).

Baumeister, A.A. (1978). Origins and control of stereotyped movements. In C.E. Meyers (Ed.), *Monographs of the American Association on Mental Deficiency* (pp. 18–23).

Baumeister, A.A., and Forehand, R. (1973). Stereotyped acts. In N.R. Ellis (Ed.), *International Review of Research in Mental Retardation, 6,* 72–91.

Bayley, N. (1969). *Bayley scales of infant development.* New York: Psychological Corporation.

Beckman, P.J. (1983). Influence of selected child characteristics on stress in families of handicapped infants. *American Journal of Mental Deficiency, 88,* 150–156.

Beisler, J., and Tsai, L. (1983). A pragmatic approach to increase expressive language skills in young children. *Journal of Autism and Developmental Disorders, 13,* 287–304.

Bennett, C.W., and Ling, D. (1972). Teaching a complex verbal response to a hearing-impaired girl. *Journal of Applied Behavior Analysis, 5,* 321–328.

Bernheimer, L.P., Young, M.S., and Winton, P. (1983). Stress over time: Parents with young handicapped children. *Journal of Developmental and Behavioral Pediatrics, 4,* 177–181.

Berns, J.H. (1980). Grandparents of handicapped children. *Social Work, 25,* 238–239.

Bijou, S. (1973). Behavior modification in teaching the retarded child. In C. Thorensen (Ed.), *Behavior modification in education* (pp. 39–52). Chicago: University of Chicago Press.

Birenbaum, A. (1971). The mentally retarded child in the home and the family cycle. *Journal of Health and Social Behavior, 12,* 55–65.

Birnbrauer, J.S. (1968). Generalization of punishment effects: A case study. *Journal of Applied Behavior Analysis, 1,* 211–221.

Birnbrauer, J.S. (1979). Applied behavior analysis, service, and the acquisition of knowledge. *The Behavior Analyst, 2,* 15–21.

Blankenship, C.S. (1985). Using curriculum-based assessment data to make instructional decisions. *Exceptional Children, 52,* 233–238.

Bonvillian, J.D., Nelson, K.K., and Rhyne, J.M. (1981). Sign language and autism. *Journal of Autism and Developmental Disorders, 11,* 125–138.

Borkowski, J.J., and Varnhagen, C.K. (1984). Transfer of learning strategies: Contrast of self-instructional and traditional training formats with EMR children. *American Journal of Mental Deficiency, 89,* 380–387.

Bornstein, P.H., Back, P.J., McFall, M.E., Friman, P.C., and Lyons, P.D. (1980). Applications of a social skills training program to the modification of interpersonal deficits among retarded adults: A clinical replication. *Journal of Applied Behavior Analysis, 13,* 171–176.

Boucher, J. (1977). Alternation and sequencing behavior, and response to novelty in autistic children. *Journal of Child Psychology and Psychiatry, 18,* 67–72.

Boyle, T.D. (1985). *The relationship between marital satisfaction and the distribution of parent involvement with developmentally disabled children.* Unpublished master's thesis, Rutgers University, Piscataway, NJ.

Breiner, J., and Young, D.L. (1985). Social interaction: A comparison of mothers with noncompliant, nondelayed and developmentally delayed children. *Child and Family Behavior Therapy, 7,* 1–7.

Breit, M., Kaplan, S.L., Gauthier, B., and Weinhold, C. (1984). The dry-bed method for the treatment of enuresis: A failure to duplicate previous reports. *Child and Family Behavior Therapy, 6,* 17–23.

Breslau, N. (1982). Siblings of disabled children: Birth order and age-spacing effects. *Journal of Abnormal Child Psychology, 10,* 85–95.

Bricker, W.A., and Bricker, D.D. (1970). A program of language training for the severely handicapped child. *Exceptional Children, 37,* 101–111.

Brightman, R.P., Baker, B.L., Clark, D.B., and Ambrose, S.A. (1982). Effectiveness of alternative parent training formats. *Journal of Behavior Therapy and Experimental Psychiatry, 13,* 113–117.

Bristol, M.M., and Schopler, E. (1983). Stress and coping in families of autistic adolescents. In E. Schopler and G.B. Mesibov (Eds.), *Autism in adolescents and adults* (pp. 251–278). New York: Plenum Press.

Brodzinsky, D.M., Pappas, C., Singer, L.M., and Braff, A.M. (1981). Children's conception of adoption: A preliminary investigation. *Journal of Pediatric Psychology, 6,* 177–189.

Brown, L., Branston, M.B., Hamre-Nietupski, S., Pumpian, I., Certo, N., and Gruenwald, L. (1979). A strategy for developing chronological age appropriate and functional curricular content for severely handicapped adolescents and young adults. *Journal of Special Education, 13,* 81–90.

Browning, E. (1983). A memory pacer for improving stimulus generalization. *Journal of Autism and Developmental Disorders, 13,* 427–432.

Brulle, A.R., Barton, L.E., and Foskett, J.J. (1983). Educator/physician interchanges: A survey and suggestions. *Education and Training of the Mentally Retarded, 18,* 313–317.

Bryer, D.N., and Joyce, D.G. (1985). Language intervention with the severely handicapped: A decade of research. *The Journal of Special Education, 19,* 7–39.

Buckhalt, J.A., Rutherford, R.B., and Goldberg, K.E. (1978). Verbal and non-verbal interaction of mothers with their Down's syndrome and nonretarded infants. *American Journal of Mental Deficiency, 82,* 337–343.

Buckle, J.R. (1984). The extra costs of mentally handicapped living. *International Journal of Rehabilitation Research, 7,* 78–80.

Burgemeister, B.B., Blum, L.H., and Lorge, I. (1972). *The Columbia mental maturity scale* (3rd ed). New York: Harcourt Brace Jovanovich.

Burr, W.R. (1970). Satisfaction with various aspects of marriage over the life cycle: A random middle-class sample. *Journal of Marriage and the Family, 32,* 29–37.

Cantwell, D.P., Baker, L., and Rutter, M . (1977). Families of autistic and dysphasic children. 2. Mother's speech to the children. *Journal of Autism and Childhood Schizophrenia, 7,* 313–327.

Cardoso-Martins, C., Mervis, C.B., and Mervis, C.A. (1985). Early vocabulary acquisition by children with Down syndrome. *American Journal of Mental Deficiency, 90,* 177–184.

Carr, E.G. (1981). Sign language. In O.I. Lovass (Ed.), *Teaching manual for parents and teachers of developmentally disabled children: The me book* (pp. 153–160). Baltimore: University Park Press.

Carr, E.G. (1982a). Sign language. In R.L. Koegel, A. Rincover, and A.L. Egel (Eds.), *Educating and understanding autistic children* (pp. 142–157). San Diego: College-Hill Press.

Carr, E.G. (1982b). *How to teach sign language to developmentally disabled children.* Austin, TX: Pro-Ed.

Carr, E.G. (1985). Behavioral approaches to language and communication. In E. Schopler and G.B. Mesibov (Eds.), *Communication problems in autism* (pp. 37–58). New York: Plenum Press.

Carr, E.G., and Durand, V.M. (1985). Reducing behavior problems through functional communication training. *Journal of Applied Behavior Analysis, 18,* 111–126.

Carr, E.G., Newsom, C.D., and Binkoff, J.A. (1976). Stimulus control of self-destructive behavior in a psychotic child. *Journal of Abnormal Child Psychology, 4,* 139–153.

Carr, J. (1975). *Young children with Down's syndrome: Their development, upbringing, and effect on their families.* New York: Butterworth.

Carrow-Woolfolk, E., and Lynch, J. (1982). *An integrative approach to language disorders in children.* New York: Grune and Stratton.

Carter, E.A., and McGoldrick, M. (1980). *The family life cycle: A framework for family therapy.* New York: Gardner Press.

Carter, L., Alpert, M., and Stewart, S.M. (1982). Schizophrenic children's utilization of images and words in performance of cognitive tasks. *Journal of Autism and Developmental Disorders, 12,* 279–293.

Casey, L.O. (1978). Development of communicative behavior in autistic children: A parent program using manual signs. *Journal of Autism and Childhood Schizophrenia, 8,* 45–59.

Cataldo, M.F., and Harris, J. (1982). The biological basis for self-injury in the mentally retarded. *Analysis and Intervention in Developmental Disabilities, 2,* 21–40.

Chalfant, J.C., and Scheffelin, M.A. (1969). *Central processing dysfunctions in children: A review of research* (NINDS Monograph No. 9). Bethesda: US Department of Health, Education, and Welfare.

Charlop, M., Schreibman, L., and Thibodeau, M. (1985). Increasing spontaneous verbal responding in autistic children using a time delay procedure. *Journal of Applied Behavior Analysis, 18,* 155–166.

Cheseldine, S., and McConkey, R. (1979). Parents' speech to young Down's syndrome children: An intervention study. *American Journal of Mental Deficiency, 83,* 612–620.

Ciaranello, R.D., Vandenberg, S.R., and Anders, T.F. (1982). Intrinsic and extrinsic determinants of neuronal development: Relation to infantile autism. *Journal of Autism and Developmental Disorders, 12,* 115–146.

Clements, J., Evans, C., Jones, C., Osborne, K., and Upton, G. (1982). Evaluation of a home-based language training programme with severely mentally handicapped children. *Behavior Research and Therapy, 20,* 243–249.

Cleveland, D.W., and Miller, N. (1977). Attitudes and life commitments of older siblings of mentally retarded adults. *Mental Retardation, 15,* 38–41.

Cohen, D.J., and Shaywitz, B.A. (1982). Preface to special issue on neurobiological research in autism. *Journal of Autism and Developmental Disorders, 12,* 103–108.

Coleman, M. (Ed.). (1976). *The autistic syndromes.* Amsterdam, Holland: North Holland.

Coleman, P.D., Romano, J., Lapman, L., and Simon, W. (1985). Cell counts in cerebral cortex of an autistic patient. *Journal of Autism and Developmental Disorders, 15,* 245–255.

Colletti, G., and Harris, S.L. (1977). Behavior modification in the home: Siblings as behavior modifiers, parents as observers. *Journal of Abnormal Child Psychology, 1,* 21–30.

Connelly, J.B. (1985). Published tests—which ones do special education teachers perceive as useful? *The Journal of Special Education, 19,* 149–155.

Cook, A.R., Anderson, N., and Rincover, A. (1982). Stimulus overselectivity and stimulus control: Problems and strategies. In R.L. Koegel, A. Rincover, and A.L. Egel (Eds.), *Educating and understanding autistic children* (pp. 90–105). San Diego: College-Hill Press.

Cramblit, N.S., and Siegel, G.M. (1977). The verbal environment of a language impaired child. *Journal of Speech and Hearing Disorders, 42,* 474–482.

Cromer, R.F. (1981). Developmental language disorders: Cognitive processes, semantics, pragmatics, phonology and syntax. *Journal of Autism and Developmental Disorders, 11,* 57–74.

Cummings, S.T. (1976). The impact of the child's deficiency on the father: A study of fathers of mentally retarded and chronically ill children. *American Journal of Orthopsychiatry, 46,* 246–255.

Cummings, S.T., Bayley, H.C., and Rie, H.E. (1966). Effects of the child's deficiency on the mother: A study of mothers of mentally retarded, chronically ill, and neurotic children. *American Journal of Orthopsychiatry, 36,* 595–608.

Cunningham, C.C., Morgan, P.A., and McGucken, R.B. (1984). Down's syndrome: Is dissatisfaction with disclosure of diagnosis inevitable? *Developmental Medicine and Child Neurology, 26,* 33–39.

Cunningham, C.E., Reuler, E., Blackwell, J., and Deck, J. (1981). Behavioral and linguistic developments in the interactions of normal and retarded children with their mothers. *Child Development, 52,* 62–70.

Dahlquist, L.M., Gil, K.M., Kalfus, G.R., Blount, R.L., and Boyd, M.S. (1984). Enhancing an autistic girl's cooperation with gynecological examinations. *Clinical Pediatrics, 23,* 203.

Davies, R.R., and Rogers, E.S. (1985). Social skills training with persons who are mentally retarded. *Mental Retardation, 23,* 186–196.

DeLaCruz, F.F. (1985). Fragile X syndrome. *American Journal of Mental Deficiency, 90,* 119–123.

Delprato, D.J., Pappalardo, P.A., and Holmes, P.A. (1984). The role of response-reinforcer relationship in discrimination learning of mentally retarded persons. *American Journal of Mental Deficiency, 89,* 267–274.

DeMyer, M.K. (1979). *Parents and children in autism.* New York: Wiley & Sons.

DeMyer, M.K., and Goldberg, P. (1983). Family needs of the autistic adolescent. In E. Schopler and G.B. Mesibov (Eds.), *Autism in adolescents and adults* (pp. 225–250). New York: Plenum Press.

Deno, E.N. (1973). *Instructional alternatives for exceptional children.* Reston, VA: Council for Exceptional Children.

Deno, S.L. (1985). Curriculum-based measurement: The emerging alternative. *Exceptional Children, 52,* 219–232.

Devany, J., and Rincover, A. (1982). Self-stimulatory behavior and sensory reinforcement. In R.L. Kogel, A. Rincover, and A.L. Egel (Eds.), *Educating and understanding autistic children* (pp. 127–141). San Diego: College-Hill Press.

Diorio, M.S., and Konarski, E.A. (1984). Evaluation of a method for teaching dressing skills to profoundly mentally retarded persons. *American Journal of Mental Deficiency, 89,* 307–309.

Doherty, M.B., and Rosenfeld, A.A. (1984). Play assessment in the differential diagnosis of autism and other causes of severe language disorder. *Journal of Developmental and Behavioral Pediatrics, 5,* 26–29.

Donnellan, A., Gossage, L.D., LaVigna, G.W., Schuler, A., and Traphagen, J. (1977). *Teaching makes a difference.* Sacramento, CA: California State Department of Education.

Donnellan, A.M., Mesaros, R.A., and Anderson, J.L. (1985). Teaching students with autism in natural environments: What educators need from researchers. *Journal of Special Education, 18,* 505–522.

Dumas, J.E., (1984). Interactional correlates of treatment outcome in behavioral parent training. *Journal of Consulting and Clinical Psychology, 52,* 946–954.

Dunlap, G., and Egel, A.L. (1982). Motivational techniques. In R.L. Koegel, A. Rincover, and A.L. Egel, *Educating and understanding autistic children* (pp. 106–126). San Diego: College-Hill Press.

Dunlap, G., and Koegel, R.L. (1980). Motivating autistic children through stimulus variation. *Journal of Applied Behavior Analysis, 13,* 619–627.

Eason, L.J., White, M.J., and Newsom, C. (1982). Generalized reduction of self-stimulatory behavior: An effect of teaching appropriate play to autistic children. *Analysis and Intervention in Developmental Disabilities, 2,* 157–169.

Edelson, S.M. (1984). Implications of sensory stimulation in self-destructive behavior. *American Journal of Mental Deficiency, 89,* 140–145.

Edmundson, K. (1985). The "discovery" of siblings. *Mental Retardation, 23,* 49–51.

Egel, A.L. (1982). Programming the generalization and maintenance of treatment gains. In R.L. Koegel, A. Rincover, and A.L. Egel (Eds.), *Educating and understanding autistic children* (pp. 281–300). San Diego: College-Hill Press.

Egel, A.L., Richman, G.S., and Koegel, R.L. (1981). Normal peer models and autistic children's learning. *Journal of Applied Behavior Analysis, 14,* 3–12.

Egel, A.L., Shafer, M., and Neef, N. (1985). Receptive acquisition and generalization of prepositional responding in autistic children: A comparison of two procedures. *Analysis and Intervention in Developmental Disabilities, 4,* 285–298.

Eheart, B.K., and Nakamura, J. (1984). A step-by-step approach to parent involvement programs for handicapped children. *Child Care Quarterly, 13,* 30–41.

Eme, R.F. (1979). Sex differences in childhood psychopathology: A review. *Psychological Bulletin, 86,* 574–595.

Fantino, E. (1973). Emotion. In J.A. Nevin (Ed.), *The study of behavior* (pp. 107–121). Glenview, New York: Scott Foresman.

Favell, J.E., McGimsey, J.F., and Schell, R.M. (1982). Treatment of self-injury by providing alternate sensory activities. *Analysis and Intervention in Developmental Disabilities, 2,* 83–104.

Featherstone, H. (1980). *A difference in the family.* New York: Basic Books.

Fenske, E., Zalenski, S., Krantz, P., and McClannahan, L. (1985). Age at intervention and treatment outcome for autistic children in a comprehensive intervention program. *Analysis and Intervention in Developmental Disabilities, 5,* 49–58.

Ferleger, D., and Boyd, A. (1979). Anti-institutionalization: The promise of the Pennhurst case. *Stanford Law Review, 3,* 717–752.

Ferrari, M. (1982). *Chronically ill children and their siblings: Some psychosocial implications.* Unpublished doctoral dissertation, Rutgers University, Piscataway, NJ.

Figley, C.R., and McCubbin, H.I. (1983). *Stress and the family: Vol. 2. Coping with catastrophe.* New York: Brunner/Mazel.

Fish, B., and Ritvo, E.R. (1978). Psychoses of childhood. In J.D. Noshpitz and I. Berlin (Eds.), *Basic handbook of child psychiatry.* New York: Basic Books.

Fischler, R.S., and Tancer, M. (1984). The primary physician's role in care for developmentally disabled children. *Journal of Family Practice, 18,* 85–88.

Foxx, R.M. (1977). Attention training: The use of overcorrection avoidance to increase the eye contact of autistic and retarded persons. *Journal of Applied Behavior Analysis, 10,* 489–499.

Foxx, R.M. (1984). The use of a negative reinforcement procedure to increase the performance of autistic and mentally retarded children on discrimination training tasks. *Analysis and Intervention in Developmental Disabilities, 4,* 253–265.

Foxx, R.M., McMorrow, M.J., and Mennemier, M. (1984). Teaching social/vocational skills to retarded adults with a modified table game: An analysis of generalization. *Journal of Applied Behavior Analysis, 17,* 343–352.

Frank, S.M., Allen, D.A., Stein, L., and Meyers, B. (1976). Linguistic performance in vulnerable and autistic children and their mothers. *American Journal of Psychiatry, 133,* 909–915.

Fraser, C., Bellugi, U., and Brown, R. (1963). Control of grammar in imitation, comprehension and production. *Journal of Verbal Behavior, 2,* 121–135.

Frederick, H.D., Buckley, J., Baldwin, V.L., Moor, W., and Stremel-Campbell, K. (1983). The educational needs of the autistic adolescent. In E. Schopler and G.B. Mesibov (Eds.), *Autism in adolescents and adults* (pp. 79–110). New York: Plenum Press.

Frolik, L.A. (1983). Legal needs. In E. Schopler and G.B. Mesibov (Eds.), *Autism in adolescents and adults* (pp. 319–334). New York: Plenum Press.

Fuqua, R.W., Hegland, S.M., and Karas, S.C. (1985). Processes influencing linkages between preschool handicap classrooms and homes. *Exceptional Children, 51,* 307–314.

Fygetakis, L., and Gray, B.B. (1970). Programmed conditioning of linguistic competence. *Behavior Research and Therapy, 8,* 153–163.

Gadow, K.D. (1982). Problems with students on medication. *Exceptional Children, 49,* 20–27.

Galagan, J.E. (1985). Psychoeducational testing: Turn out the lights, the party's over. *Exceptional Children, 52,* 288–299.

Gallagher, J.J. (1972). The special education contract for mildly handicapped children. *Exceptional Children, 38,* 527–535.

Gang, D., and Poche, C.E. (1982). An effective program to train parents as teaching tutors for their children. *Education and Treatment of Children, 5,* 211–232.

Garcia, E.E. (1974). The training and generalization of a conversational speech form in nonverbal retardates. *Journal of Applied Behavior Analysis, 7,* 137–149.

Garcia, E.E., Guess, D., and Byrnes, J. (1973). Development of syntax in a retarded girl using procedures of imitation, reinforcement and modeling. *Journal of Applied Behavior Analysis, 6,* 299–310.

Garreau, B., Barthelemy, C., Sauvage, D., Leddet, I., and LeLord, G. (1985). A comparison of autistic syndromes with and without associated neurological problems. *Journal of Autism and Developmental Disorders, 14,* 105–112.

Gath, A. (1973). The school age siblings of mongol children. *British Journal of Psychiatry, 123,* 161–167.

Gath, A. (1974). Sibling reations to mental handicap: A comparison of the brothers and sisters of mongol children. *Journal of Child Psychology and Psychiatry, 15,* 187–198.

Gath, A. (1978). *Down's syndrome and the family: The early years.* New York: Academic Press.

Gath, A., and Gumley, D. (1984). Down's syndrome and the family: Follow-up of children first seen in infancy. *Developmental Medicine and Child Neurology, 26,* 500–508.

Gelfand, D.M., and Hartmann, D.P. (1980). *Child behavior analysis and therapy.* Elmsford, NY: Pergamon Press.

German, M.L., and Maisto, A.A. (1982). The relationship of a perceived family support system to the institutional placement of mentally retarded children. *Education and Training of the Mentally Retarded, 17,* 17–23.

Germann, G., and Tindal, G. (1985). An application of curriculum-based assessment: The use of direct and repeated measurement. *Exceptional Children, 52,* 244–265.

Gersten, R.M., White, W., Falco, R., and Carnin, D. (1982). Teaching basic discriminations to handicapped and non-handicapped individuals through a dynamic presentation of instructional stimuli. *Analysis and Intervention in Developmental Disabilities, 2,* 305–318.

Gilhool, T. (1978). *Habilitation of developmentally disabled persons in a small group community setting versus a large group institutional setting.* Philadelphia: PILCOR, N.D.

Glass, R.M., and Meckler, R.S. (1972). Preparing elementary teachers to instruct mildly handicapped children in regular classrooms: A summer workshop. *Exceptional Children, 38,* 152–156.

Gold, M.W. (1976). Task analysis of a complex assembly task by the retarded child. *Exceptional Children, 43,* 78–84.

Goldstein, S.B., and Lanyon, R.I. (1971). Parent-clinicians in the language training of an autistic child. *Journal of Speech and Hearing Disorders, 36,* 552–560.

Griffiths, H., and Craighead, W.E. (1972). Generalization in operant speech therapy for misarticulation. *Journal of Speech and Hearing Disorders, 37,* 485–494.

Grossman, F.K. (1972). *Brothers and sisters of retarded children: An exploratory study.* Syracuse, NY: Syracuse University Press.

Grossman, H.J. (Ed.). (1983). *Classification in mental retardation.* Washington, DC: American Association on Mental Deficiency.

Guess, D., and Baer, D.M. (1973). An analysis of individual differences in generalization between receptive and productive language in retarded children. *Journal of Applied Behavior Analysis, 6,* 311–329.

Guess, D., Sailor, W., and Baer, D. (1974). To teach language to retarded children. In R. Schiefelbusch and L. Lloyd (Eds.), *Language perspectives: Acquisition, retardation, and intervention* (pp. 529–564). Baltimore: University Park Press.

Gutmann, A.J., and Rondal, J.A. (1979). Verbal operants in mothers' speech to nonretarded and Down's syndrome children matched for linguistic level. *American Journal of Mental Deficiency, 83*, 446–452.

Hamilton, J. (1966). Learning of a generalized response class in mentally retarded individuals. *American Journal of Mental Deficiency, 71*, 100–108.

Handleman, J.S. (1979a). Generalization by autistic-type children of verbal responses across settings. *Journal of Applied Behavior Analysis, 12*, 273–282.

Handleman, J.S. (1979b). Transition of autistic-type children from highly specialized programs to more "normal" educational environments. *Journal for Special Educators, 15*, 273–279.

Handleman, J.S. (1981a). A model for a self-contained class for autistic-type children. *Education and Treatment of Children, 4*, 61–70.

Handleman, J.S. (1981b). Transfer of verbal responses across instructional settings by autistic-type children. *Journal of Speech and Hearing Disorders, 46*, 69–76.

Handleman, J.S. (1984). Mainstreaming the autistic-type child. *The Exceptional Child, 31*, 33–38.

Handleman, J.S. (1986). Severe developmental disabilities: Defining the term. *Education and Treatment of Children, 9*, 153–167.

Handleman, J.S., Arnold, M., Veniar, F.A., Kristoff, B., and Harris, S.L. (1982). Assessment and remediation of hearing loss in an autistic youngster. *Hearing Instruments, 33*, 10–11.

Handleman, J.S., and Harris, S.L. (1980). Generalization from school to home with autistic-type children. *Journal of Autism and Developmental Disorders, 10*, 323–333.

Handleman, J.S., and Harris, S.L. (1983). Generalizations across instructional settings by autistic children. *Child and Family Behavior Therapy, 5*, 73–84.

Handleman, J.S., and Harris, S.L. (1984). Can summer vacation be detrimental to learning? An empirical look. *The Exceptional Child, 31*, 151–159.

Handleman, J.S., Powers, M.D., and Harris, S.L. (1984). The teaching of labels: An analysis of concrete and pictorial representations. *American Journal of Mental Deficiency, 88*, 625–629.

Haring, N.G. (1982). *Exceptional children and youth.* Columbus, OH: Merrill Publishing Co.

Haring, N.G., and Gentry, N. (1976). Direct and individualized instructional procedures. In N. Haring and R. Schiefelbush (Eds.), *Teaching special children* (pp. 112–134). Columbus, OH: Merrill Publishing Co.

Haring, T. (1985). Teaching between class generalization of toy play behavior to handicapped children. *Journal of Applied Behavior Analysis, 18*, 127–139.

Harris, S.L. (1975). Teaching language to nonverbal children with emphasis on problems of generalization. *Psychological Bulletin, 82*, 565–580.

Harris, S.L. (1983). *Families of the developmentally disabled: A guide to behavioral intervention.* New York: Pergamon Press.

Harris, S.L., and Handleman, J.S. (1980). Programming for generalization: Educating autistic children and their parents. *Education and Treatment of Children, 3,* 61–83.

Harris, S., Handleman, J., and Palmer, C. (1985). Parents and grandparents view the autistic child. *Journal of Autism and Developmental Disorders, 15,* 127–137.

Harris, S.L., and Wolchik, S.A. (1979). Suppression of self-stimulation: Three alternative strategies. *Journal of Applied Behavior Analysis, 2,* 185–198.

Harris, S.L., Wolchik, S.A., and Weitz, S. (1981). The acquisition of language skills by autistic children: Can parents do the job? *Journal of Autism and Developmental Disorders, 11,* 373–384.

Hart, B.M., and Risley, T.R. (1968). Establishing use of descriptive adjectives in the spontaneous speech of disadvantaged preschool children. *Journal of Applied Behavior Analysis, 1,* 109–120.

Hawkins, R.P. (1979). The functions of assessment: Implications for selection and development of devices for assessing repertoires in clinical, educational, and other settings. *Journal of Applied Behavior Analysis, 12,* 501–516.

Hawkins, R.P., and Dobes, R.W. (1975). Behavioral definitions in applied behavior analysis: Explicit or impicit. In B.C. Etzel, J.M. LeBlanc, and D.M. Baer (Eds.), *New developments in behavioral research: Theory, methods and application* (pp. 59–75). New York: Wiley & Sons.

Hermelin, B. (1971). Rules of language. In M. Rutter (Ed.), *Infantile autism: Concepts, characteristics, and treatment* (pp. 98–111). London: Churchill Livingstone.

Hill, J. (1982). Vocational training. In L. Sternberg and G.L. Adams (Eds.), *Educating severely and profoundly handicapped students* (pp. 260–312). Rockville, MD: Aspen.

Hinerman, P.S., Jenson, W.R., Walker, G.R., and Petersen, P.B. (1982). Positive practice overcorrection combined with additional procedures to teach signed words to an autistic child. *Journal of Autism and Developmental Disorders, 12,* 253–263.

Ho, C., Glanville, S., and Brave, J.C. (1980). Challenges in evaluating young developmentally disabled children. *Journal of Clinical Child Psychology, 9,* 233–235.

Hollis, J.H., and Sherman, J.A. (1967). *Operant control of vocalizations in profoundly retarded children with normal hearing and moderate bilateral loss* (No. 167). Lawrence, KS: Parsons Research Center.

Holmes, N., Hemsley, R., Rickett, J., and Likierman, H. (1982). Parent's as cotherapists: Their perceptions of a home-based behavioral treatment for autistic children. *Journal of Autism and Developmental Disorders, 12,* 331–342.

Holroyd, J., and McArthur, D. (1976). Mental retardation and stress of the parents: A contrast between Down's syndrome and childhood autism. *American Journal of Mental Deficiency, 80,* 431–436.

Horner, R.D., and Keilitz, I. (1975). Training mentally retarded adolescents to brush their teeth. *Journal of Applied Behavior Analysis, 8,* 301–309.

Howlin, P. (1978). The assessment of social behavior. In M. Rutter and E. Scholper (Eds.), *Autism: A reappraisal of concepts and treatment* (pp. 63–70). New York: Plenum Press.

Howlin, P.A. (1981). The effectiveness of operant language training with autistic children. *Journal of Autism and Developmental Disorders, 11,* 89–105.

Howlin, P., Cantwell, D., Marchant, R., Berger, M., and Rutter, M. (1973). Analyzing mother's speech to autistic children: A methodological study. *Journal of Abnormal Child Psychology, 1,* 317–339.

Hudson, A.M. (1982). Training parents of developmentally handicapped children: A component analysis, *Behavior Therapy, 13,* 325–333.

Hull, J.T., and Thompson, J.C. (1980). Predicting adaptive functioning of mentally retarded persons in community settings. *American Journal of Mental Deficiency, 85,* 253–261.

Intagliata, J., and Doyle, N. (1984). Enhancing social support for parents of developmentally disabled children: Training in interpersonal problem solving skills. *Mental Retardation, 22,* 4–11.

Isaac, W., Thomas, R., and Goldiamond, I. (1960). Application of operant conditioning to reinstate verbal behavior in psychotics. *Journal of Speech and Hearing Disorders, 25,* 8–12.

Ivancic, M.T., Reid, D.H., Iwata, B.A., Faw, G.D., and Page, T.J. (1981). Evaluating a supervision program for developing and maintaining therapeutic staff-resident interactions during institutional care routines. *Journal of Applied Behavior Analysis, 14,* 95–107.

Jackson, D.A., and Wallace, R.F. (1974). The modification and generalization of voice loudness in a fifteen-year-old retarded girl. *Journal of Applied Behavior Analysis, 7,* 461–471.

Janicki, M., Lubin, R., and Friedman, E. (1983). Variations in characteristics and service needs of persons with autism. *Journal of Autism and Developmental Disorders, 13,* 73–86.

Janicki, M.P., and MacEachron, A.E. (1984). Residential, health, and social service needs of elderly developmentally disabled persons. *Gerontologist, 24,* 128–137.

Jeffree, D.M., and Cheseldine, S.E. (1984). Programmed leisure intervention and the interaction patterns of severely mentally retarded adolescents: A pilot study. *American Journal of Mental Deficiency, 88,* 619–624.

Jenkins, J.R., Speltz, M.L., and Odom, S.L. (1985). Integrating normal and handicapped preschoolers: Effect on child development and social interaction. *Exceptional Children, 52,* 7–17.

Johnson, J., and Koegel, R.L. (1982). Behavioral assessment and curriculum development. In R.L. Koegel, A. Rincover, and A.L. Egel (Eds.), *Educating and understanding autistic children* (pp. 1–33). San Diego: College-Hill Press.

Johnson, W.L., Baumeister, A.A., Penland, M.J., and Inwald, C. (1982). Experimental analysis of self-injurious, stereotypic, and collateral behavior of retarded persons: Effects of overcorrection and reinforcement of alternative responding. *Analysis and Intervention in Developmental Disabilities, 2,* 44–66.

Joyce, K., Singer, M., and Isralowitz, R. (1983). Impact of respite care on parents' perceptions of quality of life. *Mental Retardation, 21,* 153–156.

Kale, R.J., Kaye, J.H., Whelan, P.A., and Hopkins, B.L. (1968). The effects of reinforcement on the modification, maintenance and generalization of social responses of mental patients. *Journal of Applied Behavior Analysis, 1,* 307–314.

Kaslow, F.W., and Cooper, B. (1978). Family therapy with the learning disabled child and his/her family. *Journal of Marriage and Family Counseling, 4,* 41–49.

Kazdin, A.E., and Bootzin, R.R. (1972). The token economy: An evaluative review. *Journal of Applied Behavior Analysis, 5,* 343–372.

Kazdin, A.E., and Polster, R. (1973). Intermittent token reinforcement and response maintenance in extinction. *Behavior Therapy, 4,* 386–391.

Keogh, D., Faw, G., Whitman, T., and Reid, D. (1984). Enhancing leisure skills in severely retarded adolescents through a self-instructional treatment package. *Analysis and Intervention in Developmental Disorders, 10* 259–271.

Kidwell, J., Fischer, J.L., Dunham, R.M., and Baranowski, M. (1983). Parents and adolescents: Push and pull of change. In H.I. McCubbin and C.R. Figley (Eds.), *Stress and the family. Vol. 1: Coping with normative transitions* (pp. 74–89). New York: Brunner/Mazel.

Kirk S., and Gallagher, J. (1979). *Educating exceptional children* (3rd ed.). Boston: Houghton, Mifflin.

Kirk, S., and Gallagher, J. (1983). *Educating exceptional children* (4th ed.). Hopewell, NJ: Houghton Mifflin.

Koegel, R. (1982). *How to integrate autistic and other severely handicapped children into a classroom.* Austin, TX: Pro-Ed.

Koegel, R.L., Dunlap, G., Richman, G.S., and Dyer, K. (1981). The use of specific orienting cues for teaching discrimination tasks. *Analysis and Intervention in Developmental Disabilities, 1,* 187–198.

Koegel, R.L., and Felsenfeld, S. (1977). Sensory deprivation. In S. Gerber (Ed.), *Audiometry in infancy.* New York: Grune & Stratton.

Koegel, R.L., Firestone, P.B., Kramme, K.W., and Dunlap, G. (1974). Increasing spontaneous play by suppressing self-stimulation in autistic children. *Journal of Applied Behavior Analysis, 7,* 521–528.

Koegel, R.L., and Rincover, A. (1977). Some research on the difference between generalization and maintenance in extra-therapy settings, *Journal of Applied Behavior Analysis, 10,* 1–16.

Koegel, R.L., Rincover, A., and Russo, D.C. (1982). Classroom management: Progression from special to normal classrooms. In R.L. Koegel, A. Rincover, and A.L. Egel (Eds.), *Educating and understanding autistic children* (pp. 203–241). San Diego: College-Hill Press.

Koegel, R.L., Russo, D.C., and Rincover, A. (1977). Assessing and training teachers in the generalized use of behavior modification with autistic children. *Journal of Applied Behavior Analysis, 10,* 197–205.

Koegel, R.L., Russo, D.C., Rincover, A., and Schreibman, L. (1982). Assessing and training teachers. In R.L. Koegel, A. Rincover, and A.L. Egel (Eds.), *Educating and understanding autistic children* (pp. 178–202). San Diego: College-Hill Press.

Koegel, R.L., and Schreibman, L. (1976). Identification of consistent responding to auditory stimuli by a functionally "deaf" autistic child. *Journal of Autism and Childhood Schizophrenia, 6,* 147–156.

Koegel, R.L., Schreibman, L., Britten, K.R., Burke, J.C. and O'Neill, R.E. (1982). A comparison of parent training to direct child treatment. In R.L. Koegel, A. Rincover, and A.L. Egel (Eds.), *Educating and understanding autistic children* (pp. 260–279). San Diego: College-Hill Press.

Koegel, R.L., Schreibman, L., O'Neill, R.E., and Burke, J.C. (1983). The personality and family-interaction characteristics of parents of autistic children. *Journal of Consulting and Clinical Psychology, 51,* 683–692.

Koegel, R.L., and Williams, J.A. (1980). Direct vs. indirect response reinforcer relationships in teaching autistic children. *Journal of Abnormal Child Psychology, 8,* 537–547.

Kolko, D.J., Anderson, L., and Campbell, M. (1980). Sensory preference and overselective responding in autistic children. *Journal of Autism and Developmental Disorders, 10,* 259–271.

Konstantareas, M.M. (1984). Sign language as a communication prosthesis with language impaired children. *Journal of Autism and Developmental Disorders, 14,* 9–25.

Kornblatt, E.S., and Heinrich, J. (1985). Needs and coping abilities in families of children with developmental disabilities. *Mental Retardation, 23,* 13–19.

Kotsopoulos, S., and Matathia, P. (1980). Worries of parents regarding the future of their mentally retarded adolescent children. *International Journal of Social Psychiatry, 26,* 53–57.

Kozloff, M.A. (1975). *Reaching the autistic child: A parent-training program.* Champaign, IL: Research Press.

Lagomarcino, A., Reid, D.H., Ivancic, M.T., and Faw, G.D. (1984). Leisure-dance instruction for severely and profoundly retarded persons: Teaching an intermediate community-living skill. *Journal of Applied Behavior Analysis, 17,* 71–84.

Lamb, M. (1983). Fathers of exceptional children. In M. Seligman (Ed.), *The family with a handicapped child: Understanding and treatment* (pp. 125–146). New York: Grune & Stratton.

Lancioni, G.E. (1982). Normal children as tutors to teach social responses to withdrawn mentally retarded schoolmates: Training, maintenance and generalization. *Journal of Applied Behavior Analysis, 15,* 17–40.

Lancioni, G.E. (1983). Using pictorial representations as communication means with low-functioning children. *Journal of Autism and Developmental Disorders, 13,* 87–105.

Largo, R.H., and Stutzle, W. (1977). Longitudinal study of bowel and bladder control by day and at night in the first six years of life: Epidemiology and interactions between bowel and bladder control. *Development Medicine and Child Neurology, 19,* 598–606.

Lavigne, J.V., and Ryan, M. (1979). Psychologic adjustment of siblings of children with chronic illness. *Pediatrics, 63,* 616–627.

Lederberg, A. (1980). The language environment of children with language delays. *Journal of Pediatric Psychology, 5,* 141–160.

Lehr, D., and Haubrich, P. (1985). Legal precedents for students with severe handicaps. *Exceptional Children, 52,* 358–365.

Lerner, J.W. (1976). *Children with learning disabilities.* Boston: Houghton Mifflin.

Li, A.K. (1985). Toward more elaborate pretend play. *Mental Retardation, 23,* 131–136.

Litt, M.D., and Schreibman, L. (1981). Stimulus-specific reinforcement in the acquisition of receptive labels by autistic children. *Analysis and Intervention in Developmental Disabilities, 1,* 171–186.

Lobato, D. (1983). Siblings of handicapped children: A review. *Journal of Autism and Developmental Disorders, 13,* 347–364.

Lockyer, L., and Rutter, M. (1969). A five to fifteen year follow-up study of infantile psychosis: 3. Psychological aspects. *British Journal of Psychiatry, 115,* 865–882.

Lonsdale, G. (1978). Family life with a handicapped child: The parents speak. *Child Care, Health and Development, 4,* 99–120.

Lord, C., Merrin, D.J., Vest, L.O., and Kelly, T. (1983). Communicative behavior of adults with an autistic four-year-old boy and his nonhandicapped twin brother. *Journal of Autism and Developmental Disorders, 13,* 1–17.

Lovaas, O.I. (1981). *Teaching developmentally disabled children: The me book.* Baltimore: University Park Press.

Lovaas, O.I., Berberich, J., Perloff, B., and Schaefer, B. (1966). Acquisition of imitative speech by schizophrenic children. *Science, 151,* 705–707.

Lovaas, O.I., Koegel, R.L., and Schreibman, L. (1979). Stimulus overselectivity in autism: A review of research. *Psychological Bulletin, 86,* 1236–1254.

Lovaas, O.I., Koegel, R.L., Simmons, J.Q., and Long, J.S. (1973). Some generalizations and follow-up measures on autistic children in behavior therapy. *Journal of Applied Behavior Analysis, 6,* 131–166.

Lovaas, O.I., Schreibman, L., Koegel, R.L., and Rehm, R. (1971). Selective responding of autistic children to multiple sensory input. *Journal of Abnormal Psychology, 77,* 211–222.

Lovaas, O.I., and Simmons, J.Q. (1969). Manipulation of self-destruction in three retarded children. *Journal of Applied Behavior Analysis, 2,* 143–157.

Luiselli, J.K. (1984). Effects of brief overcorrection on stereotypic behavior of mentally retarded students. *Education and Treatment of Children, 7,* 125–138.

Luiselli, J.K., Myles, E., Evans, T.P., and Boyce, D.A. (1985). Reinforcement control of severe dysfunctional behavior of blind, multihandicapped students. *American Journal of Mental Deficiency, 90,* 328–334.

Lynch, A., and Singer, T. (1980). Vocational programing for the severe and profound in the public schools. In C.L. Hansen and N.G. Haring (Eds.), *Expanding opportunities: Vocational education for the handicapped* (pp. 62–78). Washington, DC: Department of Education.

MacDonald, J.D., Blott, J.P., Gordon, K., Spiegel, B., and Hartmann, M. (1974). An experimental parent-assisted treatment program for preschool language-delayed children. *Journal of Speech and Hearing Disorders, 39,* 395–415.

MacMillan, D.L., and Turnbull, A.P. (1983). Parent involvement with special education: Respecting individual preferences. *Education and Training of the Mentally Retarded, 18,* 4–9.

Mahoney, G.J. (1975). Ethological approach to delayed language acquisition. *American Journal of Mental Deficiency, 80,* 139–148.

Marcus, L. (1984). Coping with burnout. In E. Schopler and G.B. Mesibov (Eds.), *The effects of autism on the family* (pp. 311–326). New York: Plenum Press.

Margalit, M., and Raviv, A. (1983). Mothers' perceptions of family climate in families with a retarded child. *Exceptional Child, 30,* 163–169.

Marholin, O., and Siegel, L.J. (1978). Beyond the law of effect: Programming for the maintenance of behavioral change. In D. Marholin (Ed.), *Child be-*

havior therapy (pp. 201–225). New York: Gardner Press.

Martin, E.W. (1974). Some thoughts on mainstreaming. *Exceptional Children, 40,* 150–153.

Matson, J.L., and Andrisak, F. (1982). Training leisure-time social-interaction skills to mentally retarded adults. *American Journal of Mental Deficiency, 86,* 533–542.

Matson, J.L., and Earnhart, T. (1981). Programming treatment effects to the natural environment. *Behavior Modification, 5,* 27–37.

Maurer, R.G., and Damasio, A.P. (1982). Childhood autism from the point of view of behavioral neurology. *Journal of Autism and Developmental Disorders, 12,* 195–206.

McCarthy, D. (1972). *McCarthy scales of children's abilities.* New York: Psychological Corporation.

McClannahan, L.E., Krantz, P.J., and McGee, G.G. (1982). Parents as therapists for autistic children: A model for effective parent training. *Analysis and Intervention in Developmental Disabilities, 2,* 223–252.

McCormack, J., and Chalmers, A. (1978). *Early cognitive instruction for the moderately and severely handicapped* (Vols. 1 and 2). Champaign, IL: Research Press.

McCubbin, H.I., and Figley, C.R. (1983). *Stress and the family: Vol. 1: Coping with normative transitions.* New York: Brunner/Mazel.

McDonald, A., Carlson, K., Palmer, D., and Slay, T. (1983). Special education and medicine: A survey of physicians. *Journal of Learning Disabilities, 16,* 93–94.

McKeever, P. (1983). Siblings of chronically ill children: A literature review with implications for research and practice. *American Journal of Orthopsychiatry, 53,* 209–218.

McMichael, J.K. (1971). *Handicap: A study of physically handicapped children and their families.* Pittsburgh: University of Pittsburgh Press.

Meryash, D.L., Szymanski, L.S., and Gerald, P.S. (1982). Infantile autism associated with the fragile X syndrome. *Journal of Autism and Developmental Disorders, 12,* 295–302.

Mesibov, G.B. (1983). Current perspectives and issues in autism and adolescence. In E. Schopler and G.B. Mesibov (Eds.), *Autism in adolescents and adults* (pp. 37–53). New York: Plenum Press.

Minuchin, S. (1974). *Families and family therapy.* Cambridge, MA: Harvard University Press.

Mithaug, D.E., and Hanawalt, D.A. (1978). The validation of procedures to assess prevocational task preferences in retarded adults. *Journal of Applied Behavior Analysis, 11,* 153–162.

Mithaug, R. (1981). *How to teach prevocational skills to severely handicapped persons.* Austin, TX: Pro-Ed.

Miyashita, T. (1985). Visual discrimination learning with variable irrelevant cues in autistic children. *Journal of Autism and Developmental Disorders, 15,* 399–408.

Moore, B.L., and Bailey, J.S. (1973). Social punishment in the modification of a pre-school child's "autistic-like" behavior with a mother as therapist. *Journal of Applied Behavior Analysis, 6,* 497–507.

Murdoch, J.C. (1983). Communication of the diagnosis of Down's syndrome and spina bifida in Scotland 1971–1981. *Journal of Mental Deficiency Research, 27,* 247–253.

Murdoch, J.C. (1984a). Experience of the mothers of Down's syndrome and spina bifida children on going home from hospital in Scotland 1971–1981. *Journal of Mental Deficiency Research, 28,* 123–127.

Murdoch, J.C. (1984b). Immediate post-natal management of the mothers of Down's syndrome and spina bifida children in Scotland 1971–1981. *Journal of Mental Deficiency Research, 28,* 67–72.

Murphy, G. (1982). Sensory reinforcement in the mentally handicapped and autistic child: A review. *Journal of Autism and Developmental Disorders, 12,* 265–278.

Murphy, G., Callias, M., and Carr, J. (1985). Increasing simple toy play in profoundly mentally handicapped children: 1. Training to play. *Journal of Autism and Developmental Disorders, 15,* 375–388.

Nelson, G.L., Cone, J.D., and Hanson, G.R. (1975). Training correct utensil use in retarded children: Modeling vs physical guidance. *American Journal of Mental Deficiency, 80,* 114–122.

Neugarten, B.L., and Weinstein, K.K. (1964). The changing American grandparent. *Journal of Marriage and the Family, 26,* 199–204.

Nicolich, L.M. (in press). Toward symbolic functioning: Structure of early pretend games and potential parallels with language. *Child Development.*

Nietupski, J.A., Welch, J., and Wacker, D. (1983). Acquisition, maintenance, and transfer of grocery item purchasing skills by moderately and severely handicapped students. *Education and Training of the Mentally Retarded, 18,* 279–286.

Nordquist, V.M., and Wahler, R.G. (1973). Naturalistic treatment of an autistic child. *Journal of Applied Behavior Analysis, 6,* 79–87.

Odom, S.L., Deklyen, M., and Jenkins, J.R. (1984). Integrating handicapped and nonhandicapped preschoolers: Developmental impact on nonhandicapped children. *Exceptional Children, 51,* 41–48.

O'Gorman, G. (1967). *The nature of childhood autism.* New York: Appleton-Century-Crofts.

O'Leary, K.D., O'Leary, S., and Becker, W.C. (1967). Modification of a deviant sibling interaction pattern in the home. *Behaviour Research and Therapy, 5,* 113–120.

Olshansky, S. (1962). Chronic sorrow: A response to having a mentally defective child. *Social Casework, 43,* 190–193.

Pace, G.M., Ivancic, M.T., Edwards, G.L., Iwata, B.A., and Page, T.J. (1985). Assessment of stimulus preference and reinforcer value with profoundly retarded individuals. *Journal of Applied Behavior Analysis, 8,* 249–255.

Parks, S. (1983). The assessment of autistic children: A selective review of available instruments. *Journal of Autism and Development Disorders, 13,* 255–268.

Patterson, G.R., and Anderson, D. (1964). Peers as social reinforcers. *Child Development, 35,* 951–960.

Patterson, G.R., Chamberlain, P., and Reid, J.B. (1982). A comparative evaluation of a parent-training program. *Behavior Therapy, 13,* 638–650.

Peterson, R. (1968). Some experiments on the organization of a class of imitative behavior. *Journal of Applied Behavior Analysis, 1,* 225–235.

Pollard, S., Ward, E.M., and Barkley, R.A. (1983). The effects of parent training and Ritalin on the parent-child interaction of hyperactive boys. *Child and Family Behavior Therapy, 5,* 51–69.

Poorman, C. (1980). Mainstreaming in reverse with a special friend. *Teaching Exceptional Children, 12,* 136–142.

Powell, T.H., Salzberg, C.L., Rule, S., Levy, S., and Itzkowitz, J.S. (1983). Teaching mentally retarded children to play with their siblings using parents as trainers. *Education and Treatment of Children, 6,* 343–362.

Powers, M.D., and Handleman, J.S. (1984). *Behavioral assessment of severe developmental disabilities.* Rockville, MD: Aspen.

Price-Bonham, S., and Addison, S. (1978, July). Families and MR children: Emphasis on the father. *The Family Coordinator,* pp. 221–230.

Ptacek, L.J., Sommers, P.A., Graves, J., Lukowicz, P., Kenna, E., Haglund, J., and Nycz, G.R. (1982). Respite care for families of children with severe handicaps: An evaluation study of parent satisfaction. *Journal of Community Psychology, 10,* 222–227.

Pueschel, S.M., and Bernier, J.C. (1984). The professional's role as advocate. In E. Schopler and G.B. Mesibov (Eds.), *The effects of autism on the family* (pp. 117–128). New York: Plenum Press.

Resnick, L.B., Wang, M.C., and Kaplan, J. (1973). Task analysis in curriculum design: A hierarchially sequenced introductory mathematics curriculum. *Journal of Applied Behavior Analysis, 6,* 679–710.

Rhoades, E.A. (1975). A grandparents' workshop. *The Volta Review, 77,* 557–560.

Rhode, G., Morgan, D.P., and Young, R.K. (1983). Generalization and maintenance of treatment gains of behaviorally handicapped students from resource rooms to regular classrooms using self-evaluation procedures. *Journal of Applied Behavior Analysis, 16,* 189–202.

Riguet, C.B., Taylor, N.P., Benaroya, S., and Klein, L.S. (1981). Symbolic play in autistic, Down's and normal children of equivalent mental age. *Journal of Autism and Developmental Disorders, 11,* 439–448.

Rincover, A. (1978). Sensory extinction: A procedure for eliminating self-stimulatory behavior in psychotic children. *Journal of Abnormal Child Psychology, 6,* 299–310.

Rincover, A., and Koegel, R.L. (1975). Setting generality and stimulus control in autistic children. *Journal of Applied Behavior Analysis, 8,* 235–246.

Rincover, A., and Koegel, R.L. (1977). Research on the education of autistic children: Recent advances and future directions. *Advances in Clinical Psychology, 1,* 113–126.

Rincover, A., Koegel, R., and Russo, D. (1978). Some recent behavioral research on the education of autistic children. *Education and Treatment of Children, 1*(4), 31–45.

Rincover, A., and Newsom, C.D. (1985). The relative motivational properties of sensory and edible reinforcers in teaching autistic children. *Journal of Applied Behavior Analysis, 18,* 237–248.

Rincover, A., Newsom, C.D., and Carr, E.G. (1979). Using sensory extinction procedures in the treatment of compulsive-like behavior of developmentally disabled children. *Journal of Consulting and Clinical Psychology, 47,* 695–701.

Risley, T.R. (1968). The effects and side effects of punishing the autistic behaviors of a deviant child. *Journal of Applied Behavior Analysis, 1,* 21–34.

Romanczyk, R.G., Diament, C., Goren, E.R., Trunell, G., and Harris, S.L. (1975). Increasing isolate and social play in severely disturbed children:

Intervention and postintervention effectiveness. *Journal of Autism and Childhood Schizophrenia, 5,* 57–70.

Romanczyk, R.G., and Lockshin, S. (1981). *How to create a curriculum for autistic and other handicapped children.* Austin: TX: Pro-Ed.

Rosenbaum, M.S., and Brieling, J. (1976). The development and functional control of reading-comprehension behavior. *Journal of Applied Behavior Analysis, 9,* 323–334.

Runco, M.A., and Schreibman, L. (1983). Parental judgements of behavior therapy efficacy with autistic children: A social validation. *Journal of Autism and Developmental Disorders, 13,* 237–248.

Rusch, F.R., and Kazdin, A.E. (1981). Toward a methodology of withdrawal designs for the assessment of response maintenance. *Journal of Applied Behavior Analysis, 14,* 131–140.

Russell, T. (1984). Respite care: A means of rest and recuperation for parents of retarded individuals. *The Pointer, 28,* 4–7.

Russo, D.C., Carr, E.G., and Lovaas, O.I. (1980). Self-injury in pediatric populations. In J. Ferguson and C.B. Taylor (Eds.), *Comprehensive handbook of behavioral medicine* (pp. 118–146). Holliswood, NY: Spectrum.

Rutter, M. (1970). Autistic children: Infancy to adulthood. *Seminars in Psychiatry, 2,* 435-450.

Rutter, M. (1979). Diagnosis and definition. In M. Rutter and E. Schopler (Eds.), *Autism: A reappraisal of concepts and treatment* (pp. 1–25). New York: Plenum Press.

Sailor, W., and Guess, D. (1983). *Severely handicapped students: An instructional design.* Boston: Houghton Mifflin.

Sailor, W., and Mix, B.J. (1975). *The TARC assessment system.* Lawrence, KS: H & H Enterprises.

Salvia, J., and Ysseldyke, J. (1978). *Assessment in special and remedial education.* Boston: Houghton Mifflin.

Sanford, A.R. (Ed.). (1974). *The learning accomplishment profile.* Winston-Salem, NC: Kaplan Press.

Schepis, M.M., Reid, D.H., Fitzgerald, R., Faw, G.D., van den Pol, R.A., and Welty, P.A. (1982). A program for increasing manual signing by autistic and profoundly retarded youth within the daily environment. *Journal of Applied Behavior Analysis, 15,* 363–379.

Schleien, S.J., Certo, N.J., and Muccino, A. (1984). Acquisition of leisure skills by a severely handicapped adolescent: A data based instructional program. *Education and Training of the Mentally Retarded, 19,* 297–305.

Schleien, S.J., Wehman, P., and Kiernan, J. (1981). Teaching leisure skills to severely handicapped adults: An age-appropriate darts game. *Journal of Applied Behavior Analysis, 14,* 513–519.

Schloss, P.J., and Schloss, C.N. (1985). Contemporary issues in social skills research with retarded persons. *The Journal of Special Education, 19,* 270–282.

Schneider, H.C., and Salzberg, C.L. (1982). Stimulus overselectivity in a match-to-sample paradigm by severely retarded youth. *Analysis and Intervention in Developmental Disabilities, 2,* 273–304.

Schopler, E. (1966). Visual versus tactual receptor preference in normal and schizophrenic children. *Journal of Abnormal Psychology, 71,* 108–114.

Schopler, E. (1978). National Society for Autistic Children definition of the syndrome of autism. *Journal of Autism and Childhood Schizophrenia, 8,* 162–169.

Schopler, E., and Mesibov, G.B. (1985). Introduction to communication problems in autism. In E. Schopler and G.B. Mesibov (Eds.), *Communication problems in autism* (pp. 3–13). New York: Plenum Press.

Schopler, E., and Reichler, R.J. (1971). Parents as co-therapists in the treatment of psychotic children. *Journal of Autism and Childhood Schizophrenia, 1,* 87–102.

Schopler, E., and Reichler, R.J. (1980). *Individualized assessment and treatment for autistic and developmentally disabled children: Vol. 1. Psychoeducational profile.* Baltimore: University Park Press.

Schopler, E., Reichler, R.J., DeVellis, R.F., and Daly, K. (1980). Toward objective classification of childhood autism: Childhood autism rating scale (CARS). *Journal of Autism and Developmental Disorders, 10,* 91–103.

Schopler, E., Reichler, R.J., and Lansing, M. (1980). *Individualized assessment and treatment for autistic and developmentally disabled children: Vol. 2. Teaching strategies for parents and professionals.* Baltimore: University Park Press.

Schreibman, L., and Koegel, R.L. (1981). A guideline for planning behavior modification programs for autistic children. In S.M. Turner, K.S. Calhoun, and H.E. Adams (Eds.), *Handbook of clinical behavior therapy* (pp. 54–73). New York: Wiley & Sons.

Schreibman, L., O'Neill, R.E., and Koegel, R.L. (1983). Behavioral training for siblings of autistic children. *Journal of Applied Behavior Analysis, 16,* 129–138.

Schroeder, S.R., Schroeder, C.S., Rojahn, J., and Mulick, J.A. (1981). Self-injurious behavior: An analysis of behavior management techniques. In J.L. Matson and J.R. McCartney (Eds.), *Handbook of behavior modification of the mentally retarded* (pp. 136–164). New York: Plenum Press.

Scott, M. (1980). Ecological theory and methods for research in special education. *Journal of Special Education, 14,* 279–294.

Seltzer, M.M., and Krauss, M.W. (1984). Family, community residence, and institutional placements of a sample of mentally retarded children. *American Journal of Mental Deficiency, 89,* 257–266.

Shea, V. (1984). Explaining mental retardation and autism to parents. In E. Schopler and G.B. Mesibov (Eds.), *The effects of autism on the family* (pp. 265–288). New York: Plenum Press.

Shea, V., and Mesibov, G.B. (1985). Brief report: The relationship of learning disabilities and higher-level autism. *Journal of Autism and Developmental Disorders, 15,* 425–435.

Sherman, B.R., and Cocozza, J.J. (1984). Stress in families of the developmentally disabled: A literature review of factors affecting the decision to seek out-of-home placements. *Family Relations, 33,* 95–103.

Sherman, J.A. (1965). Use of reinforcement and imitation to reinstate verbal behavior in mute psychotics. *Journal of Speech and Hearing Disorders, 28,* 398–401.

Sherman, S.R., Frenkel, E.R., and Newman, E.S. (1984). Foster family care for older persons who are mentally retarded. *Mental Retardation, 22,* 302–308.

Simeonsson, R. (1985). Efficacy of early intervention: Issues and evidence. *Analysis and Intervention in Developmental Disabilities, 5,* 203–209.

Simeonsson, R.J., Buckley, L., and Monson, L. (1979) Conceptions of illness causality in hospitalized children. *Journal of Pediatric Psychology, 4,*

77–84.

Simic, J., and Bucher, B. (1980). Development of spontaneous manding in language deficient children. *Journal of Applied Behavior Analysis, 13,* 523–528.

Singh, N., and Winton, A. (1985). Controlling pica by components of an over-correction procedure. *American Journal of Mental Deficiency, 90,* 40–45.

Skinner, B.F. (1957). *Verbal behavior.* New York: Appleton-Century-Crofts.

Smith, C., and Knoff, H. (1981). School psychology and special education students' placement decisions: IQ still tips the scale. *Journal of Special Education, 15,* 55–64.

Smith, D., Smith, J., and Edgar, E. (1976). Prototypic model for the development of instructional materials. In N.G. Haring and L.J. Brown (Eds.), *Teaching the severely handicapped* (pp. 83–102). New York: Grune & Stratton.

Smith, M., and Belcher, R. (1985). Teaching life skills to adults disabled by autism. *Journal of Autism and Developmental Disorders, 15,* 163–175.

Snell, M.E., and Renzaglia, A.M. (1982). Moderate, severe and profound handicaps. In N.G. Haring (Ed.), *Exceptional children and youth* (3rd ed., pp. 143–172). Columbus, OH: Charles Merrill.

Solomon, R.W., and Wahler, R.G. (1973). Peer reinforcement control of classroom problem behavior. *Journal of Applied Behavior Analysis, 6,* 49–56.

Song, A.Y., and Jones, S.E. (1980). *The Wisconsin behavior rating scale.* Madison, WI: Central Wisconsin Center for the Developmentally Disabled.

Sosne, J.B., Handleman, J.S., and Harris, S.L. (1979). Teaching spontaneous-functional speech to autistic-type children. *Mental Retardation, 17,* 241–245.

Sowers, J., Rusch, F.R., Connis, R.T., and Cummings, L.T. (1980). Teaching mentally retarded adults to time-manage in a vocational setting. *Journal of Applied Behavior Analysis, 13,* 119–128.

Sparrow, S.S., Balla, D.A., and Cicchetti, D.V. (1984). *Vineland adaptive behavior scales.* Circle Pines, MN: American Guidance Service.

Spinetta, J.J. (1974). The dying child's awareness of death: A review. *Psychological Bulletin, 81,* 256–260.

Stainback, W., Stainback, S., Courtnage, L., and Jaben, T. (1985). Facilitating mainstreaming by modifying the mainstream. *Exceptional Children, 52,* 144–152.

Sternberg, L. (1982). Perspectives on educating severely and profoundly handicapped students. In L. Sternberg and G.L. Adams (Eds.), *Educating severely and profoundly handicapped students* (pp. 3–10). Rockville, MD: Aspen.

Stevens-Long, J., and Rasmussen, M. (1974). The acquisition of simple and compound sentence structure in an autistic child. *Journal of Applied Behavior Analysis, 7,* 473–479.

Stokes, T., Baer, D., and Jackson, L. (1974). Programming the generalization of a greeting response in four retarded children. *Journal of Applied Behavior Analysis, 7,* 599–610.

Stoneman, Z., Cantrell, M.L., and Hoover-Dempsey, K. (1983). The association between play materials and social behavior in a mainstreamed preschool: A naturalistic investigation. *Journal of Applied Developmental Psychology, 4,* 163–174.

Strain, P.S. (1983). Generalization of autistic children's social behavior change: Effects of developmentally integrated and segregated settings. *Analysis and Intervention in Developmental Disabilities, 3,* 23–34.

Stremel, K. (1972). Language training: A program for retarded children. *Mental Retardation, 10,* 47–49.

Sullivan, R.C. (1979). Parents speak: The burnout syndrome. *Journal of Autism and Developmental Disorders, 9,* 111–117.

Sutter, P., Mayeda, T., Call, T., Yanagi, G., and Yee, S. (1980). Comparison of successful and unsuccessful community placed mentally retarded persons. *American Journal of Mental Deficiency, 85,* 262–267.

Swanson, H.L., and Watson, B.L. (1982). *Educational and psychological assessment of exceptional children.* St. Louis: C.V. Mosby.

Tager-Flushberg, H. (1981). On the nature of linguistic functioning in early infantile autism. *Journal of Autism and Developmental Disorders, 11,* 45–56.

Tager-Flushberg, H. (1985). Psycholinguistic approaches to language and communication in autism. In E. Schopler and G.B. Mesibov (Eds.), *Communication problems in autism* (pp. 69–84). New York: Plenum Press.

Tausig, M. (1985). Factors in family decision making about placement for developmentally disabled individuals. *American Journal of Mental Deficiency, 89,* 352–361.

Tew, B.J., and Laurence, K.M. (1973). Mothers, brothers, and sisters of patients with spina bifida. *Developmental Medicine and Child Neurology, 15* (Suppl. 29), 69–76.

Thompson, R., and O'Quinn, A. (1979). *Developmental disabilities: Etiologies, manifestations, diagnoses and treatments.* New York: Oxford.

Thompson, T.J., Braam, S.J., and Fugua, R.W. (1982). Training and generalization of laundry skills: A multiple probe evaluation with handicapped persons. *Journal of Applied Behavior Analysis, 15,* 177–182.

Tinbergen, E.A., and Tinbergen, N. (1972). Early childhood autism: An etiological approach. *Journal of Comparative Ethology, 10* (supplement, Advances in ethology), 63–92.

Townsend, P.W., and Flanagan, J.J. (1976). Experimental preadmission program to encourage home care for severely and profoundly retarded children. *American Journal of Mental Deficiency, 80,* 562–569.

Treffry, D., Martin, G., Samuels, J., and Watson, C. (1970). Operant conditioning of grooming behavior of severely retarded girls. *Mental Retardation, 8,* 29–33.

Tucker, J.A. (1985). Curriculum-bases assessment: An introduction. *Exceptional Children, 52,* 199–204.

Twardosz, S., Nordquist, V.M., Simon, R., and Botkin, D. (1983). The effect of group affection activities on the interaction of socially isolate children. *Analysis and Intervention in Developmental Disabilities, 3,* 311–338.

Upshur, C.C. (1982a). An evaluation of home-based respite care. *Mental Retardation, 20,* 58–62.

Upshur, C.C. (1982b). Respite care for mentally retarded and other disabled populations: Program models and family needs. *Mental Retardation, 20,* 2–6.

Vac, N.A. (1968). A study of emotionally disturbed children in regular and special classrooms. *Exceptional Children, 34,* 197–204.

Vadasy, P., Meyer, D., Fewell, R., and Greenberg, M. (1985). Supporting fathers of handicapped young children: Preliminary findings of program effects. *Analysis and Intervention in Developmental Disabilities, 5,* 151–163.

Van Etten, G., Arkell, C., and Van Etten, C. (1980). *The severely and profoundly handicapped: Programs, methods, and materials.* St. Louis: C.V. Mosby.

Wacker, D., and Berg, W. (1984). Use of peer instruction to train a complex photocopying task to moderately and severely retarded adolescents. *Analysis and Intervention in Developmental Disabilities, 4,* 219–234.

Wacker, D., Berg, W., Wiggins, M., and Cavanaugh, J. (1985). Evaluation of reinforcer preferences for profoundly handicapped students. *Journal of Applied Behavior Analysis, 18,* 173–178.

Wahler, R.G. (1969). Setting generality: Some specific and general effects of child behavior therapy. *Journal of Applied Behavior Analysis, 2,* 239–246.

Wahler, R.G. (1980). The insular mother: Her problems in parent-child treatment. *Journal of Applied Behavior Analysis, 13,* 207–219.

Waisbren, S.E. (1980). Parents reactions after the birth of a developmentally disabled child. *American Journal of Mental Deficiency, 84,* 345–351.

Walker, H.M., and Buckley, N.K. (1972). Programming generalization and maintenance of treatment effects across time and across settings. *Journal of Applied Behavior Analysis, 5,* 209–224.

Walker, J.E., and Shea, T.M. (1980). *Behavior modification: A practical approach for educators.* St. Louis: C.V. Mosby.

Wallace, G., and Larsen, S.C. (1978). *Educational assessment of learning problems: Testing for teaching.* Boston: Allyn and Bacon.

Wallace, G., and McLoughlin, J.A. (1979). *Learning disabilities: Concepts and characteristics.* Columbus, OH: Charles Merrill.

Waters, J.M., and Siegel, L.V. (1982). Parent recording of speech production of developmentally delayed toddlers. *Education and Treatment of Children, 5,* 109–120.

Webster-Stratton, C. (1984). Randomized trial of two parent-training programs for families with conduct-disordered children. *Journal of Consulting and Clinical Psychology, 52,* 666–678.

Webster-Stratton, C. (1985). Predictors of treatment outcome in parent training for conduct-disordered children. *Behavior Therapy, 16,* 223–243.

Wehman, P. (1983). Recreation and leisure needs: A community approach. In E. Schopler and G.B. Mesibov (Eds.), *Autism in adolescents and adults* (pp. 111–132). New York: Plenum Press.

Weitz, S. (1982). A code for assessing teaching skills of parents of developmentally disabled children. *Journal of Autism and Developmental Disabilities, 12,* 13–24.

Wetherby, A., and Koegel, R.L. (1982). Audiological testing. In R.L. Koegel, A. Rincover, and A.L. Egel (Eds.), *Educating and understanding autistic children* (pp. 33–52). San Diego: College-Hill Press.

Wetzel, R.J., Baker, J., Roney, M., and Martin, M. (1966). Outpatient treatment of autistic behavior. *Behaviour Research and Therapy, 4,* 169–177.

Wheeler, A.J., and Sulzer, B. (1970). Operant training and generalization of a verbal response form in a speech deficient child. *Journal of Applied Behavior Analysis, 3,* 139–147.

White, K., and Casto, G. (1985). An integrative review of early intervention efficacy studies with at-risk children: Implications for the handicapped.

Analysis and Intervention in Developmental Disabilities, 5, 7–31.

Wiesler, N.A., Hanson, R.H., Chamberlain, T.P., and Thompson, T. (1985). Functional taxonomy of stereotypic and self-injurious behavior. *Mental Retardation, 23,* 230–234.

Wikler, L. (1981). Chronic stress of families of mentally retarded children. *Family Relations, 30,* 281–288.

Wikler, L., Wasow, M., and Hatfield, E. (1981). Chronic sorrow revisted: Parent vs. professional depiction of the adjustment of parents of mentally retarded children. *American Journal of Orthopsychiatry, 51,* 63–70.

Wilbur, R.B. (1985). Sign language and autism. In E. Schopler and G.B. Mesibov (Eds.), *Communication problems in autism* (pp. 229–250). New York: Plenum Press.

Williams, J.A., Koegel, R.L., and Egel, A.L. (1981). Response-reinforcer relationships and improved learning in autistic children. *Journal of Applied Behavior Analysis, 14,* 53–60.

Williams, W. (1975). Procedures of task analysis as related to developing instructional programs for the severely handicapped. In L. Brown, T. Crowner, W. Williams, and R. York (Eds.), *Madison's alternative for zero exclusion: A book of readings* (Vol. 5). Madison, WI: Madison Public Schools.

Wing, L., and Wing, J. (1971). Multiple impairments in early childhood autism. *Journal of Autism and Childhood Schizophrenia, 1,* 256–266.

Wolchik, S.A. (1983). Language patterns of parents of young autistic and normal children. *Journal of Autism and Developmental Disorders, 13,* 167–180.

Wolfensberger, W. (1975). *Normalization.* Toronto: National Institute on Mental Retardation.

Wulbert, M. (1974). The generalization of newly acquired behaviors by parents and child across three different settings. *Journal of Abnormal Child Psychology, 2,* 87–98.

Wulff, S. (1985). The symbolic and object play of children with autism: A review. *Journal of Autism and Developmental Disorders, 15,* 139–148.

Wynne, M.E., and Rogers, J.J. (1985). Variables discriminating residential placement of severely handicapped children. *American Journal of Mental Deficiency, 89,* 515–523.

Young, J.G., Kavanagh, M.E., Anderson, G.M., Shaywitz, B.A., and Cohen, D.J. (1982). Clinical neurochemistry of autism and associated disorders. *Journal of Autism and Developmental Disorders, 12,* 147–166.

Author Index

Subject Index